VICTORIA
THE WIDOW AND
HER SON

By

HECTOR BOLITHO

D. APPLETON-CENTURY COMPANY
INCORPORATED

NEW YORK   LONDON

1934

THE LEADER OF SOCIETY

TO A. V. B.

Through the nobleness of his mind and the example of his character, I first came to comprehend the Victorians.

ACKNOWLEDGEMENTS

I wish to thank the Dowager Countess of Jersey, Lady Horner and Mr. H. B. Batchelor for reading the proofs of my book. I am indebted to them for their patience, their encouragement and their many suggestions. I wish also to thank Major-General H. Karslake, C.B., C.M.G., D.S.O., for reading the chapters of the book referring to the South African War.

H. B.

INTRODUCTION

THIS BOOK was contemplated five years ago, when I was writing *Albert the Good,* a life of the Prince Consort. I had told the story of Queen Victoria and her husband in one book and I wished also to write the story of the Queen and her son. There have been five or six biographies of the Queen and of King Edward since then. This was discouraging, for some of them were greeted as scholarly and distinguished books. I decided to pursue my plan and not to read any of the new biographies until I had completed my own manuscript. In this way they would help me to criticise my own deductions without influencing my approach to the original sources of information. I decided also to gather as much information as possible through interviews with descendants of the Queen and surviving contemporaries, allowing this first hand evidence to be the main influence upon my choice of material and my points of view.

One night at dinner, I sat next to a descendant of the Queen who talked of the many new biographies which were being published. She said to me, "All these books are interesting, but they have a common fault. The books about King Edward are written at the expense of the Queen and the books about the Queen at the expense of King Edward. Some day there may be a book which will bring out, in fairness, the faults and merits of both. This would be more true to human nature."

This chance remark encouraged me since it was in line with the conviction which first made me want to write the story of mother and son, without personal prejudices to influence my selection of evidence.

The astonishing truth about Queen Victoria is that her palpable errors, her stubbornness and her limitations do not detract from the central, strong-willed, righteous figure. One finds this most sharply defined in Lytton Strachey's brilliantly written study. He came, rather as a scoffer, allowing his personal bitterness to influence his choice of material and his dangerous talent to distort evidence to suit his own ends as a story teller. No matter how much he derided some of the facets, he was obliged to admit the qualities of the complete gem.

A close examination of almost every important contemporary book and document relating to the Queen leaves one with this impression: that all her mistakes grew out of her social isolation. This isolation sadly limited her knowledge of human nature. Except in her childhood and the twenty-odd years of her married happiness, she was without an equal who could call her by her Christian name. She cried again and again, "I am alone," and it was piteously true. Her story must be studied in the light of this limitation. Her acts were sometimes in error, but never her motives. This, I think, was the steady light of her greatness.

I have tried to tell the story of the Queen and her son, struggling with the unique relationship which exists only between a sovereign and the heir to a throne. I feel that many writers have failed to realise the most important aspect of this relationship between Queen Victoria and the Prince of Wales. They have not realised the great change which came to the Queen after Lord Beaconsfield's death. Many of the early causes of friction between mother and son disappeared when the Queen forsook the more morbid forms of bereavement and came out into the world again.

The touches of self-pity which mar the letters written by the Queen in the sixties and seventies disappear and both courage and affection give force and light to the letters of the last twenty years of her reign. During these years, mother and son faced their differences more generously and their relationship was made happier by confidence and graciousness. The Queen's support of her son in his quarrel with the young German Emperor in 1888-1889 confirms this.

Queen Victoria ruled in a land which had already disposed of the divine right of Kings, at least in the Constitution. But it was still alive in Europe and not wholly dead in the Queen's personal devotion to her position. Mother and son ruled the country during the hundred years in which the mystery of the "divine right" was destroyed in Europe. They fought the battle for Kingship in a different way from their European cousins and they won. The adaptability of the Coburg blood and the temperament of the British people made it possible for a new kind of Sovereign to evolve in England. The change began in earnest with Queen Victoria, it was further moulded by King Edward and it is perfected in the present King: a Sovereign and his subjects who seem to be outside the political excesses which shake the rest of the world. We see now the fulfilment of Queen Victoria's dictum, "... that it was not the duty of a Constitutional Sovereign to govern a country, but to set an example." One must smile and admit that her belief in the "divine right" was still sufficiently alive in her to make her wish to do both. But it is rigidly true that she set an example.

People on pedestals attract brickbats. This has been true of both the Queen and her son. But I think the fault in most criticisms of their lives has been this: that critics have viewed them as exalted people, marred by human faults, instead of as ordinary mortals, struggling with an extraordinary problem. If there is any justification for my telling the story of the Queen and her son again I would ask my readers to approach this book, not as the story of great people upon whose faults we may pounce, but rather as the story of two human beings cursed with the same failings, the same weaknesses, as their subjects, but born to the most ghastly responsibility that could be put upon a human being, and struggling to fulfil it as best they can.

HECTOR BOLITHO.

Park House, Marden, Kent.

CONTENTS

CONTENTS

CONTENTS

CONTENTS

CONTENTS

CONTENTS

ILLUSTRATIONS

VICTORIA, THE WIDOW
AND HER SON

Chapter One

§ 1 — 1861–1862

THE PRINCE CONSORT died at Windsor on December 14th.
Five days afterwards, the bereaved Queen was taken to
her quiet house in the Isle of Wight. In the hour of his
death she had made a vigorous effort at self-control: she
had sent for the doctors to thank them and to console
them for their failure. Then her grief became terrible and
unreasoning. For many days her Ministers and her Ladies
watched her anxiously; sometimes, in her paroxysms of
crying, they were afraid lest she should lose her reason.
The gardens of Osborne were stark and dead, for it was
winter. The Queen looked out of the windows, over the
expanse of cold earth, to the wind-troubled stretches of the
Solent. The scene held the mirror up to her own desolation. The little black-dressed figure, with what her un-
comprehending children called her 'sad cap' on her head,
was suddenly estranged from her kingdom and from her
own family. Her grief made her still more alone. 'There
is nobody to call me Victoria now,' she cried. '...The
things of this life are of no interest to the Queen.' [1] Without her 'dear angel' she had no wish to live.

February passed and the delicate changes of spring
came to the gardens of Osborne: the wind on the Solent
was more gentle, and sunlight came to the sullen winter
tide. The trees *he* had planted were gay with the first pale
buds of the new season. The Queen's sorrow did not abate
with the change. She hung his portrait, wreathed with

I

immortelles, over the empty pillow beside her: when her Prime Minister came to see her, she received him with the bust of Prince Albert on the table next to her. Sometimes she hung a wreath of flowers about the white marble throat. His image was in the bracelet upon her plump wrist. At Osborne, at Buckingham Palace, at Windsor and at Balmoral, his rooms were to remain as he had left them, his books in their place, his clothes ready for him to wear. She walked into the study at Osborne where she had sat with him so often. She saw the books he had been reading when they were there only a few months before; the meticulously arranged lists and papers and the few wistful souvenirs of his boyhood. Nothing was to be touched. All, *all* was to be a memorial to *him.*

She might have paused in her grief to see her Ministers tapping their feet impatiently at her door; she might have been more conscious of the young children who were now all the more a call upon her resources. There was the Civil War in America to keep the nation on tenterhooks and there was the disturbing figure of Garibaldi to draw the eyes of the people towards the Mediterranean. But the Queen turned her back on the living with an obsession which might seem selfish if we did not know the depth of her unreasoning love; she devoted her mind and her energies to the dead.

During these first months of bereavement, the Queen saw the nation only in the light of her own tragedy. She could not yet see her grief in relation to her responsibilities as Queen. The black edges on her handkerchiefs were wide: her sorrow became a focus for every conversation, every document and every sensation. She had shared her family happiness with her people with almost

2

childlike pleasure during her married life. She had been pleased to know that her comfortable, unassuming domestic life and her happiness were open to the public eye. Now, in the same way, she expected her subjects to be identified with her misery. She wrote to the Leader of the Conservative Party,[2] telling him of Windsor, where she had once been so happy. Now, she said, the castle was a *living grave*. Every feeling was swallowed up in one of unbounded grief. 'She feels,' she wrote, 'as though *her life* had ended on *that* dreadful day when she lost that bright Angel who was her idol, the life of her life: and the time seems to have passed like *one long, dark day!*

'*She* sees the trees budding, the days lengthen, the primroses coming out, but *she thinks* herself in the month of December...she wastes and pines...with a broken and bleeding heart, and with but *one* consolation—*to rejoin him* again—*never* to *part.*'[3]

Eighteen days after Prince Albert's death, the Queen made her first entry in her Journal. She was already planning memorials for him. She wrote, 'Went down to see the sketch for a statue of my beloved Albert in Highland dress.' At Windsor his body was to be buried in a great romanesque mausoleum, brilliant with mosaics within, crowned by copper without. It was to be near to the pond upon which he had skated so elegantly in the first winters of their marriage. Four bronze angels would extend their wings to support his marble effigy upon the sarcophagus: a wide sarcophagus, wide enough for her to join him when her unhappy life should end. Over the door of the mausoleum would be written, '...*Farewell, well beloved. Here, at last, I will rest with thee.*' In London, near to the Palace in Kensington where she was born, he was to be sculptured in gold, holding the cata-

3

logue of his wonderful exhibition, beneath a lofty canopy of unsurpassed, oriental-gothic beauty. Henry the Third's Chapel at Windsor, where Wolsey had planned to be buried, was to be transformed with mosaics and portraits of her children in marble: all in *his* memory. His statue was to rise in the public parks: never, never would the British people be allowed to forget him. When the Lord Mayor of London wrote, offering the memorial of the people, she said 'yes,' it could be built, providing it was 'on a scale of sufficient grandeur.'[4] She wrote that his memorials should be 'numberless.'

The pitiless storms of winter were still moving about Osborne House when the Queen went out into the garden for the first time. For half an hour each day she walked among the leafless trees, supported by two of her Ladies. Her stumbling steps were watched anxiously by her servants from the windows: she already seemed to be bent and old, remote from them, behind the walls of her grief. The effort was made against her will. She would go back to the house and to his room again, to sit there in the icy twilight, bewildered in her melancholy. She saw and spoke and moved like one in a dream. This darkness stayed with her for a long time before she saw reason. When Lord Canning died, soon after his wife and six months after her own bereavement, the Queen wrote to his sister, 'How enviable to follow so soon the partner of your life! How I pray it may be God's will to let me follow mine soon.'[5] Her obsession was dangerous in its influence, but it was deeply sincere.

§ II — 1862

QUEEN VICTORIA was forty-two years old when her husband died. She had lost the slim grace of the girl who had married him in 1840. Of her nine children, one was already married. Indeed, the Crown Princess of Prussia now had two children of her own; the elder was the boy who was to become German Emperor and the enemy of England. Princess Alice, the Queen's second daughter, was betrothed to Prince Louis of Hesse, and Prince Alfred, later to be Duke of Saxe-Coburg, was a promising youngster in the Navy. Five of the children were still young: Princess Beatrice was an enchanting little girl of four. Here were enough duties and tasks to have awakened the Queen from her despair. But the troubles from the younger children were nothing to the anxiety of training the Prince of Wales.

He was twenty, a charming and respectful son, devoted to normal pleasures. He had a taste for amusing people, light music and luxury. The Queen, who ate roast beef almost every day of her life and who went to bed at ten o'clock, failed to understand him. To her, he was his father's son and she wished nothing more than that he should grow up in Prince Albert's image. She wished him to be sober in behaviour, guarded in his humour, prone to philosophy rather than frolic and to early hours rather than the theatre and the gaming table. One of the Queen's limitations was that sometimes she could not understand the motives and tastes of other people being different from her own. No instance is more remarkable than her attitude towards the marriage of her Woman of the Bedchamber, Lady Augusta Bruce. The Queen wrote that Lady Augusta had, 'most unnecessarily, de-

cided to *marry* (*!!*).' She had observed that the bridegroom was 'a very unselfish man' so she added, 'I should
stipulate that she shall be a great deal with me.'

She made a mistake in seeking for the meticulous Spartan in her son, for he was a pleasure-loving Guelph, as
she had been in the beginning. She forgot the girlhood
nights of dancing at Buckingham Palace, before Prince
Albert came to curb her revels. She had enjoyed kicking
over the traces then. But twenty years of married life had
calmed her spirit. Nothing of the Coburg disciplinarian
had descended to her son and he was abashed before the
curriculum which his father had prepared for him. He
showed how little he cared for scholarship and sober behaviour when he was taken to the Pyramids and to the
tombs of Egypt. Arthur Stanley, who guided him, was
delighted when the young Prince scrambled up the slope
of a Pyramid, unaided. Even the little Egyptian guide
was amazed at his nimbleness. He turned his wide open
eyes to Stanley and said, '. . . that little chap—why he go
up alone?' But Dean Stanley was forlorn afterwards,
when he found the Prince sitting in front of his tent,
smoking a pipe and reading a novel.[6] He had not minded
climbing the Pyramids—that was good fun. But he had
withdrawn from the party when the tombs were suggested. 'Why should we go and see the tumbledown old
Temple?'[7] he said on another day, when they were meandering down the Nile. All that he wanted to do was
to shoot crocodiles.

The Queen was not alone in her anxiety. Others observed that the father did not live again in the son. Lord
Palmerston, still Prime Minister, still the hated *Pilgerstein* who had made her so unhappy through his rudeness
to her, went down to Osborne within a few weeks of the

Prince Consort's death, to express the official concern over the Prince of Wales. He could hardly speak for emotion when he first saw the Queen. But his sympathy did not prevent him from talking about the Prince, and the desirability of his travelling, which would be such a good thing for him.[8] Palmerston added that it was most important that he should marry. He went so far as to say, with his blunt candour, that *the* difficulty of the moment' was the Prince of Wales. The Queen, with a flash of motherly loyalty, told her Prime Minister that he was a very good and dutiful son. But when she recorded the interview in the pages of her Journal, she confessed that she 'felt the same.'[9]

In the old days the Queen might have been advised in her perplexity. Lord Melbourne could have indicated her error to her with gentle subtlety. The Duke of Wellington might have helped her, or Sir Robert Peel, in the later years when she came to like and to trust him. All these were gone now. Uncle Leopold was still in Brussels, but he was old and in the withering days of his power. The once vigorous and ruthless Stockmar had also withdrawn from his place of influence. His voice might have helped her as it had in the beginning. But Stockmar was now a shade, retired to a humble life in Coburg. His hand had lost its cunning and his eyes were dim. There was not one man in England whom the Queen both loved and respected. Only such a man could have guided her, as the Prince Consort had guided her, away from the follies of her first years as Queen. She was passionate and devoted, and the way to cajole her in official problems was through her heart. She neither liked nor trusted Palmerston. Albert and King Leopold had called him *Pilgerstein,* because *Pilger* was the German form of Palmer

and because they were able to pour a little of their dislike and derision into the nickname. At the heels of Lord
Palmerston were Lord Russell, who was Foreign Minister, and Lord Derby, who was Leader of the Conservative
Opposition. Neither of them inspired the Queen to more
than official regard and respect. She could pour out her
woe to them in italicised phrases which were incongruously mixed up with her views upon Schleswig-Holstein
and the American Civil War, but when it came to the
cold questions of Government, she suspected their advice
and she doubted their ability.

A curious personal humility is traced through the story
of Victoria, the woman. She wrote in the secret pages of
her diary that it was a 'presumption' for her to inscribe
her name in Sir Walter Scott's Journal, when his heir
asked her to do so. Those who knew her intimately have
always insisted upon this humility. But, as Queen, she
was self-willed: a rock in time of decision, a trumpet in
time of discord. Only the mind of her dead husband
would influence her now. It may seem that one is abandoning history for the realm of metaphysics if one says
that, as her deepest grief passed, the Prince Consort's
mind lived with her, guiding her and sustaining her. The
Prince was dead, but she was aware of his mind and conscious of his judgment in every hour of her widowed life.
We can trace the intellect of the Prince Consort and his
moral judgments through the Queen's letters, up to the
time of her own death. Through her love for him, she
was guided by him. Conscious of this strength coming
from the dead, she wrote to her Uncle, '*No human power*
will make me swerve from *what* he decided and wished.'
This was a warning to Leopold. He had proffered his
advice when the Prince died and, remembering his early

interference with her, when she was a girl, she made no bones about telling him once more where he stood in relation to the British Crown. She rebuffed him, graciously but firmly. 'I am *also determined,*' she added, 'that *no one* person, may he be ever so good, ever so devoted *to me.*' [10] She thought as well as wrote in italics.

She watched the affairs of the country with tear-stained eyes, but her sorrow was not to mean any abatement of her power. Lord Russell had sent a dispatch to the American Minister in London, without allowing her to see it first. She pounced upon him; a black-edged letter was sent to him from Osborne, post haste. 'Lord Russell will perhaps take care,' she wrote, 'that the *rule* should not be departed from, viz. that no drafts should be sent without the Queen's having first seen them.' [11] Some of the spirit of her girlhood was coming back again, now that the Prince's restraining hand was not with her. She would think as he had thought, but the force of her decision was to be her own. So she rapped Lord Russell over the knuckles as she had reprimanded the Duke and Sir Robert Peel, in her irresponsible twenties. The Prince Consort had curbed the rebellious spirit, but he had not killed it.

Ministers were usually well able to take care of themselves. They sweated with fear when they came to see her, just as Prince Bismarck was to do, when she received him in Germany. But Ministers could resign or they could seek excuses for the decisions which annoyed her, in the Constitution or in the machinery of politics. There was no such escape for her son, even if he had wished it. All through the story of King Edward's life this censorship of his boyhood must be remembered. The Queen sought to develop him through frustrating him. Some years before the Prince Consort's death, she had feared the increasing authority and influence of her heir so much that she had asked Palmerston to introduce a bill into Parliament, giving her husband legal precedence over her son. Palmerston's warnings and Stockmar's reluctance to abet her had thwarted her design but they had not removed her curious fear. When she first married Prince Albert in the forties, she had denied him all political secrets and she had excluded him from all conversations with Ministers. 'I am only the husband,' he had complained. Now, in her widowhood, she adopted the same tactics with her son.

Ministers and newspapers came to resent the rule the Queen exercised over the Prince of Wales. He had one friend at Court, Lord Torrington, who was a Lord-in-Waiting. Lord Torrington broke all rules by writing letters to Delane, editor of *The Times,* apprising him of what was happening within the court. In one of his letters to Delane, Lord Torrington described the Prince as 'singularly honest and truthful.' 'He deserves a little of her confidence,' he wrote; 'the pretence to consult him would have a great effect on his mind.'

It is to the Prince's credit that, during these years of dominion over him, his affection for his mother never seemed to wane. He had great capacity for respect and he had big stores of love. The Queen received both, in fullest measure, and if she had had a wider knowledge of human nature, she might have found in him some of the support and encouragement which her husband had given her.

Prince Albert had left two plans for his son's progress. He had wished him to travel in the Near East, with Dr. Stanley,[12] and he had also wished him to marry. Princess

Alexandra of Denmark was already named, before the Prince died. The Queen set about fulfilling her husband's plans and neither her grief nor her loneliness deterred her from sending the boy abroad. He left for Egypt and the Holy Land two months after his father's death.

Chapter Two

§ 1 — 1862

ON APRIL 6TH the Prince of Wales rode up the golden
slopes into Jerusalem with Arthur Stanley as his guide.
Stanley was a sincere, devout man. Young people loved
him. But he had come upon this journey reluctantly:
the shy and uncompromising priest had said 'Yes', only
because the Queen had assured him that the Prince Consort had chosen him to be her son's guide. He had been
weighed down by false preconceptions of the Prince's
character; the story of frivolity and failure had been
poured into his ears and little of the opposite picture had
been shown to him. 'I doubt whether I am the proper
person,' he pleaded, dreading the long ordeal of such a
journey. 'I should not be a suitable companion for him,'
he added.[18]

The royal wish overruled Stanley's objections: he set
out upon the journey to the East, but with little pleasure.
He went alone as far as Egypt and when the Prince met
him there, Stanley contemplated his charge and wrote to
his sister, '...nothing can be worse than I have long ago
anticipated...everything must be taken as part of an
inevitable whole.' After a few weeks had passed with excursions into the desert, grand visits to Egyptian Princes,
and donkey rides, Stanley still wrote of the Prince in depressed phrases. 'It is hardly possible to over-estimate the
difficulty of producing any impression on a mind with
no previous knowledge or interest to be awakened...I

12

cannot bring myself to pour out words into unwilling or indifferent ears.'[14]

Intimacy broke down a little of Stanley's prejudice: human nature triumphed where intellectual responses failed. Stanley slowly came to judge the Prince, not as a bored visitor to the ruins of the Near East, but rather as a normal young Briton. With this closer light, the boy was seen more pleasantly. In Stanley's later letters we come upon happy phrases which excuse the Prince for his 'levity and frivolity.' 'I certainly agree with the eulogies on his manners and from time to time he tells a good story well,' Stanley wrote from Cairo. On another day, while they were floating down the Nile in the pleasant excitement of shooting crocodiles, stuffing birds and landing to see the temples, Stanley watched the Prince again and he wrote, 'H.R.H. is perfectly friendly and easy. He set his mind on my reading *East Lynne,* which I did, in three sittings yesterday.'

They sat on the deck together, 'the Heir of half the world,' and the scholarly, affectionate priest. Their talk was all of earthly things, a penetrating examination by the Prince on the merits of *East Lynne* and a confession that temples and ruins were not interesting to him. When he was urged off the boat to see a temple, he 'treated the pillars, and the sculptures...with the most well-bred courtesy, as if he were paying a visit to a high personage.'[15]

Stanley sought beneath the surface of the pleasure-seeking youth and he came to see that the Prince was possessed by a strong desire to be all that was expected of him. He also came to know the struggle going on within the perplexed son, the struggle between his nature and his duty to his mother. Stanley softened his judgment: 'There is more in him than I thought. I do not at all despair...' he wrote from the Palace of the Citadel, where they were living in Egyptian splendour.

Early in April the cavalcade rode up from Jericho to Jerusalem. The way is from the deep shores of the Dead Sea, where Sodom and Gomorrah lie buried, up through stark and lifeless mountains, to Bethany. And then to Jerusalem. Stanley made his most sincere bid for the Prince's interest then, as they approached the Holy City. They climbed up until they came to the Inn of the Good Samaritan which rises beside the parched, dusty road. Then up again, between the flanks of the merciless, bare mountains of Judæa, until in the late afternoon, they came to Bethany. They were going by the way along which Jesus had entered Jerusalem. Stanley wrote of the afternoon:

'I then took my place close beside the Prince. Everyone else fell back by design or accident—and at the head of the cavalcade, we moved on towards the famous view. This was the one half-hour which throughout the journey I had determined to have alone with him—and I succeeded. I pointed out each stage of the triumphal entry—the "fig-trees"—the "stones," the first sight of Jerusalem—the acclamations, the palms, the olive branches—the second sight, where "He beheld the city and wept over it."
'I turned round to call the attention of the rest of the party, and as I turned, I saw and bade the Prince look round to the only detail which would have been worth noticing on such an occasion —a flock of white sheep and black goats feeding on the mountain side, the framework of the great Parable delivered also from this hillside—on the Day of Judgment. The cavalcade moved on again —and I fell to the rear—feeling that I had at least done my best, though after, I felt as if my tongue clove to the roof of my mouth.'

14

In the afternoon, when the air was cool and when the shadows were coming to the olive trees in the valleys about Jerusalem, Arthur Stanley would lead the Prince along the city walls from gate to gate, until they came to the beautiful and quiet place from which they looked out to the Mount of Olives and down into the Garden of Gethsemane. After one such day, the Prince came to Stanley in his tent, when the evening silence had come to the little camp. Sitting with him, the Prince wrote down the names of all the places he had seen. As he walked out, he turned and stood still, framed in the door of the tent. He said, 'in the most engaging manner,' 'You see that I am trying to do what I can to carry out what you said in your sermon, "Gather up the fragments—"' [16]

It might have been disappointing for Stanley to contemplate the faint intellectual response to his learning, but, as he wrote, 'It was impossible not to like him.' [17]

§ II — 1862

THE PRINCE returned to England on June 14th to the momentary delight of the Queen, for she thought him 'improved, and looking so bright and healthy.' [18] Sixteen days afterwards he still pleased her and it seemed that they were coming nearer to the sympathy and understanding which might have strengthened them both. She wrote of him as 'most affectionate, dutiful and amiable.' But she admitted his merits because he obeyed her will: because he was 'only anxious to do whatever his Mother and Father wished.' [19]

For a little time there was hope that the shadow of misunderstanding was passing from them. The Queen returned to Windsor, gathering new reasons for sorrow

15

about her through the associations with Prince Albert's life and death. Again she clung to the tangible souvenirs of the dead Prince, leaving the door open between her room and his own, with strange and morbid devotion. But she paused in 'the midst of her agony' to 'thank God for the blessed change in her son. Serious, wishing to do right, anxious to marry March or April.' Instead of 'worry and distress' there was 'love.' [20]

In celebration of his increased merits the Prince was to be given more freedom. The change was disturbed by the death of his Governor, General Bruce. General Bruce had guarded him well and with more tenderness than is usually supposed. But he was the Queen's appointed mentor, and while his death was a deep and personal sorrow to the Prince, the boy might also have come to look upon it as a release from discipline, suitable to the adventure of acquiring Marlborough House in London and Sandringham House in the country. Here, indeed, were signs of freedom, with the stretches of Norfolk for his shooting and the spacious rooms of Marlborough House for his entertainments in town. But the Queen would have none of this. The General's death caused her to look about for still another, older, balanced man, to 'keep him from doing what was hurtful to him, or unfit to his position, and who would be responsible to me.' [21] The man chosen was General Knollys, afterwards Sir W. T. Knollys, a Peninsular veteran in the autumn of his sixty-fifth year, secure from flippancy and certain to curb the Prince's taste for 'worldly, frivolous, gossiping kind of conversation.' [22] It is good to know that the Prince's taste for pleasure was sufficiently healthy and strong to survive 'the shadows of the prison house.' The Queen added one more manacle of prevention. She sent the Prince a 'little sketch' of what she wished him to do between October and the time of his marriage. All that remained now was to see that his married life was so secure and so faithful to her plan that, in the event of her death, the Prince could carry on his father's tradition and not create his own.

She signed her letter of instruction, 'Ever your affectionate and unhappy Mama, V.R.'

In September the Queen made her first journey abroad as a widow. The progress was slow and sad. She paused in Brussels to stay with King Leopold, and there the beautiful Danish Princess was brought to her. The Queen was solaced and pleased, for Princess Alexandra 'looked lovely, in a black dress, nothing in her hair, and curls on either side, which hung over her shoulders, her hair turned back off her beautiful forehead.' 'Her whole appearance,' wrote the Queen, 'was one of the greatest charm, combined with simplicity and perfect dignity.'[28] This was true, for the Princess was lovely as a flower in the gloomy world to which she came. She entranced all who saw her, by her beauty: beauty which remained until the days within our own memory, when she drove through London on Rose Day, a wistful but lovely ghost.

Six days after meeting Princess Alexandra in Brussels, Queen Victoria went to a castle near the Thuringian forest. Here she lived within sight of the places Prince Albert had known as a child. She walked out among the peasants, just as she had walked with *him* on the pleasant, first occasion when he took her to his home. Here life was simple and free from the mighty affairs of England. It was a pilgrimage of painful recollection for her, since every turret and stream, every light that fell upon the market-place or about the lofty castle was associated with him. They had wandered here like children, in the first year when their love touched the deeper wells of understanding; when he had broken down her obstinacy by the calm light of his goodness. Again her grief overwhelmed her.

On September 9th the Queen received a telegram from her son. The day before he had written, 'Now I will take a walk with Princess Alexandra in the garden and in three-quarter's of an hour I will take her into the grotto, and there I will propose, and I hope it will be to everybody's satisfaction.'[24] He had proposed and been accepted and now he wished for his mother's 'consent and blessing.' They were given readily, since his engagement was in obedience to her will. The betrothed Princess had celebrated her engagement by walking with the Prince over the battlefield of Waterloo. He hurried to his mother in Coburg with all the zest and delight of a lover. Lady Augusta, who attended the Queen, observed him with no sentimental delusions and vowed that he was truly 'in love.' He was 'too tender and so very, very dear,' facing her with a love letter of twelve pages, 'held crumpled up for fear that the zephyrs should blow upon it.'[25]

General Bruce's lessons and Arthur Stanley's sermons had not fallen upon stony ground. At least in his efforts, the Prince was facing his future honestly and we can only suspect with what happy anxiety he greeted the changes which pressed upon him by the way he turned to his most beloved sister, Princess Alice. A few months before, she had married Prince Louis of Hesse. In the north of Germany the Crown Princess was living within the rigid laws which she had so easily accepted from her father. Even the Queen had observed her assimilation of Prussian thought with concern and had once chastened her with a

18

lecture on the change. The Prince of Wales would find no deep core of sympathy and understanding from her. With his sister Alice the story was different. The Court at Darmstadt, into which she had married most happily, was so far free from the Prussian taint. 'He loves Princess Alice dearly,' Lady Augusta wrote of the brother and sister.

Princess Alice had watched her mother's grief with sensible anxiety. 'Try and gather in the few bright things you have remaining,' she had written to the Queen. 'You have the privilege...in your exalted position, of doing good and living for others...Forgive me, darling Mama, if I speak so openly....' Princess Alice was with her brother in Coburg, and in her he found a confidante and friend. 'I feel a new interest in everything, and somebody to live for,' he wrote to the wife of his old Governor. To a still closer friend he confided, 'I indeed now know what it is to be really happy.' [26]

§ III

AFTER ALMOST half a century we still seem to resent Queen Victoria's dominating power: her intolerance and her rigid pursuit of what she deemed to be 'right.' In another age, perhaps with the colour and heroics of the Elizabethans, she would have been applauded as a fine example of what a dominating Queen should be. Indeed, she had much in common with the Sovereign whom she so cordially disliked: she was never proud to be compared with Elizabeth.

One records the stories of the Queen's insistence nervously, afraid lest the picture of her should seem to be too hard and unsympathetic. We seem to lose touch with the woman whose simplicity won the devotion of those who were always near her. But she ruled with will and power and it is the story of a woman of will and power which is to be told. There were many years during her reign when she was not loved. Her own age, rude with the sounds of increasing industry and bloated by material riches, could not see her with the perspective which allows appreciation. Nor do our sophisticated eyes admit the splendour of her personal power. But it was there. If only the Prince Consort had lived to curb the occasional tempests of decision! Lady Augusta Stanley recorded her own perplexity over these matters in a letter to her sister.[27] 'The agony of anxiety about so many, many things,' she wrote, 'the feeling that the very good qualities of this blessed sufferer are liable to cause evil results and to make Her be misunderstood, the honesty, the straightforwardness, the frankness, the impulsiveness, all held in check by Him, governed, directed.'

Few women in history have been faced with such problems as those which beset the Queen in 1862. There was nobody with authority to guide her through the labyrinth of state and family affairs. Her isolation was unique and terrible, and in choosing the way of firmness and authority she may have seemed intolerant and obstinate, but she became a mighty power for security in the uncertain tides of state.

She turned from the quiet and painful memories of Coburg, the hills lit with meadow saffron and the castellated crown of Rosenau, obscured behind the chestnuts. For a moment she forgot the dead, to embrace the living. Her son had been to the Holy Land and he was engaged to be married. The two plans which Prince Albert had left behind him were now complete. The next duty was to train the guileless Danish Princess in the way she should go. This was to be the Queen's way. To guard herself from all interference and to be certain that her influence was to be the strongest in preparing the Princess, she arranged that she should come from Denmark to Osborne upon a visit. But she arranged also that the Prince of Wales should remain abroad.

The Queen's ideas would thus be the first received by the pliable young mind: they would not be confused or discounted by the more emotional anticipations of marriage. Her pupil was apt, for Princess Alexandra was neither intellectual nor worldly clever. She was beautiful, but she was obedient. And she was no doubt humble in leaving the Danish Court, in which she had made her own dresses and lived in simplicity, for the brilliance of her new life in England.

Chapter Three

§1 — 1863

As EARLY as March, those who were near to the Queen observed a change—still 'the look of sorrow and suffering,' but there was also 'calm decision and high resolve and energy.'[28] One of her Ladies was struck by the judgment that she showed. Her son was to be married on the tenth of the month: the will would not be relaxed when necessity was at the door, and the Queen threw herself into the preparations with moderate zest. She had observed Princess Alexandra closely...the books beside her bed—'all serious, pious books, all most read, underlined old copies.'[29] They had had many quiet talks together at Osborne, while the bridegroom was still abroad, and the result had been satisfying; a complete obedience to the older will on the part of the Princess. She was anxious to learn the Queen's tastes and interests and she was sensible of the immense benefit it was to be quiet with her, like this, *tête-à-tête*. There was no thought 'but of *Him*' and she was 'anxious to improve Herself in every way to be of use to Him.'[30]

The Queen, too, was pleased. 'I am sure she will do what is right fearlessly,' she said. In a splendid discipline of courage, she faced the ordeal of the wedding.

Windsor is beautiful in March. The slope between the Castle and Queen Adelaide's cottage is always sweet with primroses and a thousand birds flit among the new leaves of the chestnuts: lambs bleat in the meadows and the first

22

boats move out on the Thames. On the morning of the tenth, the sun shone valiantly. Stories of the wedding procession through London had come down to Windsor; of how the Princess had hurt her arm during the pande- monium while trying to help an old man who wished to see her. General Grey had been with them in the metropolis and when he arrived at Windsor, he told the little cluster of Ladies that he never saw anything more charming than the manner of both, so courteous, so un- affected, and simple and so anxious to respond to all the affection and loyal feeling. The Queen was delighted. There was joy in the Castle as she waited, with her Court. Indeed, the corridors and drawing-rooms buzzed with amusing gossip; talk of the little imp, Prince William of Prussia,[31] who had thrown his auntie's muff into the road as they were driving, and stories of Princess Beatrice, much shocked when she was taken to see the decorations in Windsor—*much* shocked by what she saw, because she '*never* thought there was *stays* in shops!' There was much to tell and to talk about as they waited. The slopes towards Eton were aflutter with decorations: the world seemed to be singing in adulation of the heir and his bride. The Queen moved about the Castle among smiling, happy people. Only once her courage failed her —perhaps she remembered the happy evening in February of 1840, when *she* drove down from London, a bride, in her white satin pelisse trimmed with swansdown, with a white satin bonnet and feathers. She complained only once, as the grand company waited for the wedding. '. . . all were there with their husbands. Where was Hers?' But the weakness was momentary, for she faced the noise and the excitement bravely. At dinner, she astonished them all by 'the gentle, unaffected cheerfulness of Her look and voice and smile.'[32] In the evening of this last day before the wedding ceremony, she was sitting alone in her room. She heard a gentle tap upon her door and in stole the bride. Princess Alexandra did not speak: she just knelt beside the Queen and kissed her hand.

The marriage scene in Saint George's Chapel was magnificent. The beauty and nobility of the country waited, a tide of blazing uniforms, satin dresses and diamonds, trembling with expectation beneath the soaring stone arches, the richly coloured banners of the Knights and the dark oak stalls of the choir. There was one moment of astonishment when Lord Palmerston took out his comb and combed his hoary whiskers. And there was a moment of special beauty when Lady Spencer came in, wearing a dark cerulean gown covered with magnificent lace which had belonged to Marie Antoinette. When all were seated in their stalls, there was silence. Then, like the moving crest of a wave, the diamond tiaras bowed—the Queen appeared in the high, oak closet of Catherine of Aragon, on the north side of the altar. In this pageant of colour she alone wore the black streamers of widowhood. 'At the first blast of the trumpets, she quivered all over and you could see the working of her face.' When Princess Beatrice came, the baby of the bridal procession, the Queen looked down and smiled. Then the bridegroom came, walking towards the altar over the black stone slab which marged the grave of Charles the First. The trumpets sounded three times, and the bride entered. About this time, the sun burst forth and its rays fell on the Queen's white cap. As the organ pealed forth the first anthem, to Prince Albert's own music, the Queen raised her eyes upwards and sat as if transfixed. Never once did she falter in her resolve.

THE ARRIVAL OF PRINCESS ALEXANDRA

THE QUEEN'S FIRST GRANDCHILD

Arthur Stanley was amazed at the composure of the bridegroom. He said to himself, 'Can this be the boy of last year on the Nile? Can this be the frolicsome creature, for whom all our anxiety was that this marriage should take place, and now at last it is come?' The guns were fired as the Prince put the ring on the bride's finger, and somebody, who looked up to the Queen in that moment, said that she was very much agitated by the guns, 'as if each one went through her.' But still she did not falter. She hurried back to the Castle, when all was over, and waited for them at the top of the grand staircase. When the bride and the bridegroom came, she held them, locked in her arms and, as one of the Ladies wrote, she led them upstairs, 'with that wonderful grace and dignity we know.'

Down at the Windsor station, below the Castle walls, the guests struggled for seats in the train. Ministers of State in their gilded coats, and grand ladies covered with diamonds, wrestling with the rabble for places in what was facetiously called a 'special train.' It was said that the Archbishop of Canterbury had been so pummelled in the crowd on the station that he had called to a policeman, 'I am the Archbishop of Canterbury—how can I be saved?' The policeman was said to have answered, 'The only means by which Your Grace can be saved is to cling to the next carriage that passes.' Nobody vouched for the story, but everybody repeated it. The Castle was buzzing with beauty and gossip. Little Prince Waldemar, aged four years and a half, had begged hard to be excused from the wedding as he wanted to stay in the corridor and play with his new toy donkey. The Queen went from one guest to another, commending this one for his gallantry and that one for her magnificence. But when the bride and bridegroom had driven away, the bride in a white velvet dress and ermine coat, the Queen left the Castle and the tumult. She went down the shaded walk to Frogmore. There, in the quiet gardens where her mother had walked, near to the cedar tree under which they used to drink their tea, she found the mausoleum. Here she was alone.

§ 11 — 1863

THE MARRIAGE of Princess Alexandra was not popular in Prussia, where Bismarck and his Government saw dangers in a close alliance between England and their little Northern neighbour.

More sturdy problems occupied Bismarck and the other powerful men of Europe towards the close of 1863. There were to be three years of distress. First came Poland's struggles to be free of Russia, and then Austria's fears when she suddenly realised Prussia's power. However much the Queen doted upon her bereavement and the memorials, which Gladstone gloomily said 'covered the land,' she did not allow one tittle of power to slip through her fingers, nor one opportunity for influence to pass. She took definite stands in both problems, siding with Bismarck, who believed that Poland's oppression under the Russians was no more severe than she deserved. Palmerston and Lord Russell were more prudent: they favoured Poland's cause. Now, as on other occasions when the battery of her Ministers was too much for her, the Queen turned to the memory of her dead husband. She was able to draw upon Prince Albert's judgment as if he were alive and still at her side. He had left so many memoranda for her guidance. So she was able to abash

Palmerston or Lord Russell by quoting from the opinions of her 'dear angel.'

Prince Albert had fortified the Queen with his knowledge and judgment: in the same way his daughter was increasing her influence in Prussia. The Crown Princess of Prussia was more Prince Albert's child than any of the others. She also sat up to early morning, preparing memoranda, helping her husband to write letters to the King. The energy and clear-cut judgment were alive in the daughter, and she supported and helped her husband in his quarrel with his father, for, like Queen Victoria and the Prince of Wales, they did not agree. Bismarck snubbed the Crown Prince by not answering his letters and the King was so angry with his heir that he threatened to 'take his place in the Army and the Council from him.'[33] The Crown Princess supported 'Fritz' with all her energies and she said, in disgust at the intrigue about her, 'Thank God, I was born in England.' The Queen did not see that the rift between the King and the Crown Prince was the duplicate of the rift she was engendering between herself and her own son, and that to encourage it was dangerous. King Leopold dared to advise her and she received a letter from Brussels in which he said, 'You cannot in your own position promote the disobedience of children, to which after all they are sufficiently inclined.'[34]

She found her support and help in regard to Prussia's ambitions in remembering Prince Albert's view. 'I know that our dear angel Albert always regarded a strong Prussia as a necessity, for which, therefore, it is a sacred duty for me to work.'[35] She clung to this idea with single-minded persistence, although she admitted that the Prussians were dunderheads at diplomacy, and wrote,

27

'Prussia is indeed in a sad state, and the King makes one quite miserable, for he is bent on self-ruin.' Nothing would stem the tide of Prussia's ambition. It was about this time that Bismarck used the 'tremendous phrase' that the German question would be solved only by 'blood and iron.' Prussia began the ambitious frenzies which led to the disaster of 1914. In the south, Catholic Austria stirred restlessly, fearing Prussia's demand for equality of rights 'in all Federal matters.'

In the autumn, leaning on the sacred guidance of her dead husband, the Queen set out for Germany, ostensibly to stay quietly in Rosenau where Albert had lived as a boy. For the first few days she allowed herself to forget England and Palmerston and the dangerous maelstrom of affairs. Here, in the rooms where *he* had played, where the marks of his rapier were still on the nursery wall, and where she could open the shutters of the room in which he was born to hear the thrushes in the chestnuts, as *he* had heard them, she could forget everything but her own pain. For a moment she embraced her grief again. But she was strong and capable of fierce efforts. Any suggestion that her health was better aroused her to protests so vigorous that she proved the suggestions true. 'How good Grey could give you a good account of me is indeed marvellous,' she protested to her Uncle. 'I have been very unwell ...when I talk I get excited and flushed and very feverish, and *that* THEY call being well.' This was in January. In June she wrote again, 'I think my life will *end more* rapidly than any of you think....' But her constitution was such that, coupled with her iron will, it could stand many storms. She was able to turn from her obsession as a widow and become the Queen of England in a second.

While she was resting at Rosenau, with the placid scene of autumn and the harvesters about her, there was a great Congress of reigning Princes at Frankfurt. The fissure between Prussia and the Southern Catholic countries was widening, and the King of Prussia had refused to attend the Congress. The Emperor of Austria therefore presided over the meetings. Alarmed by the estrangement between the two sovereigns, the Queen conquered her depression and attempted the role of peacemaker. For the first time she tried to impose her influence, alone, upon the other rulers in Europe: without her husband, or her Ministers, and without the advice of her Uncle Leopold. 'How beloved Albert, with his wise views and counsels, is missed at such a time!' she wrote.

First she induced the King of Prussia to come to Rosenau. In the Queen's memorandum we read of the last day in August when he accepted her invitation.[36] But the interview was doomed from the beginning. Bismarck had whispered in the King's ear, and he came prejudiced against the Queen's good intentions. She wrote in her memorandum:

'I ... said that I must be allowed to make one observation, which was, how earnestly I hoped that Prussia and Austria would go together; to which the King replied: "But how?" It had been made quite impossible for him.

'...He saw that there was pre-determination on the part of Austria to ruin Prussia, and she had so contrived it, that the odium fell now upon him of having destroyed the unity of Germany. Her conduct had been most false, he repeated. ... The King added that great efforts were made by the Austrians to increase the power of the Catholic Church, and that swarms of priests had arrived in the neighbourhood of Frankfurt, trying to influence the lower orders, in every direction, in favour of Austria.

'... In taking leave, the King's last words were: "I recommend

29

my interests to your care." To which I replied, he might rely upon me with certainty.'

Three days afterwards, Francis Joseph, Emperor of Austria, came to see the Queen in Coburg. 'He was very civil.' With the diligence and prudence learned from her husband, she hurried back to Rosenau after seeing him and wrote a memorandum:

'...the Emperor said to me how glad he was that our Governments were on so friendly a footing, which I naturally reciprocated....I then said that the present moment was one of great importance for Germany, and that I trusted it would lead to unity. To which he replied he hoped so too, but Prussia was a great difficulty.'

One cannot read the memoranda of the two conversations without trying to imagine the scenes as well as comprehend the phrases. For the first time, the Queen was attempting to assert her power and her authority alone. This second interview was in Ehrenburg Castle, in the town of Coburg—an imposing old castle disguised in a sham Gothic shell and filled with gay decoration. In the attic, high above the room in which the Queen sat with the Emperor, was Prince Albert's schoolroom. Here he had learned his first English words. One cannot withhold one's admiration before this first sign of her courage— inviting the two sovereigns and facing the ordeal of trying to impose her wishes upon them, alone. The Queen told the Emperor that she trusted 'there was no disposition to lower Prussia, for that naturally Prussia and Austria must go together,' to which the Emperor answered 'that no one dreamed in Germany of lowering Prussia, which was an impossibility, but that at Berlin great pretensions were raised.'

30

The Queen had attempted the impossible in supposing that she could reconcile the Emperor to Prussia's ambitions. But her effort proved what the later story confirmed, that however much she shunned the Courts and more superficial ceremonies of her position, she never allowed her grief to stand between her and what she considered to be her duty to the Crown, to the people, and to her relationship with the other Sovereigns of Europe. A few weeks afterwards, in a fit of depression, the Queen wrote, 'No respect is paid to *my* opinion now...."[87] But this was not true. Lord Granville had been at hand, although not present, when the Queen spoke to the King and then to the Emperor. When he read the Queen's memoranda, he said that he could not admit that the Queen had any right to feel anything but perfect self-confidence as to the perfect judgment and tact with which she conducted the interviews.[88]

Chapter Four

1863–1866

IN PRUSSIA, the Crown Princess continued to fortify her husband in his struggles against the King. If Princess Alexandra had possessed the same Coburg intellect and perseverance as her sister-in-law, she might have contributed to her husband's early revolts against his mother's authority. The Princess was gracious and beautiful and she was tender with all suffering creatures, but her conquests were made with her heart more than with her mind. Hans Christian Andersen used to tell her fairy stories when she was a child. Excited by his world of make-believe, Princess Alexandra would play among the trees with her sisters and one of their favourite games was to 'wish.' One day, Princess Dagmar said that she wished for power and influence. She became Empress of Russia. All that little Princess Alexandra asked was that she 'should like to be loved.' [39] Such gentle qualities did not give the young Prince of Wales the kind of support which he needed and he still fought a lonely fight, even when he came to the independence of married life at Marlborough House and Sandringham.

On his last journey abroad as a bachelor (while his bride was being warned at Osborne that she might still love her country, Denmark, but that she was not to make her husband a partisan against Denmark's enemy, Prussia), the Prince of Wales had contemplated his future gloomily. He had celebrated his twenty-first birthday in

32

the Bay of Naples. Here, in the bay where Lady Hamilton first met Nelson, who also had single-minded notions about an Englishman's duty, the Prince had received enough black-edged letters from Windsor to keep his attention away from frivolous celebrations of his birthday. There had been only a few garlands hung on the *Osborne* and rockets in the bay at night, with the thin flame of Vesuvius against the sky. The Prince had written, under the weight of what he felt, 'I am well aware that much is expected of me....'[40]

Now that he was married, the Prince made some attempts to fulfil the demands made upon him. But his efforts at action were curbed as much as his lethargy had been censured. He asked his mother to make the Lord Mayor of London a Baronet, because of the joyous reception the people had given him and his bride. The Queen said 'No'—only the reception of a *Sovereign* merited such an honour. When he showed his interests in affairs by going to the House of Lords, she demurred again. It must not be too often.

The letter from the Queen to her son, when his baby was born, began '...This dream is one which I like to dwell on, though it did not, could not bring back my Angel, and I am *ever, ever* lonely....I can't say *how* I love her [Princess Alexandra], how glad I shall be to do anything for that sweet dear creature....I wish now to say a few words again about the *names, sponsors,* and *christening....*I think I shall be able to be present, and hold the dear baby myself, D.V., which, trying though it will be, I *wish to do.*

'...Respecting your own names, and the conversation we had, I wish to repeat, that it was beloved Papa's wish, as well as mine, that you should be called by both, when you became King, and it would be impossible to *drop* your Father's. It would be monstrous, and *Albert alone,* as you truly and amiably say, would *not do,* as there can be only one ALBERT!'[41]

The Prince's answer was short and to the point. '...Regarding the possibility of my ever filling that high position, which God grant may be far, very far distant, I quite understand your wishes about my bearing my two names, although no English Sovereign has ever done so yet, and you will agree with me that it would not be pleasant to be like "Louis Napoleon," "Victor Emmanuel," "Charles Albert," etc., although no doubt there is no absolute reason why it should not be so....'

The Queen had written, as we already know, of her *irrevocable decision*...that Prince Albert's wishes—*his* plans—about everything, *his* views about everything were to be her *law.* '...No human power will make me swerve. ...I apply this particularly as regards our children—Bertie, etc.' The human powers attempted the impossible by trying to influence her, but if there was injustice in the Queen's plan, there was also a mountain of character to help her. The Hon. Emily Eden wrote to Lord Clarendon and said that if Prince Albert had lived, he would have found his son some work to keep him 'out of harm.' *The Times,* in the hands of Delane, who was the friend of both Lady Ely and Lord Torrington, still received secret communications from Windsor. Indeed, Lord Torrington made no bones about writing his reports to Delane upon Windsor Castle note-paper, and signing himself 'Your Windsor Special.' This irregular correspondence between courtier and editor became the inspiration of a plot to help the Prince to establish his position and increase his popularity.

Everybody was enchanted by the Prince of Wales. His parties were amusing and he was already releasing the fetters which had been upon London society for twenty years. When he received three thousand people at the levée, in his mother's name, they declared him to be most cordial—not in the least like his stiff father, who had always seemed to be a moral censor to them. *The Times,* pleading his cause, said that the time had come for entrusting the Prince with some of the duties appropriate to his place in the State. 'There are many public or semi-public duties which no one else can perform as well, and some, perhaps, which no one else, under a monarchy like our own, can perform at all.... The English people will naturally look to the Prince of Wales to give appropriate expressions to their feelings. We do not believe that they will be disappointed, and we feel sure that His Royal Highness, who has won golden opinions as the guest of foreign Sovereigns, will know how to greet the friends of England in his own country.' [42]

This first hint from Delane was mild indeed. Lord Torrington, observing the Queen at Windsor, wrote to him, 'I think your Prince of Wales article has done some good. The Queen feels that you have been very kind, and really, as no one dares to tell her the truth, it is fortunate *you* are able to do so and to be listened to also.' This correspondence was before the Prince's marriage. Delane waited two years before he openly attacked the Queen, this time basing his complaint upon her retirement. For she was shut behind the grey walls of Windsor with almost no social contacts at all. From morning to night she wrote at her desk—long, frigid letters to Lord Palmerston, reproofs for Lord Russell; the stream of correspondence was tremendous. But when her work was ended, the

Queen became the lonely widow again: she knelt beside 'that bed...in an agony of loneliness, grief and despair....' Delane, so his biographer tells us, often announced as a fact in *The Times,* what he hoped to bring about. He played this little editorial trick on, of all days, April the first. 'Her Majesty's loyal subjects,' he printed, 'will be very pleased to hear that their Sovereign is about to break her protracted seclusion. Various announcements encourage the hope that not only will Buckingham Palace resume its place in the world of life, but that Her Majesty will herself appear as its mistress.' Delane dared the Queen's anger. 'They who would isolate themselves from the world and its duties,' he wrote, 'must cease to know and to care, as well as to act, and be content to let things take their course. This in effect they cannot do; this they never do; and the only result is a struggle in which they neither live nor die—neither live as they wish, in the past, nor do their duty in the working world.'

With hasty judgment and fine courage, the Queen indulged the public privilege of 'writing a letter to *The Times.'* General Grey was sent off to London from Windsor with the letter, which was unsigned but in the Queen's own handwriting. It was addressed to Delane. The rather pathetic plea appeared on April 6th.

'An erroneous idea seems generally to prevail, and has latterly found frequent expression in the newspapers, that the Queen is about to resume the place in society which she occupied before her great affliction; that is, that she is about again to hold Levées and Drawing-rooms in person, and to appear as before at Court balls, concerts, etc. This idea cannot be too explicitly contradicted.

'The Queen heartily appreciates the desire of her subjects to see her, and whatever she *can* do to gratify them in this loyal and affectionate wish she *will* do. Whenever any real object is to be attained by her appearing on public occasions, any national interest to be promoted, or anything to be encouraged which is for the good of her people, her Majesty will not shrink, as she has not shrunk, from any personal sacrifice or exertion, however painful.

'But there are other and higher duties than those of mere representation which are now thrown upon the Queen, alone and unassisted—duties which she cannot neglect without injury to the public service, which weigh unceasingly upon her, overwhelming her with work and anxiety.

'The Queen has laboured conscientiously to discharge those duties till her health and strength, already shaken by the utter and ever-abiding desolation which has taken the place of her former happiness, have been seriously impaired.

'To call upon her to undergo, in addition, the fatigue of those mere State ceremonies which can be equally well performed by other members of her family is to ask her to run the risk of entirely disabling herself for the discharge of those other duties which cannot be neglected without serious injury to the public interests.

'The Queen will, however, do what she can—in the manner least trying to her health, strength, and spirits—to meet the loyal wishes of her subjects, to afford that support and countenance to society, and to give that encouragement to trade which is desired of her.

'More the Queen *cannot* do; and more the kindness and good feeling of her people will surely not exact from her.'

Delane waited until the end of the year (December 15th) before he replied, with his editor's 'last word':

'In all bereavements there is a time when the days of mourning should be looked upon as past. The living have their claims as well as the dead; and what claims can be more imperative than those of a great nation and the society of one of the first European capitals? ... No reigning house can afford to confirm in their views those who suggest that the Throne is only an antiquarian relic and royalty itself a ceremony.... It is impossible for a recluse to occupy the British throne without a gradual weakening of that authority which the Sovereign has been accustomed to exert.... For the sake of the Crown as well as of the public, we would therefore beseech her Majesty to return to the personal exercise of her exalted functions. It may be that in time London may accustom itself to do without the palace, but it is not desirable that we should attain that point of republican simplicity. For every reason we trust that now that three years have elapsed, and every honour that affection and gratitude could pay to the memory of the Prince Consort has been offered, her Majesty will think of her subjects' claims and the duties of her high station, and not postpone them longer to the indulgence of an unavailing grief.'

The newspapers were not alone—the once whispered suggestion that the Queen would abdicate in favour of her son became open chatter. The Paris newspapers spoke of this so openly that men of Lord Howden's [43] calm judgment began to think there might be something in it. He wrote to Lord Clarendon that it would have been well, 'for her own interest, happiness and *reputation, to* have abdicated on the day her son came of age. She would then,' he said, 'have left a great name and great regret.' [44]

The people were tiring of a mysterious, withdrawn figure who gave them no sight of the glamour which they had been brought up to expect from royalty. Gossip took on the colour of invention and *The Times* published a paragraph announcing that people employed at Woolwich were to be arrested if they looked out of the windows at the Queen as she passed in her carriage. Mrs. Bruce took the paragraph to the Queen, who was indignant. Again she sought reparation and she sent General Grey to the War Office to enquire into the story. This time he was persuaded not to go to Delane, and the stupid rumour was allowed to grow into a fabulous story. Mrs. Bruce wrote, 'During my afternoon in London...I found people so furious with the Queen that I am quite unhappy about it....' The Queen did not seem to comprehend the fading of her popularity. At Frogmore, on the anniversary which was causing less sympathy and more bitterness among her people, she went again to a short service in the mausoleum—'which we all deprecate,' wrote Lady Augusta. The sermon was to be published. 'Why?'

Chapter Five

§ 1 — 1863–1866

PRINCE ALBERT noted that his son had 'no interest for things, but all the more for persons,' when the Prince of Wales was no more than a boy. He acknowledged that this was the trait which had made the family so popular, but he deplored it. This interest and enthusiasm 'for persons' had distressed his father, but it established the Prince of Wales's popularity from the first day when he became his own master, as host at Marlborough House. His charm was so stimulating to other people that even painters and literary men, with whom he had little in common, were delighted by him. He was eager, and when he spoke to a man, he had the royal talent of making him feel that nothing else in the world mattered.

Holman Hunt has left us a pleasant picture of the Prince of Wales in the early sixties. Hunt had painted the scene of London Bridge during the royal wedding celebrations and the Prince wished to see the picture. He went, apparently, to Holman Hunt's studio. Hunt had included in the crowd the face of Combe, a face no larger than a sixpence, lost in the motley scene. 'I know that man,' said the Prince, 'I have seen him in the hunting field with Lord Macclesfield's hounds. He rides a clever pony about fourteen hands high, and his beard blows over his shoulders. He is the Head of a house of Oxford, and not a college'—as he went on following the trace in his mind—'but I'll tell you— Yes—I remember now—it's the Printing Press, and he rides in a red jacket. Am I right?' And he even remembered the man's name. This memory for faces and talent for reminiscence graced all the occasions of his life, to the end.

Seldom have sons been less like their fathers than in the last four generations of the Royal family. King Edward had risen, an eager, pleasure-loving youth, in the wake of his calm, conscientious father. He was more lenient in judging both his own morals and those of his friends. A fine, unsuspicious nature reveals itself in a letter which he wrote to Lord Granville, when he was a little older.[45] 'I may have many faults,' he said; 'no one is more alive to them than I am; but I have held one great principle in life from which I will never waver, and that is loyalty to one's friends, and defending them if possible when they get into trouble. One often gets into scrapes in consequence, but I consider the risk worth running.'

In spite of the Queen's disapproval, the Prince created his own society—a society which eschewed the conventions and barriers which had been set up by his mother and father. A friend of Lord Clarendon wrote, early in 1866, that Sandringham was 'not at all a nice young Court.'[46] The Prince frequented the houses of the opulent and, with wistful glances of reproof and regret from the stauncher social die-hards, London society became more rich and a little less well-bred. In a few years' time, brewers and actresses were to be among the Prince's friends—Jews and Americans dined with him and he dined with them. After all, no prince before him had been where he had been—America, Canada, France, Italy, Germany, Spain, Turkey, Greece, Egypt, Palestine and Syria. He was the first prince to belong to the world— the first to become tangible to the Empire. The broader

41

field was reflected in the society he chose. In 1864 he became a member of the Jockey Club, and he later raced his own horses. He created the programme for fashionable society—Epsom, Doncaster and Ascot shone again—he greeted foreign princes on the steps of the Yacht Squadron at Cowes, he gave a lead to the season on the Riviera, and, after a few years, he awakened Homburg and made it famous through his patronage. He rebuked the Lord Chamberlain for excising the daring indiscretions in Mlle. Schneider's performance of *La Belle Hélène* and he smoked cigars before ladies. The older ones were shocked, remembering the day when their menfolk withdrew to the kitchen and smoked up the chimney lest the abomination should pollute the house. The Prince travelled in hired cabs: he frequented the Garrick Club and the Savage. Every now and then he enjoyed a harmless dalliance in Paris, where restaurants and dishes were named after him. The Queen represented and sympathised with the point of view of the middle classes: all their limitations and instinct for safety. She allowed herself to be a shrine to which the gossipers brought their stories. She remonstrated with her son and likened the English aristocracy, with whom he enjoyed his leisure, to the *noblesse* of France on the eve of the French Revolution. His reply was courageous—'...they are the mainstay of the country,' he wrote, and he suggested that the alternative would be Mr. Bright's idea, of a Sovereign and the people, and no class between. As Sir Sidney Lee has said, the Prince's society was based upon 'the bracing principle of *Non unde es, sed qui sis*'—'a man's individuality counts for more than his origin.' But the note of the conversation at Marlborough House was far from being merely boisterous and ephemeral. With his rich and amusing friends the Prince

42

retained also friendships with men 'of the sedatest vocations and character.' He slowly gained influence and power through his social life—soldiers met politicians at Sandringham: sportsmen met professional citizens and found new and better ways of using their leisure and their money. The flagrantly rich were drawn into philanthropy, and, for the good of both, the scholarly and the merely human found themselves at the same table.

The Prince had a great talent as a host; his Princess was his less obtrusive, charming and beautiful companion. While the Queen hugged her grief at Windsor, the Prince and the Princess established their own kingdom in London. The changes may have ended the tradition of social pigeon-holes and they may have shaken the tenets of taste and behaviour. But the changes were inevitable and they came to Britain naturally, not in one fell swoop, as in Russia, Germany and Austria, where 'the naked sword of the proletariat' achieved in blood that which happened in England by slow evolution, with a royal lead.

The Welshman, Brinley Richards, composed *God Bless the Prince of Wales* in 1862. Slowly, it came to be sung all over the country.

§ II—1864-1866

THE QUEEN's mind was influenced by her bereavement up to the time of the first Jubilee, but early in 1864 she made valiant efforts at self-discipline. Her talents and duties sorted themselves slowly, when her paroxysms of grief had passed: her talents lay in calm censorship of ministerial hastiness, care that the public should not be gulled by knaves, and in her freedom from pettiness. Her greatness cannot be indicated in one heroic scene, for it was through her influence rather than her acts that she re-established her power. The Queen lacked the creative talents of the Prince Consort, who had conceived Alder-shot, the Great Exhibition and the museums and schools of Kensington Gore. But she possessed another quality which was rich in him: the balance of sanity which made it possible for her to calm the agitated and to be non-committal with the sour and sullen. Every apparent error must be judged in the light of her final achievement: the establishment of Constitutional Monarchy, during a century in which Government passed from the few into the hands of the many. Between 1832 and 1884, the voters in the country were increased by three and a half millions. In almost every other country this experiment in democratic government and Constitutional Monarchy failed. Queen Victoria's character and power contributed very definitely to the success of the experiment in England. She

> ... Kept her throne unshaken still,
> Based broad upon the people's will.

One sees something of the entanglement of her problems in the history of the Schleswig-Holstein invasion in 1864. Denmark and Germany both claimed the two Baltic states of Schleswig and Holstein. The Queen had already declared her German sympathies and she was stirred, every now and then, by a letter from her daughter in Prussia. In June of the previous year, the Princess had written, 'Thank God, I was born in England.' But the chameleon qualities of the Coburgs were strong in her. Her father had been able to 'make a fist' at Germany after he had been in England a few years, and King Leopold had been able to forget his Protestant upbringing and become a Belgian and a Catholic. In the same way the Princess Royal soon became intoxicated with the Prussian spirit. When the German soldiers invaded the northern States, she suddenly forgot her pride in England. 'I would almost quarrel with my real and best friends in dear England rather than forget that I belong to this country, the interest of which I have so *deeply* at heart,' she wrote to her mother in May of 1864. The comments in the British parliament made her livid, and she thought that the British newspapers were 'absurd, unjust and rude.'[47] 'I can see nothing inhuman or improper in any way in [the] bombardment of SONDERBURG: it was necessary and we hope it has been useful.' Bismarck's 'blood and iron' were already at work. With some justification, the Princess wondered what Palmerston, who was the ringleader in the agitation against the Prussian spirit, would say if *we* enquired about Admiral Kuper's[48] 'not so intensely scrupulous' bombardments in Japan. Her letter to the Queen was a fine trumpeting of Prussia's anger over 'the continued meddling and interfering of England in other people's affairs.'[49]

The Queen looked up from the Crown Princess's letters to see her Danish daughter-in-law, wistfully conscious that her country was not in favour. News came from Marlborough House that Princess Alexandra did not sleep at night for distress over her father and his people. There was a third complication: Lord Palmerston and Lord Russell were indignant at Prussia's ruthlessness. Palmerston's blood boiled at the suggestion that the Austrian fleet might sail up past the English coast to capture Copenhagen. The British fleet was summoned home in the face of such dangers. Even this action made the Queen anxious. On his death-bed, Prince Albert had

saved us from war with America over the Trent case.
Now, in imitation, the Queen raised *her* hand against the
impetuousness of the Ministers. The fleet might be summoned home: she agreed. But there were to be 'no more
orders' without consulting her—no 'threats.'

The Queen's calm decisions kept her aloof from the
extravagant excitement. She had an unerring sense of
what was right and a cold disregard for passing fancies.
She was delighted, some years later,[50] when Lord Halifax
was talking to her of the mistakes made in foreign affairs
under Lord Russell and Lord Palmerston. He said to her
that it 'was not to be told what good' she had done in
that time 'by checking their reckless course.' He was quite
vehement with the Queen and said that he would repeat
this 'to the world at large.' She was similarly calm now
that Prussia and Denmark were at war. She wrote to Lord
Russell saying that she would *never,* if she could prevent
it, allow this country to be involved in a war in which *no
English* interests were concerned.[51] Lord Russell replied
next day '…if English honour were to be concerned,
Your Majesty would no doubt feel bound to defend it.'[52]
The Queen did not pause before sending her reproof. 'She
must observe that she does not require to be reminded
of the honour of England, which touches her more nearly
than anyone else.' Then came the inevitable sentence
about the 'one wise, far-seeing and *impartial* head who
would have guided them.' The Ministers sometimes became a little tired of Prince Albert's memory: it was gall-
ing to be reminded, every day, that the only great man in
England was dead. But the Queen was never petty. There
might be an angry letter in the morning and then, because a speech had pleased her, a kind and appeasing
letter in the afternoon. She was honest with her Ministers

and, because of this, they were never in confusion or doubt as to her meaning and her intentions. The Queen of Holland, who never liked her very much, admitted that 'friend or foe' never found her 'untrue.'[53] Lord Granville admitted that her calm had 'not only saved the country, but the Government itself, from many false steps.'[54] The King of Prussia never missed an opportunity of saying how much he owed to her for her endeavours to keep peace. He even went so far as to add that peace would never have been preserved but for the Queen.[55] She may have angered the Ministers by her letters beginning 'Her Majesty will insist,' but no reminiscences or letters of the period deprecate the motives behind her judgment: she stirred up opposition and anger, but never contempt. Some of the Ministers wrote of her as 'the Missus,' but only in play.

A few of the newspapers pilloried the Queen over her Prussian sympathies and the Ministers fussed and sent her the cuttings. Her daughter fussed, too, and she wrote excited letters to her mother. The Queen, who was the object of the attacks, was as cool as a cucumber. She was the only person not disturbed. 'She must be content to see unjust remarks in obscure newspapers and must continue to disregard them,' she wrote. She believed in what she was doing and none could dismay her. When an armistice was declared and when the Queen heard of the Germans and Danes, breathless after battle, she urged that the discussions between the powers should not be hurried. 'By giving time,' she said, 'the passions on all sides will be calmed and cooled down.'

Her sense won the day. Again in April of 1864, we find the Queen restraining the politicians when they were capricious over the visit of Garibaldi to England. English people deprecate any reformers who arise in their own country, but they have an odd and perverted habit of hailing the revolutionaries who have shaken the peace of other nations. There is much slick diplomacy in this, for England gives the impression of opening her arms to the revolutionary or the oppressed, at the same time closing her doors to them. The high-falutin phrases of the politicians do not always concur with the instructions given to the immigration officers at Dover and Folkestone. The English believe that by flattering and honouring dangerous men, their power for evil is nullified. Palmerston observed that it was 'useful' that Garibaldi had been taken up by the aristocracy as it did not leave him free to be taken up by agitators. 'Garibaldi has all the qualifications for making him a popular idol in this country,' wrote Lord Granville; 'he is a goose, but that is considered to be an absence of diplomatic guile.'[56] Lord Russell thought him very frank and open in countenance and manners and even Lord Palmerston talked of his 'simplicity of character.' Some of the ladies at the Dowager Duchess of Sutherland's party went so far as to curtsey to him. The Queen was not hoodwinked by such adulation. She regretted the 'extravagant excitement,' which showed little dignity in the nation. Simple or not simple, frank or not frank, he was 'a revolutionist leader' and this label was enough to make him the enemy of the purposes of herself and England.

No phase of the Queen's reign shows how conscientiously she viewed her trust as sovereign as vividly as her distress over the freedom of the Church of Scotland. In November of 1866, she wrote a letter to Dean Wellesley [of Windsor] which shines in the volumes of her correspondence, as a proof of her devotion to the principles of constitutional rule. The Archbishop of Canterbury had countenanced and encouraged an Episcopalian movement in Scotland, and Dr. Macleod, the Queen's 'liberal-minded' and 'thoroughly Christian' friend, had come to Windsor to protest against a campaign which the Queen described as *'most serious,* and indeed *alarming* to the safety of the Church of Scotland.' Many members of the Scottish aristocracy had already been converted from Presbyterianism to Episcopalianism. The Queen wrote of the disadvantages of such conversions, 'establishing a religion for the rich, and another for the poor, and thus alienating the people from their superiors, and producing a want of sympathy between them.' The Archbishop of Canterbury had himself been to Scotland and he had permitted his Bishops to speak of *'the* Church' implying that the Scotch establishment was *'no* Church,' and her Sacraments not to be considered as such. Then come the phrases which show us the Queen's conscience. '...the Queen takes a solemn engagement, on her accession, to maintain the Established Church of Scotland, and any attempt to subvert it is *contrary* to Law, and indeed subversive of that respect for *existing Institutions* which, above all, the Archbishops and Bishops *ought* to do *everything* to maintain, and she *will* maintain it.

'But, quite apart from this, the Queen considers this movement as *most* mischievous. The Presbyterian Church is essentially *Protestant,* and, as such, *most* valuable. The Reformation in this country was *never* fully completed, and had we applied the pruning knife more severely, we should *never* have been exposed to the dangers to which the Church of England is *now* exposed, and for which the Queen thinks it will be *absolutely* necessary to take some measures.

'The Queen feels, *more strongly* than words *can* express, the duty which is imposed upon her and her family, to maintain the *true* and *real principles* and *spirit* of the *Protestant* religion; for her family was brought over and placed on the throne of these realms *solely* to maintain it; and the Queen will *not* stand the attempts made to destroy the simple and truly Protestant faith of the Church of Scotland, and to bring the Church of England as near the Church of Rome as they possibly can.'

§ III — 1864

THE FIRST great division of opinion between the Queen and the Prince of Wales was over the war between Germany and Denmark. The Prince Consort, in contemplating his son's marriage with a Danish Princess, had said, 'We take the Princess, but *not* her relations.' [57] Such cold diplomacy was all right before the wedding, but Prince Albert had not fully considered his son's character in placing this limitation on the marriage. The sight of his wife's distress unnerved the Prince of Wales and influenced him. He became pro-Danish, and while he was discreet in withholding his opinions from the public, his naturally compassionate nature made him give the Princess every sympathy. The Queen had already been reprimanded in the newspapers for abetting the Prussians: it would not do for her son to declare his allegiance to the opposite camp. She avoided speaking to the Prince herself: she chose the strange course of asking Lord Clarendon to speak to her son instead. She pointed out, in the letter of instruction to Lord Clarendon, that the Prince of Wales was 'bound by so many ties of blood to Germany' and then added, rather callously, that he was bound 'only quite lately, by marriage, to Denmark.'[58] Lord Clarendon went to the Prince of Wales and found him 'very reasonable and right-minded,' but he nevertheless 'heartily sympathised with the Princess' and there could be no doubt as to the 'feeling he must be known to entertain.' This was the beginning of a great change in the English Royal family: the slow driving of the wedge between Prussia and England. For the Prince began, at this time, to draw away more and more from friendship with Prussia. His comment on his sister's sympathies was apt. He thought her 'too German in England and too English in Germany.'

During the interview with Lord Clarendon, the Prince made his first definite effort to play the part of international mediator. The intrusion was condemned by the Queen. The Prince said to Lord Clarendon 'that occasions might arise when he could be of more use than Sir A. Paget[59] in making known to the King and Queen [of Denmark] the wishes' of the British Government and that it would be 'a great satisfaction to him to be so employed.'[60] Still communicating with her son through a secretary and a Minister, the Queen said that the Prince's offer 'must be accepted with *extreme caution.*' In June the Prince made another attempt. He spoke to Lord Russell with a view to seeing, from time to time, copies of despatches. The Ministers were on the Prince's side: they saw the advantages which would come by broadening his knowledge and his interest in the government of the country. Lord Russell said that he felt that the Queen might 'with advantage from time to time direct that despatches of interest might be sent to the Prince of Wales.' The Queen was sympathetic, but she said that she could not help 'objecting to the *principle,* which would

51

be thus admitted, of separate and independent communication between the Prince of Wales and her Government.'[61]

The Queen's care was justified, for serious Constitutional ethics were involved. But one wonders why the correspondence between mother and son should have been carried on through Ministers and secretaries. The necessary ruthless decisions might have been explained in a quiet conversation.

Chapter Six

ONE OF the most personal influences upon the Queen's widowhood was the simple domestic life at Balmoral and the fidelity of the sincere, blunt-tongued Scottish servants who attended upon her there: none more than Brown and Grant who enjoyed special privileges in the Queen's patronage and friendship.

The relationship has provided much fanciful gossip among people who do not understand the Queen's character, or the deeply personal devotion which can exist between servant and mistress in Scotland, where class distinctions are not as pernicious as in England. There has been a general rumour, persisting to this day, that the Queen's devotion to John Brown was emotional. It has even been said that they were married in the Scottish Church. If we did not know from observation of the Queen's character that this is both ridiculous and impossible, we could turn to other evidence and find satisfaction.

About a year before the death of the late Lord Davidson, the author walked with him through a beautiful park in the Thames valley. This happy experience was at the close of a visit of several days, during which he came to know the Archbishop as one of the strongest and most saintly characters of a century. Lord Davidson broke down the barriers between Queen and priest, in the later years of her reign. The Queen's childlike candour and inability to deceive made her pour out her most intimate feelings to Lord Davidson when he was Dean of Windsor. In talking of the relationship between the Queen and John Brown, Lord Davidson said that it was unwise and that it was a source of concern to all those who were close to the Queen, but that one had only to know the Queen personally to realise how innocent it was.

After Brown died, the Queen wrote a monograph upon him and wished to publish it. Any but foolish gossip seekers must see here a proof of the innocence with which she regarded her servant. The Queen consulted Lord Davidson and he told her that if she *did* publish the book, he would resign from the Deanery. His was an uncompromising honesty which would not be intimidated by the royal judgment. The book was not published. As Dean of Windsor, coming into the daily life of the Court, a man of Lord Davidson's character would not have tolerated the relationship which has been so foolishly suggested in the pages of some of the Queen's biographers.

Queen Victoria's Court was made up of people of definite character and high moral courage. It was part of her greatness that she never attracted second-rate people about her. Women like Jane Lady Churchill, Jane, Marchioness of Ely, Lady Augusta Stanley, and Mrs. Robert Bruce knew her from hour to hour. They would have retired from the Court, upon the force of their own characters, if the rumour had been true. The author has talked many times, over a period of eight years, to one Lady-in-Waiting to the Queen. She lived with the Queen in the simple domestic life of the villa in Cannes, where Brown attended upon his mistress. She has said many times that the relationship was unwise, but that it grew out of a curious ignorance in the Queen's character: an ignorance which will be explained later.

To write biography upon the basis of the reported *acts*

of a person's life is dangerous. The biographer's task is to judge, select and arrange the actions of his subject's life, according to motives and instincts. These he must discover, or fail. When we judge the Queen in the light of her motives and instincts, the accusation against her is absurd and, when disgust has passed, faintly comic.

We are still left with a desire to understand why the Queen allowed Brown to become such an intimate servant. All people are unreasonable upon some points. It was in dealing with her servants that Queen Victoria was sometimes exasperating to her family and to her Court. This has been true of so many sovereigns. The author remembers speaking to a reigning Prince with an inheritance going back to the fifth century. He said, rather extravagantly, 'Often during my reign, I have been obliged to mistrust my Ministers and to doubt my friends. But my servants I never doubt. They must be my friends. I could not live with them from day to day without this assurance.'

The hedged-in life and the estrangement from ordinary friendships which is the lot of Royal persons offers a little more help in our search for understanding this peculiar obsession. To Queen Victoria, servants could do no wrong. One recalls the early story of the drunken footman at Windsor who imperilled the Castle by dropping a lighted lamp down the steps when he stumbled. The Master of the Household had long tried to be rid of the man, for he was a sot. A long report was written upon the man's drunkenness and sent to the Queen. She returned it, with the two words 'Poor man' written in the margin.

On another day, at Osborne, some secret matter was discussed at the dinner table. It reached the London newspapers and was published. Some of the gentlemen of the

Court knew that one of the servants was in the habit of divulging information to the press. They told the Queen and she never mentioned the subject again. The drunkenness and pilfering among the servants at Windsor was an open scandal. Some of the town shopkeepers robbed the Queen so brazenly that when King Edward came to the throne, the entire shopping arrangements of the Court had to be revised. The royal servants squandered and indulged in a way which exasperated those in authority. But the Queen would never budge when the complaints were brought to her. It was an amazing, unreasonable and odd indulgence and it helps us to begin to understand her acceptance of John Brown's candour and simplicity. In some ways his character was the same as that of his mistress.

'She is absolutely the most truthful woman I have ever known,' John Bright said of the Queen. John Brown was similarly blessed. Once a lady of noble birth and exalted name went to the Palace, and somebody asked where she was. Brown answered, 'There's the woman you want.' The 'woman' heard him and complained to the Queen that John Brown had insulted her. The Queen answered, 'Well, but after all, wasn't he right? What else are you and I but women?' There was a simple, pleasant bluntness hiding behind the royal manner. Lying was anathema to her. Once at Balmoral, some musicians came to play for the Queen. Towards the end of the performance, she leaned towards one of her Ladies and said, 'What am I to do? I do not like them and I am not going to say that I do.' Nor would she. The phrases of thanks might have soothed the vanity of the singers, but they contained no word which would cause an ache to the Queen's conscience.

This honesty found its full flowering in Scotland, which was John Brown's home. He came from beside the Dee, which was the cradle and the grave of the Queen's domestic happiness. In the first years of her married life, Balmoral had been her only escape from London. Even Osborne was perlously near enough for Ministers to travel down and stay for the night. Prince Albert had loved Balmoral best, seeing something of the beauty of Thuringia in the mountains and something of the single-minded candour of the Thuringian peasants in the Scottish servants who attended him there. The purely English character, suspicious with class obsessions, had never been wholly attractive to him. When the Prince died, John Brown had already been in the Royal employ for twelve years.

Brown was singled out for a personal service at the time of the Prince's death, which gives us another reason for understanding the Queen's devotion to him. While she was melancholy at Osborne, her family and the members of the Court were distressed because she would not take any exercise. They hit upon the idea of bringing her pony from Balmoral, with Brown to lead her and to attend upon her. In the days when she wanted to be free of family and Ministers, it was Brown who went out with her upon her dismal little pony rides about the gardens of Osborne. He had been her husband's servant and she naturally saw in him a link with all the deeply personal recollections of Balmoral.

The Queen understood John Brown and he must have understood her. She might often be perplexed by the 'cleverness' of Ministers, for the Queen was not 'clever.' She might often be harassed by their trickery, for she did not understand subterfuge. But the unvarnished truths of

John Brown she did understand. One day at Balmoral she wanted a table for her sketching materials. Two or three were brought to her, but they were either too high or too low. Brown lost his patience. 'This maun dae,' he said, 'for thae canna' mak' one for ye.' On another day, he disapproved of some garment the Queen was wearing and he said, 'What's this you've got on the day?' To a woman whose character was for ever greater than her intellect, Brown must have seemed to be a rock of strength. His merits were never admitted very generously by his contemporaries, but, to the Queen, Brown could do no wrong. Only princes who have been surrounded by courtiers and servants all their lives could appreciate the refreshment and trust which could arise from such honest service.

The Queen was not saved from public insult over the friendship with her servant. '...wicked and idle lies about poor, good Brown' appeared in the Scottish newspapers. She wrote to Lord Charles Fitzroy [62] of this and of the rumours in London, as *merely* the result of *ill-natured* gossip in the higher classes' caused, she said, because they were dissatisfied at not being able to force her out of her retirement and also by 'love of ill-natured finding fault.' She ignored the gossip and announced her attitude in the last sentence of her letter. 'The Queen will quietly and firmly continue to do what she thinks and knows to be right, though it will leave a painful, bitter feeling in her heart, towards many—not easily to be eradicated.'

The simplicity of the Queen's life at Balmoral cannot be over-emphasised. She seemed to lose all consciousness of her exalted position. 'Those dreadful reporters' exasperated her when she went out on the hills for her picnic lunch, sending Brown down to a cottage to fill the kettle. She was pleased when she drove with the Duchess of

Sutherland, because the people did not recognise *her*—
excited when she ate haggis or when one of the cottagers
patted her on the arm and told her that her daughter was
'a great pet.' One day, two little children were drowned
in the burn. The Queen sat for hours on the bank with
the people from the village, waiting for the bodies to be
found. And afterwards, when she had returned to the
castle, she bethought herself of her humble neighbour.
So she went out again and 'drove up to warn Mrs. William Brown never to let dear little Albert run about alone,
or near to the burn.' Brown and the other Highland servant, Grant, understood the desire for simplicity. They
had been on all the old expeditions when the Queen and
Prince Albert would sleep in small inns, unrecognised,
enjoying their meals together. They had been from cottage to cottage at her heels, the Queen carrying a big roll
of Scottish linsey, from which she cut lengths for the old
women's petticoats. These people had no conception of
royal glory. She was their Queen in the same way that
their Lairds were the heads of their families. During the
glory of the Jubilee, when the Queen might have focussed
her eyes upon all splendour, a woman died beside the
Dee. Her friends did not even contemplate the wonder of
what was happening in London. 'The Queen will be
greetin' for she was awfu' fond of her,' they said. And
this was true, for the Queen paused in the tide of splendour to send a message to the family of Mistress
M'Donald. In return, the devotion of the Scottish people
sometimes assumed astonishing forms. When the Queen
was older, she usually went south for a winter holiday.
While in Florence one winter, she expressed her wish to
see Venice. But this was not easy, for Venetian palaces
seldom have bedrooms on the canal level and the Queen

was no longer able to walk up stairs. A loyal and rich
Scottish merchant named Malcolm coupled invention
with kindness and he wrote to Lady Layard,[63] suggesting
that as the Queen could not climb stairs and as lifts were
still almost unknown in Venice, he would lend his
palazzo to the Queen and add a special device for her
ascent to her bedroom. He proposed a crane which would
extend over the canal, and a basket in which Her Majesty
could be hoisted to her room. Nor did his hospitality end
there. He would also provide the gondolas. Because of
the Queen's love for Scotland, the gondoliers were to be
dressed in kilts.[64]

One day, on the anniversary of the Prince's birth, Grant
led the Queen to the memorial cairn near to Balmoral
Castle. He said quite simply, 'I thought you would like
to be here to-day, on *his* birthday.' To any other people
in the land, Prince Albert's birthday would have been
spoken of to her as 'His Royal Highness's birthday.' To
the people about Balmoral, it was 'his' birthday. Herein,
perhaps vaguely, one may find much to help one to understand why the Scottish servants were allowed so many
privileges.

Once, the Queen's carriage swayed from the main road,
in the dark, and Brown was obliged to walk, leading the
Queen home on her pony. It was a rainy, miserable day.
Next morning, the Queen was much distressed to find
that poor Brown's legs had been cut by the edge of his
wet kilt, just at the back of the knee. He had 'said nothing about it.' A hundred little scenes tumble out on the
pages of the Queen's Journal, to show what an affectionate, personal relationship it was between Queen and servant. None perhaps more thrilling than the account of
Brown rushing to the Queen's carriage at Buckingham

Palace and seizing the miscreant who had interrogated her with a petition and a pistol. On this occasion, it seems that he saved her life.

The judgment of those who knew the Queen was that the relationship between herself and Brown was wholly innocent, but that it would have been 'expedient' if she had moderated it. Her answer to this would have been her answer to her Prime Minister who used the word to her: 'I have been taught, My Lord, to judge between what is right and what is wrong: but *expediency* is a word I neither wish to hear again nor to understand.'

Chapter Seven

§1 — 1865

In october, Lord Palmerston died, 'in the plenitude of his political and intellectual power...plucky and Palmerston to the last moment.'[65] The Queen did not write unkindly of his death. She turned from her usual reproaches and she remembered, with feeling, that his cynical, ungracious figure was a link with the old days. He had lived for eighty-one years, and he had seemed like a shade, remaining with her from the giddy epoch before she was Queen. But there were phrases in her letters which showed that she felt Eternity's gain to be also her own. '...poor Lord Palmerston'[66] she wrote to her uncle. 'It is very *striking,* and is another link with the past—the happy past—which is gone, and in many ways he is a great loss. He had many valuable qualities, though many bad ones....But I *never* liked him, or could ever the least respect him, nor could I forget his conduct on certain occasions to my Angel. He was very vindictve, and *personal* feelings influenced his political acts very much. Still, he is a great loss! I shall have troubles and worries...I sometimes wish I could throw everything up and retire into private life....'

The Queen did not retire: she imposed her will in the reshuffling of offices with sturdy enthusiasm. She hated changes, but she watched the moves at Westminster anxiously. Only a few weeks before, she had heard from her daughter that the King of Prussia was 'under the influence of a clever, unprincipled man' who had completely changed him. This was Count Bismarck, who was arming his soldiers with the new needle-guns, to make battle still more terrible. No politician or soldier was to be allowed to usurp the Queen's rights and power in this way. She was aware of every move. Her letters to her Ministers were numerous: her wishes were emphatically expressed. Lord Russell became Prime Minister again, in his seventy-fourth year: otherwise the Ministry was not drastically changed because of Palmerston's death. Lord Russell was not as self-willed or complicated as Lord Palmerston had been. The Queen had disliked Palmerston because he was complex and unscrupulous: two aspects of human nature which she could never understand. He had once written: [67] 'When people come to the point to which you wish to bring them, you ought not to be too nice about the road they have chosen for getting there.' To a woman like the Queen, who found the simple word 'expedient' repugnant, such ethics in her Prime Minister were frankly shocking.

§ II — 1866

IT WAS not until February of 1866 that the Queen could be induced to open Parliament again. The mass of people poured over from Lambeth and from the East, past the place where Cromwell's head had been impaled upon a pike. The people from the West of London drove down, past the statue of Charles the First in Trafalgar Square. The lesson of Cromwell and the Stuarts was one that they had forgotten to heed. Their Queen was to appear from the dungeons of her bereavement. She came from Osborne, 'much exhausted,' and she drove through the

streets of London. From the pavements, the windows and
the balconies, she was seen by a new generation. This
was before the day of the press photographer: many of
the people who had waited since dawn did not even
know what their Queen looked like. For them she was a
dim oracle. '...she looked grave, but she bowed kindly
and unceasingly on all sides and sat forward as one would
have wished.'[68] Dean Stanley remarked how much more
enthusiastic the cheering for 'the Wales Couple' had been,
than for the Queen. In some places unkind things were
said and a man in the crowd was heard to say, 'If she
does not bow, I'll strike her!' But she did bow, gravely,
as the carriages rolled on, through a day so fine that it
might have been a day in May.

In her own Journal the Queen wrote, 'A fine morning.
Terribly nervous and agitated....Dressing after luncheon,
which I could hardly touch. Wore my ordinary evening
dress, only trimmed with miniver, and my cap with a
long flowing tulle veil, a small diamond and sapphire
coronet rather at the back, and diamonds outlining the
front of my cap.

'It was a fearful moment for me when I entered the
carriage *alone,* and the band played; also when all the
crowds cheered, and I had great difficulty in repressing
my tears...the people seemed to look at me with sympathy. We had both windows open, in spite of a very
high wind. When I entered the House, which was very
full, I felt as if I should faint. All was silent and all eyes
fixed upon me, and there I sat alone....'[69]

The Lord Chancellor read the Queen's Speech as she
sat upon the throne. Her Empire was growing in territory and in people, and most of her subjects were living
in peace. The mad Irish were up to their old tricks again,

but the Maoris in New Zealand were more obedient and European neighbours were comparatively quiet. Her Uncle Leopold had died at the end of a successful, constructive career: her daughter Helena was engaged to marry Prince Christian of Schleswig-Holstein. On the West Coast of Africa and in the Persian Gulf, commerce and morality were sailing hand in hand, for the trade in slaves was going down and the trade in merchandise was going up. The American Civil War was past. At the end of the address, there was a hint at Parliamentary Reform.

When the speech was over, the Lord Chancellor turned to the Queen and bowed his obeisance. She 'slightly but courteously returned the salute.' Then she rose from the throne, stepped down and kissed the Princess of Wales, and walked out, with the poise and grace which thrilled people, even when she was old. Delane softened. Although he referred to the grief 'which everyone hoped would have been more speedily lessened,' he allowed his journalist to write in *The Times* of 'the loftiest and most beloved head in the realm.'

One can guess the tumult of emotions which assailed the Queen. She walked out, past the stiff figures, on the arm of her son. She hurried back to Osborne—almost alone, 'terribly shaken, exhausted, and unwell from the violent *nervous shock* of the effort she made....' Princess Helena watched her anxiously and wrote of her mother more calmly, as being 'softened and gratified and in a good frame.' [70]

§ III — 1866

THE YEAR 1866 saw a turning of the tide in the Queen's widowhood, for she made still more efforts to calm the public restlessness over her retirement. After the opening of Parliament in February, which she likened to 'an execution,' she seemed to recover and to find a little of her old courage. She held Courts at Buckingham Palace and she went to Aldershot: she attended two Royal weddings, one the marriage of her daughter, Princess Helena. She even looked on at the Highland games at Braemar, full of conversation, and she opened the Aberdeen waterworks. She drove through the crowded streets of Wolverhampton to unveil still another memorial to Prince Albert. These busy appearances seemed to help to conquer her obsession. The change manifested itself in her private life, and when Lady Augusta Stanley went into waiting, in December, she saw the signs of the new courage: the Queen 'most sweet,' no longer repining, talking, not as one unique in sorrow, but as 'one of ourselves,' and, an eminently good sign, she spoke 'of no affairs of her own.' The brighter prospect went out beyond the Castle in its influence. People began to talk of the Queen more kindly, as one alive and near to them, and not as one estranged in sorrow. The last public protest against her seclusion was made early in December, at a Reform meeting in St. James's Hall. Then her champion was none other than her political enemy, John Bright. He astounded everybody by saying, 'I am not accustomed to stand up in defence of those who are the possessors of crowns; but I could not sit here and hear that observation without a sensation of wonder and pain. I think there has been, by many persons, a great injustice done to the Queen in reference to her desolate and widowed position. And I venture to say this, that a woman—be she Queen of a great realm, or be she the wife of one of your labouring men—who can keep alive in her heart a great sorrow

66

for the lost object of her life and affection, is not at all likely to be wanting in a great and generous sympathy with you.' [71] John Bright had touched the main-spring of the Queen's despair. Her womanly instincts needed male support and encouragement. When these were taken from her, she was at sea, and she fell into the sin of self-pity. Only a man could help to divert her attention from the dead to the living. It was in this year that she began her friendship with Benjamin Disraeli, finding in him the safety and kindness none of her English Ministers had given her since Melbourne and Peel. Even if the Queen did not wholly comprehend the field of creative talent, she knew it by instinct, as being different from pure efficiency. Disraeli was a creator as Prince Albert had been. Also, both Prince and Jew had suffered from the same bitter accusation of the English—they were not 'gentlemen' according to the accepted tenets. The Queen knew the complacency and the ordered talents of Palmerston, Lord Russell and Gladstone, but her woman's instinct allowed her to search more deeply into the heart of Mr. Disraeli. She admired courage and she knew creative talent, even if it spoke in a language which she did not wholly comprehend. She had seen it before.

Somebody has already made the obvious and interesting division of the Queen's life into three separate stories. First, the girlhood, in which her innocent devotion to Lord Melbourne made it possible for him to guide her over the first cataracts of her reign. Then the matron, radiant in the security of her married life. Then, as the third story, the romantic friendship with Disraeli which gave pleasure, confidence and even purpose to her widowhood. We find, with this division, the gap of years of which we have been reading, between 1861, when the

Prince Consort died, and 1866, when Disraeli came into the Royal circle again, as Chancellor of the Exechequer. These were the empty years in which she made her greatest mistakes as a mother and as a Queen. She needed male guidance, without any reckoning of emotions or sex: she was incomplete without the different kinds of help which she received from Lord Melbourne, Prince Albert and Benjamin Disraeli, in the three seasons of her reign. She admitted the desolation which overwhelmed her when she was not thus supported. Some years later she wrote, with curious humility, in her Journal:

'I feel how sadly deficient I am, and how over-sensitive and irritable, and how uncontrollable my temper is, when annoyed and hurt. But I am so overcome, so vexed, and in such distress about my country, that that must be my excuse. I will pray daily for God's help to improve.' [72]

There was another reason why the Queen came to find that Disraeli was a friend after her own heart. When his wife died in 1873, he was alone. This allowed the Queen to see more deeply into his nature, for she also knew the exile of bereavement. However confident Disraeli may have seemed as a statesman, however ruthless in forcing the issues of his life, nobody can read his letters without discovering the wistful, Jewish sense of inferiority and loneliness which no achievement or power could kill. As he said, power came to him 'twenty years too late' to represent fulfilment.

Mr. Disraeli had another string to his bow. He was so very different from the tiresome Mr. Gladstone. There were no half shades in the Queen's likes and dislikes: she was governed by definite affections and equally healthy antipathies. Mr. Gladstone did not 'fit in': he was a

stranger in the Court when he came down to Windsor,
the sort of man who made people self-conscious by the
way he mumbled grace before dinner. When he first
came down from London to stay with them all in the
Castle, the Ladies had thought him very agreeable. 'And
oh! What a charming voice!' But the charm had faded.
Next month, when he departed, they were sad, but they
dubbed him 'a thought too systematic.' The same witness
said in November of 1866, that he had 'no possible understanding of a joke.' This excluded him from the homely
relationships at Windsor and the Queen was glad when
the Government collapsed at the end of the year. With
Mr. Disraeli, the story was different. Prince Albert had
said that 'the Jew had not one single element of a gentleman in his composition.' This was forgotten in 1866.
The success which came to him in his parleys with the
Queen stirred older statesmen to cruel gibes. Lord Clarendon wrote, 'The Jew, "the most subtle beast in the field,"
has, like Eve's tempter, ingratiated himself with the
Missus.' Benjamin Disraeli was a talented, sophisticated
and entertaining man of the world and the Queen's character and power prospered again under his influence. She
was never petty in her judgments, even when she was unjust. The House of Commons still cried at the memory
of Disraeli's flamboyant waistcoats. Prince Albert had
been one with them in this prejudice. But even Prince
Albert was capable of pettiness which could never have
been awakened in the Queen. Lord Palmerston had come
to see her the first time after the Prince Consort's death,
wearing a brown greatcoat, light grey trousers, green
gloves and blue studs. Others had commented upon the
strange get-up, but not the Queen. Her dislike for Cromwell would not have been because of the wart on his face.

§ IV — 1866

LORD RUSSELL's Ministry retired from office in the summer. Lord Derby's Conservative Ministry came into power, with guarded views on the Parliamentary Reforms for which the country was clamouring. The Queen wished that Reform could be avoided for one more year, but the public impatience and the political pressure were too great, after fifteen years of procrastination. Mr. Gladstone considered that Parliament and the Legislature had been dishonoured and lowered by this prolonged delay. Mighty changes had come to England since the day of the Queen's accession. Science and industry were causing strange splits in the crust of the English system. Chemical processes were giving the poor people cheap soap, glass and paper. Artisans and miners could afford lamps to read by and books which gave them a glimpse of scenes beyond their drab, smoke-dimmed windows. Great parks, where tranquil oaks shaded ancient lawns, were molested by railways: chimneys rose with the elms, against the English sky. Old houses, built from the oak of Elizabeth's ships, were being torn down and factories built in their place. The industrial plague was upon the land: wages were increased and the poorest children learned to read and to write. Slowly, the peasant and the labouring man came to know their own power. When the cry for Parliamentary Reform became louder, the people were tipsy over the sudden realisation of their own strength. Londoners crowded into Hyde Park on July 23rd: they trampled over the lawns and flower beds to hear the many speakers who rose above their heads to damn the Tory Government and to speak of the freedom and the rights of the masses. But the masses became apathetic again in the face of the Communist promises. There were eighteen hundred policemen, a company of Grenadier Guards and a troop of Life Guards in Hyde Park but they made no attempt to quell the speakers. A few 'roughs' threw stones and they were arrested. At Marlborough Street next morning, when they were brought before the magistrate, he found that only six of them were respectable working men. *The Times* of the next day tells us that 'The fatigued audience were glad to get back as soon as possible to the various public-houses which served as their headquarters.'[78] When Parliament was opened in February of the following year (the Queen drove out once more, this time through rain and mud), a Reform Bill was more or less promised in her speech. She announced also that a commission would be appointed to enquire into and report upon the organisation of Trades Unions, because of the discontent between employer and working man. The Reform Bill was passed —the most liberal change in franchise since 1832. Ratepayers and small men of respectable industry and substance found that they were active figures, with the power to vote in their hands. A hundred signs of the emancipation and education of the people appeared in the life of London and the countryside. New schools were opened and the educational policies of Eton, Harrow and Winchester were made more liberal. The Duchess of Sutherland held a meeting at Stafford House in support of the Saturday Half-Holiday Movement. Ten thousand people attended the South Kensington Museum every day and the business of the Post Office grew, especially with the advent of the halfpenny post card. With enlightenment came cures for cholera and other pestilences. There was already a venereal disease hospital in London, although the secretary considered that 'the special character' of its mission made it 'not easy to plead in public' for support. In all the small details of day-to-day life it was apparent, at the end of 1866, that Britain was moving along the road of social reason and prosperity.

§ v — 1866

ONE OF the reasons for England's greatness has been her firm belief in her own high moral purpose. She has usually established her trading stations hand in hand with her missions. She captured New Zealand's trade on the wings of religious conversion, and the South Sea Islands in the cause of respectability, manifested in petticoats for the natives. She captured the trade of the Red Sea and the Persian Gulf from the Turks, in the name of anti-slave traffic. These conquests have blessed the English with a glow of self-righteousness and they have never understood the stirring of similar, mercenary ambitions in other countries: especially Prussia. There was this difference between the English and the Prussian system. The English truly believed that it was as much in the cause of the Bible as the ledger when they gave their belated support to Clive's plea that India should be freed from the mercenary power of the East India Company. They believed, too, that they were rescuing the Kaffirs from the cruel Dutchmen during the Boer War. Being the worst diplomats in the world, the Prussians did not pause to throw any of the dust of high purpose into their eyes when they too began to desire territory and Imperial magnificence. Bismarck was candid enough to confess Prussia's ambition and to use the phrase which was so shocking to his English contemporaries—that the problems of Germany would be satisfied only through 'blood and iron.' The Queen believed in Prussia's destiny but not in the way Bismarck wished to pursue it. What Prince Albert had said in 1847 was still wisdom to her in 1866. He had said, 'My own view is that the political reformation of Germany lies entirely in the hands of Prussia.' The Queen accepted this as law. 'A strong united, liberal Germany would be a most useful ally to England,' she wrote to Lord Stanley. She did not remember that Prince Albert had also written a private letter to his brother, asking for one of the celebrated needle-guns with which Prussia was to wage her war, so that England too could be up-to-date in methods of destruction.

In March the Crown Princess wrote from Berlin, in a fever, about 'the wicked man' and his power over the King. On April 10th, remembering her attempts at mediation between the King of Prussia and the Emperor of Austria in Coburg, Queen Victoria wrote a private letter to the King of Prussia, begging him to pause before he succumbed to Bismarck's ambitions. 'You are deceived,' she said. But the thundering machine of Prussia went on. Bismarck sought to complete what had been thought of in 1848: a country which was one country, not thirty-six little states. Europe needed one strong master and it was right and good that Germany should assume the role. In June, the first openly hostile step was taken when the Prussians drove the Austrians out of Holstein. The Prussians turned then to Hanover. If it were not for the clause prohibiting female succession, Victoria would have been Queen of Hanover, as well as Queen of England. The blind King of Hanover was driven from his throne and he became an exile in Paris. Victory followed victory, and on July 3rd the Austrians were defeated at Königgrätz, in Bohemia. Among the wounded was a young officer named Hindenburg. Bismarck's needle-gun, the ambassador of more terrible machines of war, was too much for the Austrian muzzle loaders. Austria fell back, defeated and discouraged, and the Catholic priests in Vienna trembled lest the hard-fisted religion of Luther should sweep south, with Prussia's soldiers, and assail the Roman power. Peace came to a fattened, prosperous Prussia and to a humiliated Austria. Queen Victoria pleaded with the victors for the poor King of Hanover, and for the family of her own daughter in Darmstadt. The letter from the Crown Princess of Prussia, in answer to her mother's compassionate plea, was no less than astounding. 'I cannot, and will not, forget that I am a Prussian,' she wrote, forgetting her recent thanks to God that she was English. She continued '...as rivers of blood had flowed and the *sword* decided this contest, the victor *must* make his own terms and they *must* be hard ones for the many....We have made *enormous* sacrifices, and the nation expects them not to be in vain. I fear this is all the answer I can give you at present....' [74]

Chapter Eight

§ 1 — 1865–1868

THERE IS a school of commentators who say of Queen Victoria, 'She lost us Ireland.' Perhaps it would be nearer to the truth to say that she failed to *hold* Ireland—she failed to answer, in full, the plea of the Irish woman who called out to her from the tide of people in Dublin, when she saw the Royal children, 'Oh! Queen, dear! Name one of them Patrick, and all Ireland will die for you.' It has been said that the reason for the Queen's coldness—coldness which froze her feeling for Ireland to the end of her reign—was that the Irish had been rude to Prince Albert. In all the years of her rule the Queen spent less than five weeks in Ireland and almost seven years in Scotland. The affection she denied to Ireland she gave to Balmoral and to the Deeside—it was enshrined in the *Leaves from the Journal of our Life in the Highlands* which was published in 1866. There was a chorus of praise in the newspapers. The naïve record of the day to day life of the Queen, of her picnics and of her health, her servants and her dogs, gave the people a peep into the seclusions of life at Balmoral. Lady Augusta Stanley was sceptical over the success of the book and she said that if the Queen had settled on Ireland instead of Aberdeenshire, 'the ecstasies and interests that would have grown up would have been just as great' and that 'Fenianism would never have existed.' Lady Augusta realised the perils in the Queen's antipathy and, when she went her-

75

self to Ireland in the summer, she wrote to her mistress, gently trying to draw her interest towards the rejected country. 'How much I hope that Your Majesty may some day be able to see some of the peculiar beauties of Irish scenery....I am certain that Your Majesty in no degree over-estimates the good that would result from it. The people are very sensitive and so alive to anything that honours them and their country and *raises them and it* in their own estimation and in the scale of nations....' Lady Augusta sowed her seed cleverly, but upon stony ground.

The Queen saw Ireland in the terms of unbending diplomacy, and the Irish people as so many dangerous, vexing insurgents. The Prince of Wales was attracted to a more simple and human side of the problem and he supported the views of both Mr. Disraeli and Mr. Gladstone, together with the Lord Lieutenant of Ireland,[75] that the one way to hold the distressful country would be to give it some form of royal patronage. The division of the people into those who left Ireland, embittered, for America, and those who stayed, in the anxiety of famine—appalled them. The passions of the Irish had always been a thorn in the Englishman's side and, in Westminster, thin-lipped Anglo-Saxons tried to understand the fierce and unreasoning Celts with as much success as a Colonial Office clerk attempting to comprehend the witch-dances in a Kraal in Bechuanaland. The division between Anglo-Saxon, Protestant landlords and their Celtic, Catholic peasantry was no less a tragedy. The Queen had been agitated when the Archbishop of Canterbury sanctioned an Episcopalian campaign in Scotland because, she said, it would lead to the rich being Episcopalian and the poor Presbyterian: a division which would bring disaster. She did not see the disaster already upon Ireland, where land-owners and peasants were divided by race and religion, already living in the antagonism and misunderstanding which she feared would rise in Scotland. In September of 1866, armed Fenians rescued two prisoners from a van in Manchester. A police sergeant was killed and three of the Fenians were afterwards hanged. On December 13th, the Fenians blew up Clerkenwell prison, rather incongruously, since two of their own 'martyrs' were inside. How could the English understand these mad creatures, who cut off their noses to spite their own faces? The one hope, it seemed, was to give Ireland the Royal patronage she wished by appointing the Prince of Wales as Lord Lieutenant.

Mr. Disraeli wrote, a little dreamily, in March of 1868, that a house for the Prince in Ireland—in a hunting county—would combine pleasure and duty in the way 'which befits a princely life.' The last thing that the Queen wished was this picture of a gallant Prince, away from her control, free to hunt and amuse himself on the other side of the Irish Channel. She already thought him too much of a gadabout. 'The country and all of *us,* would like to see you a little more stationary,' she wrote to him in October of 1866. This further threat of freedom was 'not to be thought of.' Perhaps it is true, as she told Gladstone, that 'she doubted the Prince's fitness for high functions of State.' She was almost alone in this belittling of her son's talents. Three Prime Ministers, the Lord Lieutenant and the Prince pleaded in vain. Even General Grey, her secretary, was 'very angry with her about the Irish matters.'[76] We may turn again to Lady Augusta Stanley, who knew the Queen's mind so well, for a searching comment. 'I believe she is so afraid lest any of them should be taken up by, or take up the Irish so as to throw Balmoral into the shade, now or later. I really do.'

The Queen remained so adamant that these champions of Ireland's need simply fell back, breathless and discouraged. Lord Spencer, who had been Lord Lieutenant, was so forlorn at the rejection of his design that he wrote frankly to the Queen's Secretary, saying that he felt inclined 'to throw up the sponge and retire to his plough in Northamptonshire.' [77] The Queen was isolated and there was nobody to penetrate past the formality of address to help her. In such situations as this, one realises the full tragedy of the Prince Consort's death, for he alone could have guided her from this mistake. Even her secretary complained about her lack of graciousness at times ... times in which she stood aloof, unguided, not knowing which of the many advisers she could trust. Thus confused, the Queen trusted none of them. Unfortunately the Queen trusted her own instinct and prejudice. Even the Prince, who so much wished that the Irish could be 'humoured a little and taken notice of,' at last fell back into torpor, under his mother's assurance that his plan for living in Ireland was 'quite out of the question.' He had to be content with a few, hurried visits, grudgingly sanctioned by the Queen. She gave her consent more generously when Mr. Disraeli asked her. Lord Palmerston had been blunt enough to point out that it was 'politic and useful.' Indeed, he had frankly and stupidly described the Prince's proposed visit to Ireland as a 'journey for a political purpose in place of Her Majesty.' Mr. Gladstone, who thought that the Prince had 'much natural intelligence,' had sharply announced to the Queen that the question of the Prince's residence in Ireland was to come before Parliament. The Queen was alternately suspicious and angry. Mr. Disraeli was more subtle when he became Prime Minister, in February of 1868. He pleaded to the Queen only for 'the tranquilisation of the disturbed country.' He reminded her, too, that her son might be installed as a Knight of Saint Patrick. He showed none of his political axes: the novelist turned to history for his argument and he told the queen that. during two centuries, the sovereign had passed only twenty-one days in Ireland.

In April of 1868 the Fenian prisoners were released from Irish gaols in celebration of the visit of the Prince of Wales. He crossed the Irish Channel with England's olive branch in his hand. A few Irishmen in the streets saw the olives as aloes and there were slight hisses as he drove in an open carriage from Kingstown to Dublin Castle. This was his first attempt at reconciliation among his mother's people. His smile and his gallant manner won the day. With Princess Alexandra sitting beside him in Dublin Castle—with the Irish multitude still waiting out-side—he wrote a letter to his mother. 'There were an enormous quantity of people in the streets who cheered very lustily, and with the exception of a very few and slight hisses, the people seemed determined to give us a thoroughly cordial reception.' St. Patrick's Cathedral was made glorious for the ceremony on the eighteenth, when he was installed as a Knight of Saint Patrick. There was a State dinner at the Castle in the evening and the Prince spoke, without any notes—a straightforward, sincere message of goodwill. The Duke of Cambridge, the Prince and the Princess, and the Lord Lieutenant sat in Dublin Castle after it was all over, planning to soften the Queen's heart. The Prince wrote, 'I only wish, dear Mama, that you could have been here instead of us.' The Lord Lieutenant wrote that he was 'hardly prepared for the progressive increase of welcome.' Even the Fenian sympathisers had cheered. The Duke of Cambridge wrote, 'Come over to convince and satisfy yourself of the force of the affectionate feeling.'

The Queen was not moved. She seemed to exclude her son still more from her confidence and a few months later, when she wanted to express her views about his proposed journey to Greece, she avoided writing to him, and she asked Lord Clarendon to send a letter in her place. She thought it 'more likely ... to produce an effect.'

For her the Irish revealed themselves in full in two incidents which she never forgot. In March of 1868 her son, Prince Alfred, was shot in the back by a Fenian, in Australia. In March of 1871, Lord Spencer unveiled a statue of Prince Albert on Leinster Lawn, in Dublin. Two months after the ceremony, the Fenians tried to blow it up. The incident in Australia made the Antipodes ring with expressions of loyalty, but these viciously personal insults closed the Queen's heart against Ireland for ever.

There was another reason behind the Queen's suspicion of Ireland and love for Scotland. She was rigidly Protestant, as Prince Albert had been. Luther had translated the psalms in a room in the Coburg Castle in which he had played. The memorials of Lutheranism had surrounded Prince Albert when he was a boy. Popery and devilry were synonymous to the Queen, and her cold religion drew her away from all sumptuousness in worship. Many times it drew her away from the Anglican Church, for she liked the simple services of the Scottish Kirk. No matter how much she made friends of Dean Stanley of Westminster, Dean Wellesley or Dean Davidson, it was to Dr. Macleod that she was wholly devoted. She cried when she was told that he was dead. *His* religion she understood. On religious matters, she 'could ask him anything.' She saw the difference between the state worship—the confusion between the functions of Abbey and Parliament at Westminster, and the services on the Deeside, where the sacraments were rare and simple. In November of 1873, her anxiety over the Church reached the point of protest. She wrote to Dean Stanley of the state of the *English* Church, '... its Romanising tendencies.' 'She thinks a complete *Reformation* is what we want,' she wrote, with honest motives, but little knowledge of what complete Reformations involved. She was against 'dressing, bowings... and, *above all, all* attempts at *confession.*' She attacked the *bigotry* and *self-sufficiency* of the Church and added that she thought it should 'bethink itself of its dangers from Papacy, instead of trying to widen the breach with *all* other Protestant Churches.' 'The Church will *fall,*' she threatened.

If she was so violent in her fear of the feeble attempts at Popery in the English Church how much more was she afraid of the out and out Roman Catholicism of Ireland? She had refused to allow her son to be alone in the room with the Pope, in Rome, in case a word might be distorted, a phrase exploited, by the Holy Father of bigotry. The Queen was equally antagonised by the extreme of Evangelism and when the Sankey and Moody Mission came to England in 1875, she deplored the 'sensational style of excitement' associated with the movement. She thought theirs was 'not the religion which *can last.*' In this unreasonable Lutheranism, there may lie still another reason why the Queen looked upon Ireland as the black sheep of her Imperial family.

Queen Victoria may have been intolerant in her dismissal of Ireland and the Irish, but there was courage in her scorn of the strength of the Fenians, as well as of their spirit. *Guelph courage* is a phrase among European historians. In the English line, George the Fourth was the only Sovereign who lacked it. Queen Victoria had laughed when a miscreant shot at her as she was driving past the Green Park, and, when a second attempt was made on her life, she drove out of Buckingham Palace immediately afterwards, to draw the assassin out of hiding, so that he should be caught. She was little more than twenty then. She was able 'to sit quite still' in later years, when a madman cut her face with a whip. In this she was magnificently brave. She did not know fear, and when the Fenians threatened to kill her, in Ireland's name, the Queen perplexed everybody by her calm and fearlessness. She was almost fifty when, in the summer of 1867, a telegram arrived at Balmoral, saying that a party of Fenians had set out from Manchester to seize her. She said it was 'too foolish,' [78] and she continued her long drives, unprotected, into the surrounding country. As Fenian passions became stronger, Ministers and friends were more and more anxious for the Queen's safety. She alone was calm. When her servants saw her driving out into the wooded country at Osborne, there was mild panic, for rumours of plots came to the island almost every day. At last General Grey, her secretary, wrote her a letter indicating the dangers she courted. Everybody was afraid for her. He would go *on his bended knees,* he wrote, and asked her to leave Osborne, with its open shore and woods, and live safely at Windsor. The Queen defied all. She continued to drive in the woods and to walk down, past the pines and ilexes, to the shore of the Solent and she told General Grey, with fine anger, that she would *not* go to Windsor and that she would not 'have it mentioned again.'

§ II — 1865–1868

ONE OF the reasons given by the Queen for not wishing the Prince of Wales to visit Ireland in 1868 was that there were to be races at Punchestown. '...it strengthens the belief,' she wrote to her son, 'already too prevalent, that your chief object is amusement; and races have become so bad of late, and the connection with them has ruined so many young men, and broken the hearts thereby of so many fond and kind parents.'[79]

Two daughters and two sons were already born to the Princess of Wales and while Marlborough House was the scene of vivid parties and unrestrained fun, there was no neglect of the nursery. The Prince was aware of the faults in his own training and he tried not to repeat them. In 1873, we have a simple picture of him, which shows his regard for his children more sharply than a searching psychological analysis could do. He had been to the House of Lords, to hear Lord Granville's speech and he was obliged to leave before it was ended. The note he sent to Lord Granville reveals his relationship both with statesmen and with his children. He apologised for hurrying away—he was celebrating the birthday of his 'eldest little girl' he wrote. 'The Princess and I are going to take four of the children to the circus at 7.15, and it is now 6.30. I have not a moment left.'[80] 'There is another engaging picture of him about this time, in a letter which he sent to Mrs. Bruce.[81] He wrote from Sandringham, where his improved estate and jolly hospitality attracted shooting parties of his cosmopolitan friends almost every week-end. 'Fancy, on Saturday last a reporter from Lynn actually joined the beaters while we were shooting, but as I very nearly shot him in the legs, he very soon gave me a wide berth. General Knollys then informed him that his presence was not required and he "skidaddled," as the Yankees call it.' This young Prince, who took his children to the circus and who used the word 'skidaddled,' in a time of sedate phrases, was intensely human and his faults were human too. Sir Sidney Lee likens him to Anthony, 'Our courteous Anthony,'

> Whom ne'er the word of 'No' woman heard speak.

We have already seen how the British public could be bored by a virtuous Prince, in the story of the Prince Consort. He was torn to ribbons by the Press for keeping the Ten Commandments. In the sixties, his son was assailed for breaking them. He lived in a time when Royal persons were still the prey of *Punch* and *The Times*. Both papers pilloried the Prince, in line and word, and his love of frivolity was exaggerated and condemned. There was no satisfying the English taste, it seemed. George the Fourth had almost lost his crown through his sins. Prince Albert recovered it and exalted royalty again, through his virtue. But he did not gain esteem for his pains. When Prince Albert Edward showed that the Hanoverian blood had not faded from the family, in one generation, he was also set upon by gossips and newspapers and, at last, by the perpetrator of an action for divorce. Sir Charles Mordaunt brought a petition against his wife, citing two co-respondents, who were friends of the Prince and also making an allegation against the Prince of Wales, upon the authority of his demented wife's confession. Lady

Mordaunt was hopelessly insane before the case came into the Courts, but the Prince's name was so unhappily dragged into the affair that he volunteered to go into the witness-box to clear his honour. The evidence against him hung on eleven letters, written to Lady Mordaunt, scattered over a period of two years. None of them began with phrases more affectionate than 'My dear Lady Mordaunt.' When a provincial newspaper published the letters, the most incriminating phrase was, 'I hope when I come back from Paris to meet your husband.' *The Times* described them as 'simple, gossiping, everyday . . . stupidly honest letters.'

The trial opened in February of 1870 and the Prince went into the witness-box and cleared his name enough to earn the congratulations of Mr. Gladstone, the Lord Chancellor and *The Times*. Mr. Gladstone wrote, rather gloomily, '. . . so long as the nation has confidence in the personal character of its sovereign the throne of this Empire may be regarded as secure.' For some time the Prince suffered as much as if he had been proven guilty. He went to a theatre and he was insulted. At Epsom there was hissing when he appeared. Few people paused, in the fever for dangerous gossip, to realise that there was a more serious aspect of his life, such as his yearly manœuvres with the 10th Hussars. Here the Prince of Wales rose at six o'clock in the morning and faced the rigours of camp life. Nobody remembered that if he gambled at night, he also worked all day, denying his help to no charity or cause. Wellington College, the Royal Agricultural Society, the Society of Arts and the building of the Royal Albert Hall were helped through his zeal. He was not lazy. He was no gilded patron, free with his name and tardy with his energies. There was a fine, class-free acknowledgment of the ordinary citizens' rights in all that he did and in every cause which he supported. His father, who had built the first ideal workmen's flats in Kensington with bathrooms, and who had publicly reprimanded the employers and *not* the employees, when he was asked to speak upon Labour questions, might have been pleased with his son if he had heard the address the young Prince prepared for the Trade Unionists Exhibition. He annoyed the capitalists, as his father had done, by saying that he hoped that the increase in manufactures would mean 'a corresponding increase of sympathy and friendly relations between employers and their workmen.' The Prince Consort would have welcomed this strain of sane sympathy in his son, however much he might have wept because of the scandals over amorous adventures and hours squandered at the gambling tables. No matter how much he played, to give vent to his store of fun, the Prince of Wales did not neglect his duties as a husband and a father.

'Class can no longer stand apart from class,' he once said. Although he was inviolate in protecting and sustaining the dignity of Princes, he was a democrat, and he worked successfully for the broadest good. His theories on democracy never permitted any lapse of dignity or any offence against law and order. He was kind, but punctilious.

The truth was that the members of the old-fashioned London society, discontented as all city society must be, were as annoyed by the Prince's easy habits as they had been exasperated by the Queen's withdrawal from their drawing-rooms. The Prince's vagaries of behaviour were indications of a change. The century was slowly shaking off the lull which had settled upon it during the Prince

Consort's worthy and wholly noble reign. The country was rich and the standard of living was passing the point of reason. London was substantially rebuilt, richness gilded everything and society tended to forsake elegance for vulgarity.

The Prince was identified with the changes. With the material transformations there came also revolutions against morbid hero-worship and history-worship. The scene of his mourning mother caused the Prince to turn, almost ruthlessly, from the past. He had complained in Rome, 'You look at two mouldering stones and are told that it's the temple of something.' When news of the death of a distant relative reached him one evening in Paris just as he was going to the theatre with some friends, he did not hesitate in saying, 'Put on black studs and go to the play.' Nor was he loth to have the Duke of Wellington's statue on the top of the Arch moved to the entrance to Constitution Hill, when the increase of traffic demanded more space at Hyde Park Corner. It was the Prince's letter which gave Gladstone his plan for the change and the Prince was wholly and sensibly pleased when the space was cleared and the statue was given to Aldershot. 'We had a very pretty and successful ceremony at Aldershot yesterday,' he wrote to a friend, in August of 1885, '... I handed over to the General Commanding the troops there ... the old statue of the great "Dook".'

Sudden flashes help one to imagine the character and personality of the Prince of Wales. One sees in the lists of his friends that he was what is described as a 'man of the world.' The development of his family proves his qualities as a father and his kindly and chivalrous attention to his wife show that this other side of his domestic life was decorous to the end. But a hearty sense of fun was left over, with no outlet within his family circle. He was no prude and he liked risqué stories and gay songs. The truant never died in him. He liked to run away from the shadow of his mother's crown. Yvette Guilbert tells us in her reminiscences of the day in Paris, when she first sang for the Prince. She had been warned by her hostess to sing only the most delicate and irreproachable songs in her repertoire. 'He continued to smile at me in a friendly fashion during my first "select songs",' she writes. The hostess crossed the room and said to her, 'The Prince has heard about a song, *Le Fiacre;* he'll speak to you about it himself.' 'And as a matter of fact, the Prince took my arm, and then, speaking low so that no one else could hear: "Dear Mlle. Guilbert, why don't you let me hear your songs of Montmartre? I have read so many articles about your way of interpreting the spirit of the *Chat Noir.*"

' "Your Highness, I am somewhat puzzled at what you say, for Mrs. Goelet has asked me on your account to sing only songs — *pour jeunes filles.*"

'The Prince laughed so heartily that there was a sudden silence among the guests; he took advantage of it to say that he would ask to be allowed to suggest the songs he would like to hear. Everyone heartily agreed and the Prince, leaning on the piano, asked for the most delightfully Parisian items of my repertoire.'

The public habit of denying Princes the right to human frailties is inhuman. The fierce light in which royalty lives makes one wonder why any reigning Prince or heir does not abdicate, in defence of his own soul. Prince Albert Edward stayed, fighting the accusations against him. 'This damned morality will be the ruin of us,' Lord

Melbourne said of the Prince's father and his discipline in the forties. The cry was changed when the Prince was changed.

It is singular that Queen Victoria made no comments during the scandal of the Mordaunt divorce case. Nor were there reproaches for her son. With all her rigid standards of behaviour, the Queen was not a prude. This has been the easy and inaccurate accusation made against her by so many writers. Indeed, the much talked of Hanoverian blood was strong in the Queen and if Prince Albert curbed her boisterousness, he did not kill it. Having no equals, being curiously alone, she was removed from the contacts which engender fun. But there are records of the Queen's enjoyment of a faintly risqué story. One night at dinner, somebody was talking of the Zulu War and they said that the Zulus came over the top of the hill 'like a swarm of cockroaches.' A man at the table in the zest of his spontaneous wit corrected the speaker and offered another simile in place of the cockroaches, frankly phallic and very funny. The company became rigid. After a moment the Queen laughed—alone. Even upon the subject of sex, aspects of which we might imagine to be unknown to her, the Queen was not as intolerant as we would expect. Once it is said, the subject came up in conversation, during a time when there was a public scandal to excite the moralists. The Queen said, 'I am not concerned with what my subjects do, providing they do what I wish.'

Chapter Nine

§ 1 — 1868

THE QUEEN's letters became more lively during Mr.
Disraeli's short term of office in 1868. Reading through
the great volumes of her correspondence, one comes upon
the happy change in their tone in February, after Lord
Derby was obliged to retire because of his pestilential
gout. The Queen's secretary went to Mr. Disraeli, then
Chancellor of the Exchequer, in the moment of crisis,
and found him 'very cordial and *most* practical in all he
said; going straight to the point and showing a most
sincere desire to do nothing that could look presumptuous
on his part, or unhandsome towards Lord Derby.' [82] The
Queen was waiting anxiously at Windsor, still hating all
changes, but pleased that the Chancellor of the Exchequer
was coming to her in still closer relationship. The spirit
of her political correspondence changed over night. In
his first letter Disraeli showed that he knew how to please
the Queen as neither Lord Derby nor Mr. Gladstone had
ever done. Disraeli was humble: he asked for her guidance, since he was so young and inexperienced. He wrote,
'Your Majesty's life has been passed in constant communication with great men...this rare and choice experience must give your Majesty an advantage in judgment which *few* living persons and probably no living
Princes can rival.' [83] In one isolated line of the letter,
Disraeli wrote that he 'could only offer devotion.' The
Queen's reply was warm and friendly, and when their

90

relationship as Sovereign and Prime Minister was established, the correspondence between them became jolly at times. Instead of long, gloomy arguments, Mr. Disraeli's letters gave her pictures which she could comprehend. Sometimes, when Mr. Gladstone wrote her, she had to ask her secretary to help her to disentangle his meaning: she was confused by the lugubrious moralising. Not so Mr. Disraeli, who wrote of Gladstone, '... it is marvellous how so consummate an orator should, the moment he takes the pen, be so involved and cumbersome and infelicitous in expression.' When Mr. Disraeli had an appointment to recommend he used the craftsmanship of the novelist to give the Queen an unerring picture of his man. One of his first duties was to appoint a new Chancellor of the Exchequer, to take his place. He wrote to the Queen of Mr. Ward Hunt whom he proposed. His appearance was 'rather remarkable, but anything but displeasing. He is more than six feet four inches in stature, but does not look so tall from his proportionate breadth; like St. Peter's, no one is at first aware of his dimensions. But he has the sagacity of an elephant, as well as the form. The most simple, straightforward, and truthful man Mr. Disraeli ever met....' [84]

Here was a Prime Minister after her own heart, for the Queen disliked bores and she never used her pomposity except as a defence against fools. Disraeli's letters from the House, even when they were written by a tired hand late at night, were entertaining to receive: his little pictures of the speakers—'Mr. Lowe, who raised his crest, and hissed like an adder.'

In September the friendship between the Queen and her Prime Minister was complete. Chivalry, humour and kindliness were its mainstays. There were little gifts: two

volumes of views of Balmoral, a box full of family photographs and a very fine, whole-length portrait of the
Prince Consort. Upon the same day the Queen sent a
Scotch shawl for Mrs. Disraeli, with the hope that 'she
would find it warm in the cold weather.' This first opportunity for friendship between the Queen and Mr. Disraeli
was short-lived: at the end of the year Mr. Gladstone
pressed the affairs of Ireland so forcibly on the House
that Disraeli was obliged to advise the Queen to dissolve
Parliament. A General Election followed, with the increased enfranchisement granted by the Reform Bill of
the previous year. The Liberals swept into power with
Mr. Gladstone triumphant in the tide, his Bill for the
Disestablishment and Disendowment of the Church of
Ireland in his hand. Mr. Disraeli suffered a momentary
eclipse: but he retired from the Royal favour as he came.
The Queen's secretary went to him again and he wrote
to her, from London, that nothing 'could have been more
proper or manly than Mr. Disraeli's way of taking what
he admits to be a total defeat.'[85]

Again the Queen had to accept a change, and Mr.
Disraeli came to take leave of her. The Queen, who
thought that he showed more consideration for her comfort than 'any of the preceding Prime Ministers since
Sir Robert Peel and Lord Aberdeen,' turned gloomily to
the Liberal reign, with all the doubts and resentments
that the word held for her. At first the glow from Mr.
Disraeli's friendly calls lent light to the new regime. She
was so forthcoming with Mr. Gladstone in their first
interview that he went away 'completely under the
spell.'[86] She thought him 'cordial and kind in his
manner.' The whole interview was 'satisfactory.' But
when the new Prime Minister returned to Downing

Street, he took the Bill for the Disestablishment and Disendowment of the Church of Ireland out of a drawer —a bill which the Queen frankly disliked. Before the end of January he sent her upwards of a dozen quarto sheets of explanations. She was at Osborne and when she came in, to find the formidable letter waiting for her on her desk, she read and re-read it, but 'found herself more and more lost in the clouds of his explanations, the more she toiled through them.'[87] She sent for Theodore Martin to help her. With his *précis* she was able to understand. But even Theodore Martin, professional editor and scholar, admitted that it 'seemed only natural' that the Queen 'should have been lost in the fog of the long and far from lucid sentences of her Prime Minister.'[88]

On July 26th Mr. Gladstone's Bill received the Royal assent, after a troublous journey through the Lords and Committees for amendment. We do not know all of what Mr. Disraeli did, in the days of his comparative leisure. But he no doubt found time, towards the end of the year, to read the glowing account of the opening of the Suez Canal in the newspapers. His early travels in the Levant had given him a lively interest in all the changes which came to the countries of the Mediterranean.

§ 11 — 1868

THE YEAR 1868 was not one of great events in the Queen's life. On March 5th, she made one of her rare visits— to the Deanery at Westminster. Lady Augusta Stanley, for ever anxious to find correctives for the Queen's loneliness, had asked Carlyle and Browning to meet her at tea. The Queen thought Carlyle 'strange-looking, eccentric,' holding forth 'in a drawling, melancholy voice upon

Scotland and upon the utter degradation of everything.'
Mr. Browning was 'very agreeable.' At first it was shy
work for her to speak to them, but afterwards, when tea
was being drunk, Lady Augusta 'got them to come and sit
near' her. Then, under the spell of her voice, they 'were
very agreeable and talked very entertainingly.' [89] Lady
Augusta's effort was akin to the Prince Consort's plan, in
the early days. He too had wished to gather the intellectuals of the day about him, but without much success,
for he was discouraged by the Queen. Lady Augusta
suffered the same fate. In 1876, she again asked the Queen
to the Deanery at Westminster to meet some notables.
The Queen went home depressed by the experience. She
thought one of them 'rather ponderous and pompous.'
Froude had fine eyes, 'but nothing very sympathetic.'
Professor Tyndall 'not very attractive' and another,
though young and pleasing, was 'very shy.' [90]

§ III — 1866-1868

THE PRINCE OF WALES and Princess Alexandra went off to
Egypt and Constantinople in the spring, so the five grand-
children went to Windsor, to stay with their grandmama.
She found 'Eddy ... very good and very sensible.'

Two years before, the Queen had made a journey to
London, to call upon Princess Mary of Teck and her new
baby. The Queen was assailed by a hundred memories
when she came to Kensington Palace—the house of her
birth and her childhood. The old courtyard, where her
pony had waited for her—the scene of the Round Pond
by which she had walked, in the shadow of a big footman—the flower border which she had watered, spilling
the water on her little white shoes. She came now, quiet,

and forlorn. She went in through the door, 'the very knockers of which were old friends.' One room, overlooking the gardens, was the scene of her first meeting with Prince Albert—she had been seventeen then. He had made a joke at breakfast and she had thought him to be most amusing. In this room they had played a duet on the piano and she had been quite certain afterwards, when they sat upon the sofa with an album of views, that she was head over heels in love with her beautiful cousin. But that was all over.

The Queen passed through the quiet palace. Here was the room to which they had come, to tell her that she was Queen: here the room in which Baroness Lehzen had first told her, as a child, that she would grow up to rule England. And here, the room in which she had slept, so many, many years ago. Now there was a cradle in the bedroom, and in it lay the new baby—Princess May, 'with pretty little features and a quantity of hair,' much too young even to dream that she, too, would some day grow up and be Queen of England.

Chapter Ten

§ 1 — 1870

THE VICTORY of 1866, when Prussia defeated Austria and extended her territory, was not enough for either Bismarck or the brilliant soldier Moltke. With her amazing army, which could be mobilised within twenty-four hours, she looked about and sought a pretext for ravishing France. Potsdam was no longer the hub of a little country, but of a growing Empire—the people became drugged: they listened to the 'Ancestral voices prophesying war' and they drilled and marched obediently. Bismarck had not allowed his needle-guns to rust after the defeat of the Austrians at Königgrätz: they were ready now, with new engines of war to support them. The Prussian soldiers were dizzy with the promise of conquest and they were confident of their strength.

The Crown Princess had written to her mother some years before of Bismarck's sinister influence over the King—the influence of a 'clever, unprincipled man.' The King had listened to the tempter: with such an army and such a Minister—a Chancellor of Iron—he would become Emperor of all Germany and no longer be merely the King of Prussia. The King, Bismarck and Moltke—the Prussian army and the Prussian people, shared the thirst for power. The sounds of the parade ground were in their ears and the stink of gunpowder was in their nostrils. All that was needed was a cause.

About this time there was a proposal to put a Hohenzollern Prince on the throne of Spain. France, forgetting

Louis Philippe's deception of England over the Spanish marriage in 1846,[91] protested against this threat of German influence in Spain. The French Ambassador was sent to speak to the King of Prussia, who was then taking the waters at Ems. The Ambassador hurried away, saying that the King of Prussia had snubbed him. Paris rose in wild pride and indignation, and the cry was, '*à Berlin!*' Everything tumbled into Bismarck's hands. The Empress—the army—all except the Emperor believed that France could march *à Berlin,* and war was declared. The ill-equipped French threw themselves against the terrible machine of Prussia's army, only to be defeated and humiliated, as the Austrians had been, four years before. The victory at Sedan was followed by the *Commune* and then the capitulation of Paris. The Emperor Napoleon, exhausted and ill, his body almost falling from his horse, was taken as a prisoner to Wilhelmshöhe, near Cassel. The French were beaten mercilessly. The old anger between Germany and France became more fierce than ever: the acid of hatred pouring from either bank into the Rhine. Prussia spread herself to new magnificence and Alsace-Lorraine, with its vine-laden valleys, was added to her territory. Catholic Bavaria and other German countries were wooed into the Prussian fold. In January the King returned to the Palace among the lakes of Potsdam, radiant: he was able now to call himself Emperor. Queen Victoria looked on, amazed. 'A peaceful Germany can never be dangerous to England, but the very reverse,' [92] she wrote, still clinging to Prince Albert's dictum. She had angered the French two years before, when she was in Paris. The Empress had come up to the Elysée Bourbon, instead of to the Tuileries, as a gracious gesture, so that it would be less distance for Queen Victoria to travel, when she returned the visit. But the Queen did not return the visit: all she did was to ask the Empress a few questions about sight-seeing in Paris. The Empress waited in vain at the Elysée Bourbon, where she had prepared flowers for the Queen's reception. Queen Victoria remained in the British Embassy, not showing herself, and keeping the gates closed.[93] The Empress had not complained, although she had remarked to Lord Cowley that she wondered why Queen Victoria did not abdicate.[94] The mass of people in Paris were not so kind. When they saw the closed gates of the British Embassy, and when they heard that Queen Victoria had not returned the Empress's compliment by calling on her, they were incensed. They hissed her and they cried, *'A bas les Anglais,'* when at last she drove out into the streets.[95]

In the beginning of the Franco-Prussian war England's sympathies went with those of the Queen against France. The Germans had been 'insulted and attacked' and Mr. Gladstone wrote, on July 15th, that it was evident 'that the sentiment of the House on both sides' was a general condemnation of 'the conduct of France.' '... The feeling of the people and country here is *all* with you, which it was not *before,'* the Queen wrote to her daughter at Potsdam.[96] The Crown Princess, so stiffened by the militarist spirit when the Prussians were battling with the Danes a few years before, softened her tone, on the eve of another war. She relaxed and wrote emotionally to her mother, 'Why continually speak of enmity and hateful conduct when, as history teaches us, national misunderstandings can be settled by rational handling of questions of common interest.... How many poor mothers will be praying with me for the lives of their dear ones. ...'[97] I cannot think of the lives that will be lost—how willingly would I give mine to save theirs.' But she tightened her grip again when victory came, in September. Germany had been drawn together in her magnificent, Imperial effort. The soldiers who had fought in 1866, north against south, Protestant against Catholic, now sang *'Die Wacht am Rhein'* in unison as they marched against their common foe.

The Germans saw a glorious purpose in their deeds. The Crown Princess changed her tone again at the end when the Emperor was a prisoner at Sedan: when he was brought to Bismarck, in the weaver's cottage at Domchéry, bereft and ill, after his surrender. Louis Napoleon crept up the back stairs. When the servant went to him, three hours after Bismarck had gone, she found Louis Napoleon still sitting at the table, with his head hidden in his hands. The Crown Princess forgot her noble charity in the hour of victory. 'We have no less than 12,000 French prisoners in Germany! Is it not marvellous?' she wrote. 'Add to that more than fifty Generals and the Sovereign himself.' [98] Then she wrote of the noble purpose behind Germany's triumph. The blow to the 'immoderate frivolity and luxury' of Paris: the victory to the 'plodding, hardworking, *serious life,* which made Germany strong and determined.' Here, indeed, was reason enough for Bismarck's mighty dreams. On September 5th, the mob surged into the Senate in Paris and proclaimed a Republic. Queen Victoria, walking among the larch trees at Balmoral, received the terrible news. 'Not one voice was raised in favour of the unfortunate Emperor!' she wrote. 'How ungrateful!' [99] She could not comprehend war or revolution. She ruled a country which had not known battle since 1745, and then only on the border. Nor had there been revolution: only once in her reign had the malcontents clutched the railings of Buckingham Palace. But they had melted away, to be next week's joke in *Punch*. Her knowledge of revolution was limited to reports from crazy Ireland. Her only knowledge of war was in the stories from the Crimea, which had been chilled and faded by the time they arrived home. Queen of a sea-girt land, she could not know the hysteria and anxiety of countries which were bounded by frontiers. She saw government in the terms of politics and war as a fault in the diplomatic machine; not as a grim physical struggle for earth and existence. She did not begin to understand the nature of the hatred between Germany and France.

The tale of the forsaken Emperor, alone in Sedan, touched her heart. She wished to telegraph to the Empress that she was not insensible to the heavy blow which had fallen on her. She was 'not forgetful of former days.' The phlegmatic calm which strengthened her when others were mad, came to her now. She telegraphed to the triumphant King of Prussia that he could afford to be generous, since victory and glory were in his hands. He had begun his reign as King of Prussia...no more than that. Now he was to stand in the Galerie des Glances at Versailles, the memorial of France's Imperial glory, and he was to be proclaimed 'Emperor.' The Queen thought that the closed hand might unclench and indulge in mercy to the vanquished.

§ II — 1870

ON SEPTEMBER 15th, Sir John Montague Burgoyne wrote to the Queen's secretary, describing the astonishing circumstances in which he had brought the Empress

Eugénie from France, to the English coast. She had sobbed, as she came from her place of hiding in Deau-ville, telling him that she was 'safe with an Englishman.' It was not until the last day of November that Queen Victoria went to see the Empress, in the refuge she found at Chislehurst, in Kent. It was a 'dull, raw and cold day.' The Queen was met at the door by the 'poor Empress, in black.' Queen Victoria wrote in her Journal [100] of the house, 'like a French house and many pretty things about.' The Empress asked her to sit down near to her, on a sofa. She looked very thin and pale, but still very handsome. 'There is an expression of deep sadness in her face, and she frequently had tears in her eyes. She was dressed in the plainest possible way, without any jewels or orna-ments, and her hair simply done, in a net, at the back.' She had remained as long as she could in Paris, she told the Queen, but the garden of the Tuileries had been already full of people and there had been no troops to resist them. 'The night before, she had lain down fully dressed, on her bed. The crossing had been fearful...' 'It was a sad visit,' wrote the Queen, 'and seemed like a strange dream.' In March, 1871, when the humiliation and pain were passing, the Queen received the Emperor at Windsor, embracing him *comme de rigueur*. As he came towards her, the Queen, with all the security of Windsor about her, thought of the last time he had come, 'in perfect triumph, dearest Albert bringing him from Dover, the whole country mad to receive him.' Now he came, bereft of all power and magnificence, 'stout and grey...his moustaches no longer curled or waxed.[101] And there were tears in his eyes.' For a little time they sat alone, and when the politenesses were passed, the Emperor alluded to the origin of the war. Just as the conversation became interesting, they were unfortunately interrupted, 'which was very provoking.'[102] When the Empress Eugénie returned the Queen's visit, she arrived at Windsor in tears. The Queen solaced her in her own inexplicable way. She took her down to the mausoleum at Frogmore, through the pouring rain.

Her visits of compassion to the exiles did not lessen the Queen's devotion to Germany. But the feelings of her people changed. While the German Crown Prince was writing to the Queen from Germany of the fine hopes in a triple alliance between Germany, England and Austria, and of his wish that England should learn to do justice to German affairs, instead of seeing only *Force and Militarism* in her ambitions,[103] a tremendous twist was coming to English feeling—a change too deep and powerful to be affected by a Royal lead or by political persuasion. The British people suddenly gave their compassion to defeated France. The sight of a vanquished Emperor, forlorn, living in a house on the edge of London, stirred them more than the distant and more frightening spectacle of a King turned Emperor, leading his soldiers through the streets—their bayonets shining in a rain of flowers. The Queen noted the change in her people and she wrote to Mr. Gladstone of the sympathies which, strange to say (for no one exactly knew why), had 'become very French.' She had been talking to Lord Derby[104] and, although he had confessed that only 'the smallest number of very foolish people' wished for England to join in a war against Germany, the admission was astonishing, when the public tenderness for the German cause, but a few months before, is recalled. The small number of 'very foolish people' formed the spring which grew into the violent river of 1914.

The Prince of Wales was drawn into the new sympathy, although he was too strongly devoted to peace to
wish for war against anybody. His love for France had
begun when he was a boy in his teens: he had said to
the Emperor Napoleon III, when he was in Paris in
1855, 'You have a nice country. I would like to be your
son.' [105] The affection slumbered in him until 1864, when
the war between Prussia and Denmark incited first his
interest, and then his hatred of the German aims. With
the experience of the Franco-Prussian war to stimulate
his feelings, he took a definite stand against Germany,
antagonising his mother, the Crown Prince, Bismarck,
and Count Bernstorff, the German Ambassador in London. He faced the indignation of the formidable array
rather splendidly.

From the day on which war was declared, the Prince
was single-minded in his devotion. On July 15th he had
entertained a party at Marlborough House. Mr. Delane,
editor of *The Times,* his mother's old enemy, was among
the guests. During dinner, a telegram arrived for Mr.
Delane—it was to tell him of the declaration of the war
between France and Germany. [106] It was in this way that
the Prince heard of the conflict which was to draw the
last shred of his love from Germany and direct his whole-
hearted affection to France. There was no hesitation in
his decision, but perhaps there was too much enthusiasm
in the way in which he declared it abroad. He wrote to
the Queen, when his sister in Berlin expressed her fears
lest France should win, that this peril would help Prussia
to realise 'what the feelings of little Denmark must have
been when they heard that the armies of Prussia and
Austria were against them.' [107] A few days after the
declaration of war, the Prince dined with the French

Ambassador. A gossip at the table hurried to the German Ambassador next day and the result was an astonishing despatch to Berlin, saying that the Prince of Wales had dined with the French Ambassador and that he had expressed his wish for Germany's defeat. The Court and the Foreign Office in Berlin boiled at the story and the Crown Princess reported her brother's crime to the Queen. She said that his words were 'quoted everywhere' in Germany. Bismarck believed the story and he declared that Germany had a foe in the heir to the British Crown. Queen Victoria defended her son and dubbed Bernstorff as 'a shocking mischief-maker,' but she was also perplexed by the Prince's frequent want of tact.[108] The Prince sent his secretary to Count Bernstorff to deny the story. Bernstorff professed to accept the assurances, but he waited his time. A few months afterwards, when the Prince's great friend, the Marquis de Galliffet, was taken prisoner, the Prince wrote a letter to the King, begging for his exchange. Count Bernstorff dismissed the letter as 'irregular' and he refused to forward it to his Sovereign. The Queen put a further curb upon the Prince's freedom: she was afraid of his enthusiasm and the candour which went with it. It was her nature, in a crisis, to be calm. It was her son's nature to wish 'to be of use.' He was at Abergeldie in August, but he was restless. He forsook his shooting party and wrote to his mother, 'I cannot be sitting here and doing nothing, whilst all this bloodshed is going on. How I wish you could send me with letters to the Emperor and King of Prussia, with friendly advice, even if it ultimately failed.'[109] Perhaps the Queen recalled her own efforts at peace-making between the King of Prussia and the Emperor of Austria, at Coburg, before 1866. She joined with her advisers in thinking her son's wish to be 'highly creditable.' Thus she patronised his enthusiasm, adding that it would be impossible, 'even if he were personally fitted for the task.'

The Prince was shown those papers which the Queen wished him to see: mostly the pro-German letters of his sister and his Prussian brother-in-law. But he was denied all true intimacy with affairs. The fear of his unguarded tongue intimidated the Queen more and more. So he tried to find his own ways of helping. When the unhappy Empress Eugénie arrived in England, he offered her Chiswick House. The Queen reprimanded him for his 'presumptuous indiscretion' and the Empress tactfully refused. Then he wished to help a fund for sending corn to French farmers, for the hungry peasants. Again he was rebuffed. The Foreign Secretary said 'No.'

The frustration by his mother and her ministers did not cool the Prince's sympathy and in June of 1878 he walked through the streets of Paris at the head of the funeral procession of George the Fifth, the blind ex-King of Hanover. Berlin was not soothed because the blind King was the Prince's cousin, nor did the Germans see any excuse for this demonstration of sympathy, when the body was taken to Windsor. To the Prussian mind, the Prince had led an anti-Prussian demonstration in Paris.

He made another gesture of sympathy when the Prince Imperial was killed by Zulus while he was fighting with the British in South Africa. The Prince of Wales thought that his 'horrible and untimely death' was a blot on the good name of the British army and he persuaded his mother to allow a British man-of-war to bring the body back to England. Through his thoughtfulness, twenty three-minute guns were fired off Spithead, one for each year of the gallant soldier's life. He paid his last tribute to the heir of the Bonapartist cause by acting as pall-bearer in the funeral at Chislehurst. These were definite manifestations of the Prince's devotion to France and they were also bitter proofs of his dislike of the 'bullying' spirit of the German government. He did not pretend to sympathise with his mother's Prussian leanings and the Queen saw her son receding from her—he was less and less within her comprehension. With him went the emotions of the English people. On January 14th, the Emperor wrote to Queen Victoria[110] regretting the 'change of popular feeling in England.' At first, it had been 'all in favour of Germany.' 'No one can regret more than I do the signs of ill-feeling which are arising between England and Germany—the two countries...in all respects destined to go hand in hand.' Then, confusing the achievements of Bismarck with those of his Creator, he wrote, 'I cannot but be proud that God has chosen to raise me...I take it with humility, as I do all God's dealings with us.'

When victory comes to armies, they thank God. When they are vanquished, they blame the government. In France where the clergy were being shot, along with the others, the people of Paris were passing through the hell of destroying an old government and forming a republic out of their mutilated people.

§ III — 1864–1892

SIR SIDNEY LEE has described the Disraeli-Gladstone years as the 'golden era in English politics.' They were certainly the years when statesmen moulded public opinion, not merely reflecting it. The Prince of Wales passed through the golden era, struggling with both Prime Ministers for diplomatic information and confidence. It was not until November, 1892, when he was a man of fifty-one years, that diplomatic trust was given to the Prince in full. In the main the exclusion of the Prince from affairs of Government involved three people: his mother, who thought him wanting in discretion, and, during their alternate seasons of power, Mr. Gladstone and Mr. Disraeli. When he was twenty-eight years old, the Queen still wrote to him *earnestly and seriously,* asking him not to go more than two days to Ascot races. She pleaded, 'I hear every true and attached friend of ours expressing *such anxiety* that you should gather round you the really good, steady, distinguished people....' He was brave and assertive enough to resent interference this time. 'I am past twenty-eight and have some considerable knowledge of the world and society,' he answered. Mr. Gladstone favoured the heir, and their relationship enjoyed moments of candour and friendliness. Gladstone thought him intelligent and, after they had played whist together at Abergeldie, the Prime Minister wrote of the Prince's 'usual good manners.' Their friendship survived even the difference of opinion over Irish Home Rule. It has been alternately stated and refuted that the Prince was drawn to the Liberal High Churchman because his mother was repelled: that he favoured Gladstone and not Disraeli, because Disraeli was his mother's friend. The Prince made an astonishing gesture when Mr. Gladstone died: he bowed and kissed the widow's hand. Mr. Gladstone admitted the Prince's talents. Mr. Disraeli did not, for he described his conversation as 'chitter-chatter.' Any normally sensitive person would discover the difference in the two responses, and this the Prince no doubt did.

He was too quick, impatient and matter-of-fact to wish to be drawn into the warm, Oriental imaginings of Mr. Disraeli.

The split between the Queen and the Prince, over State papers, began during the war between Prussia and Denmark in 1864. It was the first division of opinion which they evinced, the Queen pledging her loyalty to the Prussians and the Prince, rather naturally, following the anxious eyes of his wife, then turned towards Denmark. Had he agreed with his mother, the Prince might have been allowed to peep into the imposing, guarded, red leather boxes from Whitehall. The Foreign Secretary of the time had sponsored the Prince in his wish for more information, but the Queen, having made up her mind that not one strand of power should slip out of her grasp, had said 'No.' All she could permit was a *précis* of the papers and then, only the papers *she* might choose. The Prince was denied an active part in the government of the country so he turned to less informed channels for his information. He read the newspapers, like any other man, and he picked up relayed secrets and gossip from Westminster. It is little wonder that his opinions lagged behind what the Queen expected of him. She asked plants to grow without roots. The Prince demurred, but he waited patiently, until 1882, when he was forty-one years old. Then he protested again, telling his mother that he was denied even as much information as fell into the hands of private secretaries to Ministers. They possessed keys to the mysterious, travelling red boxes. His mother made her old reply. It would be 'quite irregular and improper': besides, he 'talked too much.' [111] Not until he was forty-four years old did the Queen go so far as to allow him to learn the 'decisions or changes of policy before they became known.' [112] The old fear still haunted the Queen: the fear that had begun when the Prince Consort was yet alive: that her son would usurp her husband's place and thus jeopardise her own. Her Prime Minister, her secretaries and friends pleaded for the Prince, but she continued to feel that her middle-aged son was not to be relied upon. She was afraid, too, that he would discuss affairs with the members of the Government and thus weave a web of political influence. 'It would not be desirable,' she admitted, 'that W. G. [Gladstone] and His Royal Highness should have discussions which she knew nothing about.' [113]

During Mr. Gladstone's term of office, in 1886, a gold key was found in the Foreign Office, where it had lain, forgotten, since 1861. It had been the Prince Consort's own key, for opening the special boxes in which only the most confidential papers were kept: the last stronghold of the Foreign Office secrets. Lord Rosebery was Foreign Secretary; he bravely handed the key to the Prince of Wales. For the first time, in his forty-fifth year, the secrets of the country he was to rule were laid bare to him. The final, wholesale participation in the Sovereign's secrets did not come until 1892. Mr. Gladstone, eighty-three years old, and the Queen, seventy-three years old, at last permitted full confidence to the Prince of Wales, whose own son was now twenty-seven years old, and to be betrothed in six months' time.

This dogged campaign against her son's participation in State affairs has been a sturdy peg for most of the Queen's biographers and critics. Here they found the proof of her selfishness and lack of vision. But there is another side to the story. The Queen looked upon her Crown as a sacred trust. Nowhere, in all the thousands of documents written during her reign, do we find any hint at a broken secret, a trick of duplicity or violated confidence. From beginning to end, she was scrupulously honest over the conversations and documents of State—never playing one man against the other—never, in fact, showing pettiness or meanness. For her, the less rigid methods of the later part of the century were disturbing. She was always haunted by stories of the parties at Marlborough House—the gay company and the late hours. The Queen saw most events in the terms of pictures—the precious red boxes, the precious documents and the precious key, upon a table at Marlborough House, during a ribald party! She shuddered at the picture and she exaggerated the dangers. But she felt them, and it was as much to guard her sacred trust as in suspicion of her son's talents and integrity, that she withheld the key from him for so long.

Chapter Eleven

§ 1 — 1871

THE SELF-CONFIDENCE of the Queen and her subjects was shaken at the end of 1871, when the Prince of Wales fell ill with typhoid fever. At the prospect of his death, the members of the Royal family were reconciled and the mass of the British people were anxious and deeply stirred. They found themselves more passionately devoted to the Royal cause than they had imagined. For there had been apathy and even demonstrations . . . echoes of the Communist fever which was upon Europe again. In April there was a mass meeting in Hyde Park to demonstrate English sympathy with the Paris Communists. While the Queen was writing naïvely of 'these horrid Communists,' they were finding in her and in the Prince of Wales a butt for their restlessness. It was suggested in both the Press and the House of Commons that the Queen and the Prince of Wales had used the Foreign Office messengers for sending letters to their relations in Germany during the Franco-Prussian War. The accusation was impertinent and silly, for the obligations of a neutral country would not require that a Sovereign should not communicate with her own daughter. The story involved the Prince of Wales: it was enlarged so that he was obliged to make a protest and an explanation. Then came a restirring of the old rumour that the Queen was to abdicate. The story persisted, and as late as 1877 one may find reports in the newspapers that 'the Queen had

III

abdicated' and that she intended 'to pass the remainder of her days in Scotland.' While these rumours disturbed the public mind, the Queen remained rock-like: even when Sir Charles Dilke attacked her personally before big audiences at Newcastle and Leeds. He wanted to know why Royal dowries should be paid, and he deplored the cost of the Court, which he estimated at one million pounds a year. He described the expense as a 'moral mischief' and added that it would perhaps be worth two million pounds to put an end to it. His remarks and the derision of his audience were all reported in *The Times* for the Queen to read: even Dilke's description of one of the officials as the 'Court undertaker,' and the quick, cruel answer of a man in the audience who said that he wished the Court undertaker had more work to do.[114] The Queen was unmoved. She read *The Times* without comment, as she lay on her sofa at Balmoral, crippled by gout. She was adamant and she never relaxed her vigilance. Her attitude was, 'I expect it,' and her solace was in her firm belief that only a stupid minority was involved. She still wrote, 'The Queen insists,' and however bitter the grumblings against her will, she usually won in the end. In April, she read the new Budget. While London was playing with the rumour of her abdication, she ignored the newspapers and she sat in the gardens of Osborne, reading the Chancellor of the Exchequer's plans for raising new revenue. One of the causes for this need was the death of the old Purchase system in the Army. Among the items was a tax upon matches. The Queen pounced upon this and she wrote to Mr. Gladstone '... the poorer *classes* will be *constantly* irritated by the increased expense and reminded of the tax by the Government Stamp on the box.' She was wise and right. This letter was written on April 23rd. From Osborne she knew the public mind better than the politicians in Westminster. Next day, as she foresaw, a procession of poor match-makers, representing the 30,000 men, women and children employed in the factories, marched to Westminster. The result of the Queen's intervention and the match-makers' protest was the withdrawal of the item from the Budget. Her agitation was never in favour of the rich. Nor did she seek protection for the upper classes. In October of 1873 she was alarmed because of the numerous accidents on the railways. She wrote to Mr. Gladstone: [115] 'In *NO* country except ours are there so many dreadful accidents, and for the poor people who have to travel constantly by rail, and who cannot have the comparative security which those who travel in first-class carriages *can* have, to be in perpetual danger of their lives is monstrous.'

There were disturbances within the Royal family also, to make the Queen anxious. She tried to allay these. In July she struggled against her feeling that only Prince Albert ever had the right to stand beside her. '... as years go on, I strongly feel that to lift up my son and heir and keep him in the place near me, is only what is right,' [116] she wrote. But she did not conquer the antipathy entirely. She still communicated with him through her Ministers. Nor did she protest when her daughter in Germany belittled his talents, resenting his French sympathies and asserting that he was jealous of her own Crown Prince, who enjoyed privileges and opportunities which were denied to the Prince of Wales.

On November 22nd, the Queen heard that the Prince of Wales 'had mild typhoid fever.' [117] She was herself recovering from an operation to her arm and a devilish attack of rheumatic gout. Her Journal, written during these days, reveals the true pluck with which she met pain or mischance. She struggled against her own weakness and set out for Sandringham. Mr. Gladstone's letters of sympathy already smelled of death: he was the last person to advise her in a time like this, when she needed anything but reminders of Mr. Gladstone's rather gloomy God. When she came to Sandringham, she was allowed to step into the bedroom, and stand 'behind a screen, to see her son sleeping or dozing.' The room was dark and only one lamp was burning, so she could not see him well—'lying rather flat on his back, breathing very rapidly and loudly.' It all reminded her, 'vividly and sadly,' of 'dearest Albert's illness.' The old tenderness was awakened in her again. Royalties are born to a damnable fate. Their children must belong to a system, a tradition and a future. The present Duke of York is said to have once declared, 'We are a firm, not a family.' The personal anxiety of the ordinary mother and father, the nurturing of simplicity rather than splendour, of character rather than ambition, are not enough. Royal persons bear their children, only to lose them, for Princes do not belong to themselves or to their parents. One must consider the story of mother and son in this cruel light. It was not enough, as it would be for any other mother, for the Queen to see her son moderately good and contented. She had to drive him with the spurs of her own will and the consciousness of how grim the struggle of kingship was to become. This she realized to the full. This fear and this unique relationship must never be forgotten when we are tempted to withhold our sympathy because of the Queen's apparent hardness of judgment. Standing behind the screen, peeping at her son upon his bed, the hardness vanished. Princess Alexandra too needed affection and help from her now. The simple, pathetic depths in her were stirred: the depths which used to be stirred in those old days when she was alone with Prince Albert in their little sitting-room at Osborne, when all the others had departed. When they sang their little songs together,

> The husband's heart is bowed unto the dust,
>   But still the wife looks up with fearless trust,
> To heaven's pure light, to the stars beyond,
>   And a tear falls, that says, 'Do not despond.'

These had been the moments in which she ceased to be Queen of England. The Prince Consort and the Queen had liked being sentimental and homely: it was the kind of life they both understood. It was to this simplicity that the Queen returned at Sandringham, when all the anxieties of being Queen were drowned by the simple fear and compassion of being a mother. She was allowed the sensation very seldom, but it was real. She was still so weak that she could not walk very far, and there were meandering letters from Gladstone every day. There was no respite for her in this dreary time of waiting, as there would have been for any other mother. She would sit behind the screen, watching, or she would observe Princess Alexandra, seeing, in her simplicity and patience, qualities which endeared her to her.

It seemed that the falling away of her life had already begun. Her sister was to die very soon. She had loved Princess Hohenlohe very dearly: her '*last* near relative' who was on 'an equality with her.' 'No one can really help me,' she wrote in her Journal. 'All, all gone.' In January of 1873 Louis Napoleon was to die at Chislehurst, and in June, Dr. Norman Macleod, her beloved friend, at Balmoral. She wept many 'bitter tears.' [118] In December,

Lady Beaconsfield died and, within a year, her dear friend
Winterhalter died—Winterhalter, who had painted her
with Prince Albert so many, many times. In October,
Sir Edwin Landseer died: he had made many excursions
with her in the Highlands, teaching her to draw stags'
heads. She possessed about forty of his beautiful oil paint-
ings and many of his drawings. Bereavement followed
bereavement; one long chronicle of death. Even her
favourite dog was to die: Dacko, with his 'funny, amusing ways' and his 'large, melancholy eyes.' He died while
she was at Sandringham. She would bury him at Windsor, with a fine bronze effigy, just below the East Terrace.
All the dogs would be there, in bronze, between the hollies
and chestnuts—especially Sharp, with a bronze glove,
just as he used to guard it when they went down to
Frogmore to tea. These were the signs of the end. She
felt it so. There were no hopeful or pleasant memories for
her to contemplate, nor events to welcome, as she sat
there. She might have paused to realise the signs of her
refreshed power. In a trice the Communists were silenced.
London forgot its impatience and the word 'abdication'
was no longer mentioned. A wave of simple dread swept
over the land, and columns of anxious messages appeared
in the newspapers. In Penzance and Hawick, in Tun-
bridge Wells and in Dover, the people stood hour after
hour in the December cold, waiting for the new bulletins
on the doors of the post offices. The telegraph had been
invented so that the far-away corners of the Queen's
Empire were able to think with her and to talk to her.
The anxiety touched the southern edge of New Zealand:
it hushed the voices of Canadians and it quietened the
disgruntled settlers of the Cape. They might grumble

against the central power which ruled them, but once the existence of that power was endangered, a curious and passionate anxiety took the place of the discontent. People telegraphed their homely remedies for typhoid to her, some, 'of the most mad kind.' On December 8th the report was so alarming that the Queen hurried down to Sandringham again, 'a melancholy journey' which exhausted her. But she sat in the darkness behind the screen, staring at the blank in front of her, peeping around the corner every now and then to watch and to listen to the troubled breathing. Hour after hour and day after day she waited. Sometimes she was so tired that she drowsed at her vigil.

At one moment during the public anxiety, Alfred Austin was said to have written, with more feeling than art:

> Flashed o'er the wires
> The fateful message came,
> He is no better;
> He is much the same.

At half-past-five on the morning of the eleventh, the Queen was awakened by Dr. Jenner. 'At any moment' Bertie might die. She hurried through the cold passages of Sandringham to the dark room, 'the candles burning, and most dreary,' expecting death. But her son did not die. On the thirteenth, she wrote in her Journal:

'I was so terribly anxious, and wanted to be of any little use I could. I went up to the bed and took hold of his poor hand, kissing it and stroking his arm. He turned round and looked wildly at me, saying "Who are you?" and then, "It's Mama." "Dear child," I replied. Later he said, "It is so kind of you to come," which shows he knew me, which was most comforting to me. I sat next to the bed, holding his hand. . . .' [119]

117

No observer of these scenes was more wise than Lady Augusta Stanley. One is always tempted to turn to her letters for the comment which is unsentimental yet wholly kind. When the Duke of Edinburgh told her of the hours in which his mother waited beside her son, Lady Augusta wrote to her sister of the Queen's patience, 'I quite long to see Her thus, Her best self, by being taken out of herself—taken out of doctors and maladies (I mean her own) and nerves and fighting off what Her own righteous conscience tells Her would be right.' [120]

The fourteenth day of December was terrible for the Queen. It was the tenth anniversary of Prince Albert's death. She sat behind the screen again and when she was allowed to go to her son's bed, at last, he kissed her hand, smiled and said, 'So kind of you to come; it is the kindest thing you could do.' The nurses said that in his fevers he whistled and raved in all languages. But when he was calm, he thanked them, never complaining. And he called his wife by endearing names. It was on the anniversary of his father's death that the Prince showed the first signs of change. 'On this *very* day,' the Queen wrote in her Journal, 'our dear Bertie is getting better instead of worse.' On January 1st when she went to him, he was able to kiss her and to give her a New Year nosegay, which he had ordered.

A season of peace came after the Prince's illness. The talk of Republics and the contempt for Crowns passed into the background. *The Times* dwelt upon the 'warm and personal' relationship between the Queen and her people. All rancour died in the face of death and Kingship won another victory in England. Again the violent influences of European politics were swept back before they could hurt us. Thiers still struggled in Paris for a rickety Presidentship. Bismarck was expelling the Jesuits from Germany: he still held the cords of power tightly in his hands.

A hardness came into the Prussian campaign which the Queen did not sanction. She protested to her daughter against the dethroning of lesser Princes and the confiscation of their palaces and estates. The Crown Princess's answer was impertinent. She wrote of the confiscated palaces, *'Those* in which *we have* been, we have as much right to inhabit as you to wear the *Kohinoor....'* [121] There was much anxiety in Europe, but the threat of the Prince's death had calmed England strangely. On February 27th the Queen, the Prince and Princess Alexandra drove through a happy, cheering London, to a thanksgiving service in St. Paul's.

The Queen wrote in her Journal:

'Luckily a fine morning.... Went to dress, and wore a black silk dress and jacket, trimmed with miniver, and a bonnet with white flowers and a white feather. Beatrice looked very nice in mauve, trimmed with swan's down.... Bertie was very lame and did not look at all well, I grieved to see. My three other sons were there, and the poor Emperor Napoleon and Empress Eugénie, who were anxious to see the procession quietly.... The boys with little George [122] went on and got into an open carriage and four, with Lord Ailesbury, and in a few minutes I followed, taking poor Bertie's arm, for he could only walk very slowly, down to the Grand Entrance. We entered an open State landau with six horses, ridden by three postilions.... The deafening cheers never ceased the whole way.... We seemed to be passing through a sea of people, as we went along the Mall.... At the corner of Marlborough House there was a stand on which stood Bertie's dear little girls, who waved their handkerchiefs.... Everywhere troops lined the streets, and there were fifteen military bands stationed at intervals along the whole route, who played "God Save the Queen" and "God Bless the Prince of Wales" as the carriages approached, which evoked fresh outbursts of cheering. I saw the tears in Bertie's eyes and took and pressed his hand.' [128]

Two days afterwards, a poor, mad boy presented a pistol at the Queen as she stepped out of her carriage. Brown, her servant, seized him. This last sensation was providential: it shook Englishmen to the core. Londoners came again to the railings of the Palace, all day and all night, to stare at the doors beyond which the symbol of their safety lay. There was not a word of complaint now, only thanksgiving. The change in public feeling was almost as unreasonable as the carping had been. When Sir Charles Dilke stood up again in the House and moved for an enquiry into the Civil List, which was the Queen's own affair, he was howled down. Mr. Gladstone opposed the motion contemptuously, and it was rejected by 276 votes to 2. England sang *God Save the Queen* again, with heart and voice.

If these were exciting days for the Queen, they were dull as far as politics were concerned. Mr. Gladstone was still in power. The people wished a change, and when Mr. Disraeli spoke to them, in June of the new year, he made the Conservative orchards seem so sweet that they were tempted to stray from the Liberal vegetable garden. They listened to Disraeli again, his phrases like an Aurora Borealis in the dull political sky. They enjoyed the sight and the promise of change: they were entranced as they had never been before.

§ 11 — 1873

MR. GLADSTONE was busy with his Irish University Bill at the beginning of 1873. It was defeated by 287 votes to

284 and Mr. Gladstone went to the Queen and resigned.
She sent again for her favourite, but Mr. Disraeli's glorious
hour had not come and he declined to take office with
such a slim majority. So Mr. Gladstone was Prime
Minister again, although his Liberals were already wilting
under the growth of Tory popularity. By-elections were
thinning out the ranks of his followers. Again, in the
moment of uncertainty between Liberal and Tory, the
Queen showed herself as a great constitutional monarch.
There do not seem to be any records of her two interviews in the Queen's Journals, but an unusual letter from
her secretary, General Ponsonby, helps us to comprehend
her calm and sense during the days when the Tories and
the Liberals were in the balance. Excepting the Queen,
General Ponsonby was the only person who knew both
sides of the story: the interview with Gladstone, heavy
under the threat of eclipse, the interview with Disraeli,
in which the Queen saw hope of a return to the regime
in which she believed and the Prime Minister whom she
liked. General Ponsonby could not contain his admiration
and he wrote [124] of her 'clear and unmistakable directions,'
of the way in which she had considered each difficulty,
promptly deciding upon it, and with an accurate knowledge of precedents. He was amazed by the way in which
she conducted the two interviews, skilfully avoiding 'taking any step that was liable to misconstruction.' He com-
mended her 'love of fairness and justice to both parties'
and her 'clear-sighted judgment.'

The government of the country jogged along. Income
tax fell from fourpence to threepence and the tax on
sugar was reduced. The country was prosperous—new
millionaires ripened in the midlands and Australian
sheepowners came home and increased the ranks of the

rich. In June the Queen celebrated the thirty-sixth anniversary of the day of her Accession. But she had no time for contemplation, for the Shah of Persia was coming to see her. Again the Windsor hill was gay with flags and covered with people. He came, like a Prince out of a fairy story. His coat was buttoned with big rubies: his sword hilt and epaulettes were all of diamonds, each with a huge emerald in the centre. His sword hilt and scabbard were adorned with jewels and an aigrette of diamonds sprayed from his astrakhan hat. Two chairs were placed in the middle of the room and upon these the Shah and the Queen sat and talked. She was shy at first, but her sense of humour conquered her. '...very absurd it must have looked,' she wrote. She gave the Shah the Order of the Garter, 'Arthur and Leopold' helping her to put the blue riband over his head. Then the Shah gave her an order, much to the danger of her cap, as he tried to put the riband over *her* head. The Grand Vizier helped this time. Before he left, the Shah took off his aigrette and put on his spectacles. The two chairs were put against the wall again. The Shah went back to London where his fine horse with the pink tail was waiting for him. The Queen sat down to a dinner of roast beef and talked of the thirty-six years in which she had ruled England. She thought it 'almost impossible.'

Chapter Twelve

1866–1874

WHEN THE Prince's efforts to help in English affairs were curbed, his energies turned to other fields. Quite naturally, it seemed, he identified himself with the other countries of the world: France, Austria, Denmark and Germany. He travelled as far east as Russia, and as far south as Egypt and India. His taste for talk with cosmopolitan people, his gift for languages and his flair for international politics increased his success in the capitals and courts of Europe. But there was another reason why he became the friend of so many princes. His mother's unwillingness to entertain royal visitors to England threw the onus and the pleasure of the host upon him. No royalties were invited within the walls of Windsor, except to lunch or dinner, for many years. The Empress Eugénie and the German Empress were the Queen's only royal guests, apart from the members of her own family.

It is astonishing to read of the growth of the Prince's friendships and influence during the eight years before 1874. In 1866, he had been to Russia for the first time. On this journey he had stayed with the new King of the Belgians and he had celebrated his twenty-fifth birthday with his sister and her family, which included the Queen's first grandchild, the future Emperor William II, in Potsdam. In 1867, he had entertained the Sultan of Turkey in London. In 1868, with Princess Alexandra, the Prince made a great journey. It began in Copenhagen, where he was wholly loved by Princess Alexandra's family. His friendliness graced all occasions. The Prince and the Princess went to Berlin, where all but Bismarck spoke cordially to them, although there were moments in which the Prince felt that he was being treated as 'a French spy.' The King of Prussia (afterwards German Emperor) gave Prince Albert Edward the order of The Black Eagle. The collar of the order which was given him had belonged to his father. From Berlin the Prince and Princess went to Vienna, where the Emperor entertained them magnificently. Here was sumptuousness which was lively and dazzling, after the solid domestic air of the Court at Windsor. Everybody was charming to them: they floated across Europe upon a tide of compliments and favours. The ramifications of their life and interests extended every day.

If the Prince was denied visits to Ireland and some voice in the Government of his own country, he could at least enjoy the dazzling experience of travel in countries where neither his mother nor Mr. Gladstone nor Lord Granville could interfere with his movements or censor his speech. Upon the same journey they crossed the Mediterranean and travelled a thousand miles on the Nile. The Near East opened its gaily painted doors to them. The Prince talked to M. de Lesseps, the designer of the Suez Canal, and when he returned to England, he showed a pleasant freedom from insularity by urging that the coveted Albert Medal should be given to the Frenchman. In April they crossed the Mediterranean again and steamed into the Bosphorus. The Princess was entranced by the scene of Constantinople—the domes of St. Sofia and the slim minarets rising from beside the water to the sky. The Sultan was half mad with joy

THE QUEEN'S FIRST GRANDCHILD

over his visitors, and he made the Moslem purists angry because of the gaiety of his entertainment. For the first time in his life, the Sultan gave a party. Up to then, nobody but the Grand Vizier had ever been allowed to eat with him. But tradition was thrown to the winds. The doors of the Palace were opened wide—the doors into the hundred white rooms—into the sacred gardens, noisy with the screeching of parakeets. But the moment of Turkey's conflict was coming. She was already beginning to forget Mecca, and the prophetic moon which had split for Mohammed. Advanced Turks were turning their faces to the west. Twenty-six guests, including women, sat at the Sultan's table. He came out from behind the hundred walls of the Palace to attend a ball at the British Embassy. The devout Moslems were furious, and the holy men from Mecca gathered in a palace on the shores of the Bosphorus and thought the end had come. The Sultan was very sorry, he said, that the dictates of the Prophet forbade his giving a similarly splendid ball in return. The Prince and Princess rambled through the bedlam of the Constantinople bazaars, in the guise of 'Mr. and Mrs. Williams.' These months abroad gave them pleasure and experience, without London's censorship of everything they did. From Turkey they travelled to Athens: from Athens, and the pleasure of being with the Princess's brother, to Paris, and then home. The world was their oyster now.

In 1873, the Prince went to stay with his sister, Princess Alice, near to Darmstadt. At Jugenheim, set in one of the prettiest parts of the country, he was completely happy. He was with his beloved sister, and he was free to speak of the big affairs of the world to the Princes who came there. His talk was eager and his plea was always for peace. There was a long conversation with the Tsar of Russia, who also came to stay. The Prince was one of the first to be told of the betrothal of his brother, Prince Alfred, to the Grand Duchess Marie: one of the first to imagine that the marriage would bury the hatchets of the Crimea. There was a more thoughtful note in the Prince's letters as these new interests awakened him. Perhaps a little extravagantly, he seemed to see himself as a friendly influence between nations. At least the beginning of the influence was already apparent. We have evidence of his powers as early as 1872, when the Prince called upon Monsieur and Madame Thiers at Versailles. The Prince had been the friend of Louis Napoleon. This allegiance, coupled with his strong belief in monarchy, made him declare beforehand, that it 'went very much against the grain' for him to have a parley with the President of the Third Republic. But Thiers, 'like most Continental politicians...believed implicitly in the Prince's political influence.'[125] The meeting was a success, much to the annoyance of Bismarck.

In 1873, the Prince met Thiers again, by accident. He was yachting on the north coast of France and he happened to land at Trouville, where Thiers was staying. At that time, Thiers's fear of German military plans was at its height. He 'begged the Prince to find an opportunity of impressing on the German Emperor and his counsellors the desire and indeed the resolve of the French Government to maintain peace.'[126] But the accidental meeting and the peaceful wishes expressed in the conversation appeared in a different light to Bismarck. One of his spies happened to be in Trouville and he reported the meeting to Berlin. Bismarck, knowing the Prince's sympathy for France and hatred for his own domineering policy, saw fresh dangers in the interview. The talk with Thiers made one more bond between French interests and England's future King. It did not wholly serve the cause of peace, as the Prince of Wales imagined, for the more France became his friend, the more Bismarck's Germany became his enemy. But it showed that the Prince was able to enjoy in Europe some of the influence and position which was denied to him in his own country. Sometimes, in his eagerness, he talked to his new friends too much. His spontaneous politics were not an expression of the more wise and careful policy of Gladstone, Granville and the Queen. The dangers that lay in such youthful eagerness may explain the anxiety which lay behind the Queen's policy of frustrating her son.

In 1873, after accompanying his brother, Prince Alfred, to the marriage in St. Petersburg, the Prince returned the Russian hospitality with princely kindness at Marlborough House. This was in June. Among the Prince's Russian guests was the young Grand Duke Nicholas, afterwards Tsar Nicholas the Second. Through some slip, the Shah of Persia arrived in London at the same time, but the Prince was as eager to greet the Oriental ruler as those European Princes who were more closely related to him. He seemed to revel in this field of responsibility, and he was radiant with smiles and little stories as he walked through the drawing-rooms of Marlborough House. Through all these celebrations his mother remained at Windsor. By this time mystery had surrounded her. The European princes spoke of her as if she were an oracle, believed in, but never seen. The story of her widowhood had become a legend in the Courts of Europe and when princes came to London, they were taken down to Windsor for luncheon, and ushered into the presence of fear.

She was always charming, and the story of her beautiful voice and the memory of her entrancing laugh were something to take away with them, back to Munich, Vienna, Paris, Potsdam ... wherever they lived. But it was the Prince of Wales who opened the glorious drawing-rooms of London to them, regaling them with good food, good music and just enough fun to prove that his court was human as well as elaborate.

When the Prince was in Europe, he moved among the Courts in friendly ease. The Tsar liked him and Louis Napoleon had been his friend. He went to stag hunts in France, he visited Winterhalter in his studio in Paris and in Stockholm the King induced him to become a Freemason. His experiences were wide and personal. All were his friends, except some of the German princes who copied their prejudices from those of Bismarck.

Opportunities for usefulness soon came to the Prince. The first was in aid of his brother-in-law, King George of the Hellenes. He was Princess Alexandra's brother: a con-scientious Dane, bewildered in trying to bring order to the tangle of Greek politics and Government. In April of 1870 a party of English people were captured by Greek brigands, and two of the men were ultimately murdered. The English newspapers began a virile attack upon the Hellenes and the name of Greece soon stank in English nostrils. King George of the Hellenes pleaded with the Prince of Wales and, in turn, the Prince pleaded with Mr. Gladstone who was then in power. Mr. Gladstone was cold in the spirit of his answer. He said that the fury of the people against Greece would pass and that 'the lapse of a short time' would 'restore the balance of the public mind.' [127]

Mr. Gladstone was no doubt right, but his decision did

not bring much solace to King George, nor did it satisfy
the Prince. The incident hinted, however, that his visits to
Europe were opening the door to usefulness. The Tsar
wished to set the seal upon his friendliness in 1873 by
making the Prince Colonel of a Russian Regiment. His
letter to his mother was an eager request that he should
be allowed to accept, but the Queen said 'No.' In a similar
conflict, in a more lusty age, Queen Elizabeth had said,
'My dogs shall wear no collars but mine own.' Lord Granville, Mr. Gladstone and the Duke of Cambridge agreed
with the Queen, that the precedent of accepting such
honours from other countries was full of foreboding.
Lord Granville threw cold water upon the Prince's ex-
uberance by writing, 'We are insular and there are many
advantages in remaining so.' The Prince pleaded once
more. Then the Tsar telegraphed to the Queen, asking
that the Prince should be allowed to accept the honour
offered him. The Queen still said 'No.' She did not
change her mind until she was offered a similar honour
herself, some years afterwards.

Chapter Thirteen

§1 — 1874

EARLY IN the year 1874, the Queen said that no one could be 'more *truly* Liberal at heart' than herself.[128] What she disliked about Mr. Gladstone's brand of Liberalism, more than Mr. Gladstone himself, was his passion for reforms, the 'many alterations and changes' which he fathered. Prince Albert had been a Liberal Reformer, and the Queen had been taught to believe that the secret of the Coburg success had been Liberalism. But she still had hankerings after the *divine right.* She would have liked reforms and lenience to appear in the shape of Royal patronage. She was compassionate but she wished to give bread to the poor, not to have it snatched out of her hand.

There was one bogey, above all others, which aggravated the Queen's dislike of Mr. Gladstone: the Romanising of the Anglican Church. She was almost inclined to agree with Dickens, that Roman Catholicism was 'the most horrible means of political and social degradation left in the world.'

It was when she came back from Balmoral that she seemed to be most anxious. She remembered the simple services at Crathie and she was appalled by the imagined increase of Popish practices in the Anglican Church. She was pledged to protect an institution of which she had small understanding, especially of its historical continuity.

Her religion was subjective; she had no comprehension of objective religion. She had been brought up on Prince

Albert's habits of worship, exemplified in his practice of always dining alone with her upon the evening before he took the Sacrament. With the inherited Lutheran principles which were strong in her, and the memory of the simple religious practices on Deeside, the Queen stood her ground against ritualism. Mr. Gladstone had been its symbol. Once he had even admitted his interest in Christian communities other than his own, 'most of all the Roman Catholic Church, within which,' he wrote, 'the largest number of Christians find their spiritual good.' The Queen had written again and again to Mr. Gladstone, warning him of the danger to the Church. But he had always reassured her. He wrote of the 'power of the Church' and of its 'tenacious vitality,' but the Queen was not convinced.

The New Year began dismally for Mr. Gladstone. On December 29th he had written in his diary: 'Sixty-four years completed to-day—what have they brought me? A weaker heart, stiffened muscles, thin hairs; other strength still remains in my frame.' But he wrote now like an old man. When he went to the theatre, earlier in December, it was to see 'how low our stage has fallen.'[129] The New Year came and, on January 8th, Mr. Gladstone wrote to Lord Granville of the disintegration of the Liberal Party. 'The signs of weakness multiply,' he wrote. He had to admit that his Government was ceasing to 'possess that amount of power which is necessary for the dignity of the Crown and the welfare of the country.' He turned restlessly in his bed in Carlton House Terrace, demoralised by bronchitis, and with the darkness of an election before him. He wrote to the Queen of 'a tightness of the chest,' and he confessed his desolation to her. He could expect indulgence, but little sympathy. In his letter he recalled the recent history of Liberal failure; the defeat of his Irish Universities Bill in the previous March, the continual snubbing of his measures by the House of Lords, and the by-elections in which his Liberal candidates had been tumbled over like nine-pins. England was tired of his reign. On January 23rd, while the Queen was reading the letters describing the dazzling beauty of her son's marriage [130] in St. Petersburg, Mr. Gladstone sent her an ominous telegram. The Cabinet had agreed to dissolve. Scene followed scene, each one intensifying the Liberal calamity. At the age of sixty-five, Gladstone had to go to Greenwich like a novice in politics, to induce his electors to vote for him. They came in thousands to listen to him, but he had to stand, bareheaded in the drizzling rain, with a cart for his platform. His voice and his powers were as wonderful as ever. He was returned to Parliament again, but he led a thinned army. The Tories surged into Westminster with a majority of eighty-three for all Great Britain.

On February 17th Gladstone set out for Windsor, carrying a copy of Thomas à Kempis in his hand, for reading in the train. He drove up the Windsor hill and into the great quadrangle of the Castle. The Queen received him kindly but there was little tenderness and less commiseration. He wished Parliament to dissolve at once. Even the Queen's suggestion of an honour for him only deepened his gloom. 'Oh! Nothing!' he said. He could not accept any honour 'in the face of such condemnation from the country.' He repeated his explanation of the Liberal decline. When he had driven down the hill again, the Queen sent for Princess Beatrice and asked her to write down her own notion of why Gladstone had failed. 'I could, of course, not tell him that it was greatly owing to his own unpopularity.'

Next day Mr. Disraeli came. Almost immediately, Windsor smiled again. Not more than a dozen sentences were exchanged between the Sovereign and the new Prime Minister before she thought something 'amusingly said.' Disraeli gave her back what she always felt to be wilting when Gladstone was in the room: her self-confidence. Gladstone made her feel that her power was shaky. Disraeli 'repeatedly said' that what she wished 'SHOULD be done, whatever his difficulties might be. ...' [131] Her capitals and italics were signs of her refreshed sense of security. A few weeks afterwards, Mr. Disraeli showed how truly he understood her and how he could awaken her to her fullest power. 'It may be unconstitutional,' he wrote, 'for a Minister to seek advice from his Sovereign, instead of proffering it.' [132] His excuse for his unconstitutional lapse was her 'unrivalled experience of public life.' The Queen blossomed again under his encouragement. The 'very grave' Mr. Gladstone was safely out of her sight. When Disraeli came to her, on February 20th, they talked about the changes and the difficulties, but he made them all seem to be so easy and so much less alarming. When the audience was over, Disraeli knelt down before her, his head bowed. The Queen extended her hands. Disraeli raised them to his lips and he kissed them. The deep, beautiful voice whispered to her, 'I plight my troth to the kindest of *Mistresses.*' His magic lay in his ability to convince her that she was still ruler of England.

§ II — 1874

MR. GLADSTONE behaved as if this were his end. He had faced the long interviews and the drizzling rain at Greenwich, while he was still weak from bronchitis. He was tired: he packed his possessions at Number 10, and he bade his room farewell. All that he wished now was to spend the remainder of his days 'in tranquillity,' providing, of course, that it was God's pleasure also.

In March he read his rival's old novel, *Vivian Grey*, and he declared the first quarter to be extremely clever. But the last three-quarters were 'trash.' Mr. Disraeli's opinion of Gladstone's 'scribblement' was no less scathing. 'Gladstone, like Richelieu, can't write,' he declared to Lady Bradford. 'Nothing can be more unmusical, more involved, or more uncouth.... He has not produced a page w^h. you can put on y^r. library shelves...' Mr. Gladstone turned to his 'scribblement' with a heavy pen. His theme was *The Vatican Decrees in their bearing on Civil Allegiance: a Political Expostulation*. One hundred and forty-five thousand copies were sold before the end of the year. Mr. Disraeli spoke generously of him in the House, praising his 'illustrious career.' The public voice was more kind than the opinions expressed in private. Disraeli wrote to Lord Derby of Gladstone as an 'unprincipled maniac ...extra-ordinary mixture of envy, vindictiveness, hypocracy and superstition...'

Mr. Gladstone behaved now as if his career were over. He sold his London house: he sold his china and his wedgwood ware. His books were packed and sent to his house in the country. There he lingered, becoming less and less inclined to be drawn into the confusion and quarrels of Parliament.

§ III — 1874

THE FINAL and dismissing criticism to be made of an English statesman by his colleague is that he is not a gentleman. The aristocracy had said this of Prince Albert. Prince Albert had said it of Disraeli. Disraeli, in turn, said that Gladstone had 'one commanding characteristic— whether Prime Minister, or Leader of Opposition, whether preaching, praying, speechifying or scribbling— never a gentleman.' This scornful judgment upon an Englishman's tongue is as a dagger in the hands of a Latin. Englishmen had said that Disraeli was not a gentleman ever since the first time he spoke in the House of Commons, when his speech was greeted by 'hisses, groans, hoots, catcalls, drumming with the feet, loud conversation, and imitations of animals': [133] ever since the day when he walked down Regent Street, wearing a blue surtout, light blue trousers, black stockings with red stripes, and shoes. Now that he was Prime Minister again, the old argument against him had become stale. The memory of his coloured waistcoats could no longer be a sane reason for snubbing him, and the fact that he had written a popular novel which made him a profit of six thousand pounds, was not sufficient evidence of his superficiality. He had dared to say, some years before, 'I am never well save in action, and then I am immortal.' The day had come for him to prove his un-English boast to be true.

Disraeli dressed less obtrusively as he grew older. There was but one criticism left for his doubters who thought him insincere in the way he inveigled himself into the Queen's confidence and affection. His letters to her became as like love letters as he dared to make them.

Without full knowledge of Disraeli's nature, the accusation of false gallantry may have seemed justified. While he was plighting his troth to the Queen, he was also writing exuberant love letters to Lady Bradford: at the same time he was proposing marriage to her sister, Lady Chesterfield. With all his artifice, Disraeli was an incurably romantic boy. At an age when other Prime Ministers become stolid and phlegmatic, he admitted that he 'sighed for the moonlight.' 'I think I could live and love in that light for ever,' he wrote. To frigid Englishmen, such notions in an old man were alarming. The good Briton, who will enter a burning building to save a woman he does not know, but who will not rise from his chair to open the door for his own wife, has little truck with gallantry. Nor does he understand or condone the harmless romantic flights of a man like Disraeli, who said, when he was a young man, 'My nature demands that my life should be perpetual love.' The nature did not change: when he was seventy years old, writing of his joy in women's company, he said, '... if, in the sunset of life, I have still a young heart, it is due to that influence.' His romances were violent but innocent. He courted affection freely and he gave it with equal freedom: if his bouquets were placed tenderly upon many doorsteps and not merely upon one, they were no less elegant and sincere in their message.

Disraeli once confessed that he was not fond of male society and that he owed everything to women. It is to be doubted if he would have shone as radiantly among the Victorians if he had served a King instead of a Queen. He admitted that he felt 'fortunate in serving a female sovereign.' [134] It is a fascinating game to imagine the form of his career if a King had been upon the throne. There

was one rare and noble emotion vouchsafed to Disraeli
which helps us to understand his devotion to his women
friends. He was grateful. Somebody once spoke to him of
his wife, for whom, it is obvious, he did not feel or profess
a passionate devotion. He is said to have answered, 'I only
possess one quality in which most men are deficient:
gratitude.' The record of all his friendships shows this to
be true. And, still more so, the record of his marriage.
Through this experience he was bound closely to the
Queen. They had both lived through a completed, wholly
beautiful term of married life, based upon the principle
of 'give and take.' They had both experienced the full
affection and understanding of another human being,
apart from all attractions of sex. This had been the blessing of both of them and they felt the terrible isolation
which comes when the blessing is withdrawn. The Queen
made her own wistful attempt at expressing this knowledge when she sent him a note with a bunch of flowers,
because she knew that there was no longer 'one' with him
to pay him these little attentions.

§ IV — 1874

MR. DISRAELI had not been in power very long when the
Queen renewed her support of the war against ritualism.
Disraeli too felt disgust at the 'finical and fastidious crew'
in the High Church, although he admitted that the Public
Worship Regulation Bill was 'the most difficult question'
that had ever been placed before him. The Bill was to
give Secular Courts the power to suppress ritualism. Time
has proved the Bill to be ineffectual, but the will that
urged it through Parliament never relaxed until August
of 1874, when it was passed. During the year, letters were

exchanged between the Queen, the Prime Minister and the Archbishop, all destined to flout the 'unwise and unprotestant' arguments of Mr. Gladstone. The Queen wrote memoranda to Mr. Disraeli, laying down her ideas of which appointments would 'strengthen the tottering fabric of the Established Church.' [135] He wrote to her, as she lived in the 'sweet stillness of Claremont' or with 'the bonnie breezes of Balmoral,' in apparent agreement with all she said. Her letters were insistent, now that she knew that she was not writing in vain. Under the deluge of her correspondence, Mr. Disraeli never became impatient. He answered gently, '... supported by Your Majesty, Mr. Disraeli is in good heart.' He once confessed his way of dealing with his Sovereign. 'I never deny; I never contradict; I sometimes forget.'

On August 6th, the Queen wrote to the Archbishop in high delight. The 'welcome news' of the passing of the Bill had reached her at Osborne. Mr. Disraeli dashed down to the Isle of Wight with fuller news of all that had passed. Mr. Gladstone and his High Church ritualists had been defeated and, as far as he knew, the Queen's people were safe from the tentacles of Rome. Mr. Disraeli recorded the scene in a letter to Lady Bradford. He wrote it from Longleat, where he was staying with Lord Bath. He pleaded that she could not expect a good letter, since the paper, 'muddy ink, pens, w^h. are made from the geese on the common,' entirely destroyed any genius he had. He wrote:

'Osborne was lovely, its green shades refreshing after the fervent glare of the voyage, and its blue bay full of white sails. The Faery sent for me the instant I arrived. I can only describe my reception by telling you that I really thought she was going to embrace me. She was wreathed with smiles, and as she tattled, glided about the room like a bird. She told me it was "all owing to my courage and tact," and then she said, "To think of you having the gout all the time! How you must have suffered! And you ought not to stand now. You shall have a chair!"

'Only think of that! I remember that *feu* Lord Derby, after one of his severest illnesses, had an audience with Her Majesty, and he mentioned it to me as proof of the Queen's favour, that Her Majesty had remarked to him "how sorry she was she could not ask him to be seated." The etiquette was so severe.

'I remembered all this as she spoke, so I humbly declined the privilege, saying I was quite well, but would avail myself of her gracious kindness if I ever had another attack!...' [136]

Not all were as pleased as the Queen with the manacles which had been put upon the forms of Anglican worship. On August 10th, Disraeli went to see a church in Frome. 'The Priest or Sacristan, or whatever he was' looked rather grimly upon him as he showed him the church. Mr. Disraeli noted that the priest refrained from exhibiting the vestments.

Chapter Fourteen

§ I

Turgot wrote gloomily of Empire building, and of colonies as being 'like fruits which cling to the tree only until they ripen.' [137] There were reasons, still not easy for us to define, why Queen Victoria was to be the sovereign of a different kind of colonial Empire. Perhaps it was that Britons gave as much to the new countries as they took from them, a principle which lay behind the schemes of soldiers like Clive and shrewd colonisers like Rhodes. The British did not plunder and intimidate quite as ruthlessly as the French. Yet one cannot trace any fixed national purpose in the campaigns by which land was taken and savages were quelled to make the Empire in the nineteenth century. The apathy which lost the American colonies and allowed England to remain deaf, for so long, to Clive's pleading for India, was still powerful in England. It allowed the chance of power in the Near East to slip through England's fingers at first, when de Lesseps placed his plans for the Suez Canal before us. The Empire seemed to fall into the Queen's hands through a series of happy accidents.

It is now a fashion to compare the Victorian age with the glory of the Elizabethans. We are told that, with added perspective, the once derided Victorians will assume a place of splendour and might in our history. If this is so, the story of the century will revolve about three achievements. The two material conquests were in industry and the gaining of territory. The third more noble conquest was in the improvement of the standards of living, education, health and morality. A century of peace at home gave Britain opportunities which were denied to Germany, France and Austria. We were spared to advance through the 'exasperatingly slow process' of evolution. We were able to pass the Public Health Acts, the Artisans' Dwellings Act, the Employees and Workmen's Act, the Trades Union Act, the Friendly Societies Act, and the Factory Act of 1878. These were all part of an advanced legislation which transferred the power of rule from the hands of the few into the hands of the many. A thousand evidences of our growth could be quoted, none more convincing than the developments in education. When the Queen was born, no Jew, Roman Catholic or Non-Conformist could take a degree in an English University. Law became more compassionate during her reign. It is unbelievable, in the light of nineteenth century reforms, to be told that a woman was hanged at Marble Arch for stealing a roll of stuff, little more than a hundred years ago. Distance became less formidable through invention and engineering. In 1875 the Queen travelled from London to Balmoral in forty-eight hours. In the same year there was already talk of a Channel tunnel. The building of the Forth bridge was begun in 1882. Engineers were changing the speed of life, but not without mishaps. There were twenty-three railway collisions in England in 1875 and five hundred people lost their lives in an emigrant ship which was bound for New Zealand.

The standard of living in the working man's home was revolutionised during the Queen's reign. Artisans were allowed annual holidays. Water and gas were carried by pipes to cottages which had relied upon tallow candles and the village pump for centuries. Before she died, the Queen used the telephone and she was photographed by the motion-picture machine. Not even the daguerreotype had been invented when she was a child. The national income grew by about three hundred per cent between 1840 and the end of the century. While success and prosperity were coming to the mother country, the Empire was growing. Yet Englishmen barely heeded its growth; they still sympathised with the men who declared that 'the niggers begin at Calais.' The wand of adventure touched only a few; these left England to pitch their tents in savage lands and to prospect for gold. Some who did not fit into the English system were shipped away to the Antipodes and other places, in the early days. A subtle wit said they left their country for their country's good. Later in the century boisterous younger sons were packed off to 'the colonies,' where they prospered in freedom from the social manacles England had set upon them. But the great mass of Englishmen remained uninterested in the lands they could not see. Even the Queen thought that the best way to be rid of an official who had been 'parsimonious, rude and tactless,' would be to send him off, rather vaguely, to some post in the colonies.[138] We cannot find much to reassure us in contemporary despatches and letters, if we seek to know why the Empire grew. But the statistics provide some sturdy evidence. In 1840, the exports to British possessions were valued at seventeen million pounds. In the year of the Queen's death, they reached their zenith for the century: more than one hundred and two million pounds. The territory in the Empire grew by one-third during the Queen's reign. The Maoris had ceded New Zealand to the British Sovereign in 1840. Twenty-seven years later the scattered

Provinces of the North were united in the Dominion of Canada. The Government of India was transferred to the Crown after the Mutiny in 1858. In the last decade, the Australian colonies were federated into a Commonwealth, and, as the outcome of the war at the end of the Queen's reign, the Union of South Africa was formed. Hers was the century of tremendous achievement. During her reign, her subjects increased from ninety-six millions to two hundred and forty millions.

The story behind the cold statistics is an epic which still waits to be written. When the Queen was a girl, slow wind-jammers stole across the Pacific and, after long months of watching, the anxious settlers came to the shores of half-known, southern lands. There they built their rude shanties, upon the edge of the silent forest. When the Queen was old, steamers made the journey, proudly, through the Suez canal. When she was a child, Australia had been wild with the tales of Botany Bay. When she was eighty a city had been built upon the land which had begun as a criminal colony: a city almost as big as Manchester. English apple trees grew, heavy with fruit, in the valleys of Tasmania.

Salmon ova from her own Deeside rivers had been taken across the world, in ice houses. The luscious fish were already being caught in the New Zealand streams by the second generation of Scottish settlers. This new generation had never seen the Highlands, but, with the chill wind of the Queen's most distant colony upon their faces, they tramped the Sutherland hills in kilts. They spoke Gaelic.

British steamers moved up from the Indian Ocean, through the magic canal, and on to the Mother England, with the produce of India and of the new southern countries. In turn, their steel bellies were filled up at the docks in the Thames with machines and clothes, glass, furniture and paper, to be carried back to the south again, for the Australians and New Zealanders to buy: or to Canada, in the eighties, to be carried by the two thousand eight hundred miles of railway through the grain prairies and over the Rockies to the land which bore the Queen's name.

One day at Windsor, the Queen went on to the lawn below the South Terrace—where Elizabeth and Anne and Mary had walked—to see a game of lacrosse, played by fourteen Canadians and thirteen Iroquois Indians. The Indians placed a tomahawk on the ground at her feet as a token of their submission.

When she came to the throne, Queen Victoria ruled an agricultural country. But the smock was forsaken for the overall and in the seventies she ruled a people who thrived on industry. The figure of John Bull was bursting with good living.

Samuel Butler had been to the new Canterbury and he had found *Erewhon* in the hills. Painters had climbed among the white hummocks of the Canadian Mountains and their water-colours were hanging upon the walls of English country houses. Mary Taylor, who had been to school with Charlotte Brontë in Brussels, had already climbed a New Zealand hill, to watch for a sailing ship to carry a letter back to her friend in the Haworth parsonage.

To the Queen, this growth, this bringing of the world to her, was more ideal than real. The brave journeys were pilgrimages of compassion to the ignorant: there was romance in the stories of trappers and soldiers, missionaries and merchants, all harnessing the wild lands of the earth to enrich her sovereignty. Her Bibles were pressed into the brown hands of the Polynesians. She sent a suit of clothes to a swaggering, black, African King, who sent her his own loin cloth back in exchange. With naïve pleasure over her power, she arranged the crowns and trophies of the subdued Indian Princes in a glass case upon the stairs of Windsor Castle. She drank colonial wine. Envoys came to her: Burmese knelt before her and placed boxes of gold and rubies at her feet.

She saw these conquests in the light of a crusade: if there was chicanery, it was hidden from her. Hindus, Kaffirs, Melanesians and Maoris were dark-skinned people, in need of the Bible and the strong, just hand of British administration. She saw herself as the Sovereign chosen to guard the brown-skinned hordes of the world on their pilgrimage out of the darkness into the light. Almost every other Englishman who bothered to think about the growing Empire seemed to agree with her. A few stout souls rose above this pardonable hoodwinking. They saw, too, the wool and the cotton and the grain, feeding and clothing the mill-workers of the Midlands, so that they could labour at the great new machines and produce cotton goods for the bazaars of Calcutta, petticoats for the native barbarians of Nukualofa and sweet biscuits for the emancipated cannibals of Fiji.

England believed in the virtue of her mission; she gave as much as she took, in produce and morale, and this no doubt prevented the colonies from fulfilling Turgot's morbid prophecy. When they ripened, the little fruits did not cease to cling to the tree.

§ II — 1875

THE CONQUEST of India and the growth of Australia and New Zealand were incongruously linked with the disintegration of the Turkish Empire. It was through the bankruptcy of Turkey and the consequent poverty of her subject princes in Egypt that it was possible for Mr. Disraeli to achieve the most melodramatic moment in his melodramatic career; when he bought the Khedive's shares in the Suez Canal, for four million pounds, in 1875.

Few problems of the century produced so much correspondence over such a length of time as the Eastern Question. It was our boast that we wished to protect Turkey from Russia, as we had done in the Crimean War. But it was also true that, while Turkey was in a state of weakness, we could gain influence over the countries which she controlled in the Near East, thereby assuring safety for our trade and shipping. In 1839 the British had occupied Aden and in 1857 they had occupied Perim. The Southern gate of the Red Sea was thus safe for them. Disraeli's clever purchase of the Canal shares in 1875 was the final stroke in the new scheme. When he wrote to the Queen in November, 'It is just settled; you have it, Madam,' he had made the greater part of her Empire safe for her. While the other European powers watched the decline of Turkey and the death of her dominion in the Mediterranean, and while the covetous sovereigns wondered what would happen to Turkey's Balkan States, Mr. Disraeli showed even greater imagination. He saw the tossing of the Near East dice with the eyes of a gambler. The world was the stake, rather than the small prizes of the Balkans. When the news of the purchase of the Canal shares came to the Queen, she was excited over the conquest of her favourite. She wrote[139] 'It is entirely the doing of Mr. Disraeli, who has *very* large ideas and *very* *lofty views* of the position this country should hold. His mind is so much greater, larger, and his apprehension of things great and small so much quicker than that of Mr. Gladstone.'

Mr. Disraeli's Faery was 'in ecstasies.'[140] When he went down to Windsor on November 26th, he described his visit as 'triumphant.' What she liked most was the 'blow at Bismarck,' because the 'terrible man' thought England's political power was dead. After dinner she was gracious, interesting and amusing. On the 30th he described 'The Faery' as being 'in the 10th heaven' because she had received a letter of felicitations from the King of the Belgians on 'the greatest event of modern politics.'[141]

During this year the Queen had showered many favours on her Prime Minister. There was an incident in May of 1874 which shows the magnitude of his power over her. The Tsar Alexander was visiting England as a compliment to the Queen, after the marriage of her son to Princess Marie. He decided to prolong his visit for two days beyond the date upon which the Queen was to leave for Balmoral. She refused to change her plans and Lord Derby, the Foreign Secretary, feared serious trouble. He wrote to Mr. Disraeli '...it will be resented by the Russians, who are as touchy as Yankees.' '...it will entirely destroy whatever good result may be expected from the marriage and the visit...what possible excuse can we make? Not health, for if the great lady can bear 5 days of ceremonies she can bear 7...Do try what you can to set the business right. Nobody can have managed the lady better than you have...'[142]

Everybody failed to induce her to stay—even the Prince

147

of Wales. On May 5th, after Mr. Disraeli had pleaded with her, he imagined that she was angry. He wrote to Lady Bradford '...she averted her head from me—at least I fancy so—at the drawing-room to-day....I have no doubt I am not in favour. I can't help it.' But it was Mr. Disraeli who won the little conflict. Two days afterwards, the Queen wrote to him, when she had consented to stay until after the Tsar's departure, 'It is for Mr. Disraeli's sake and as a return for his great kindness that she will stop till the 20th.' [143] In September of 1875 the Queen sent him a letter almost every day,[144] and when he crossed the Solent, from Osborne to the mainland, the *Victoria and Albert* was 'accorded' to him as 'a particular attention.' [145]

The favours became so embarrassing that Disraeli was sometimes obliged to refuse them. Once the Queen ordered her yacht, the *Fairy,* for him, so that he would not have to cross the Solent in the public steamer. He declined the honour because he thought that it made 'an injudicious distinction' from his colleagues who were so 'faithful and devoted' to him.

§ III — 1875

THE QUEEN's pleasure over her increased power in the Near East changed to gloom when she contemplated Germany. All through 1875, her letters italicised the "overbearing, violent, grasping and unprincipled' behaviour of Bismarck. The German Emperor's friendly letters and assurances of his peaceful motives did not appease her. She believed that Bismarck—the terrible man—was 'like the first Napoleon' [146] and that it was his ambition to crush France once more. She thought the other powers of Europe would have to join in frustrating the disasters which would undoubtedly come from his 'overbearing, insolent way.' The letters of the year show the increase of the Queen's power in Europe. Withdrawn from its frontier squabbles, and free of its military ambitions, she was able to write with detachment, which no doubt made the rulers of Russia and Germany examine their own motives as well as those of their ministers. She could not prevent wars, but she might lessen their magnitude.

An unending stream of letters passed between the Queen and her daughter in Berlin, until the end of the year, when the Queen raised her eyes towards the East again. It was suggested, much to her alarm, that her eldest son should visit India.

Chapter Fifteen

§ 1 — 1875-1876

WHEN THE Prince of Wales worked so eagerly for the success of the British section of the Paris Exhibition of 1878, he pleaded for recognition of the part played by the British Colonies. Through his intercession, his mother bestowed Knighthoods upon some of the colonial representatives who had crossed the world with their produce, 'most liberally,' [147] to enhance Britain's show in Paris. The Prince's little gesture was significant. He had talked with the merchants from his mother's colonies and their stories of minerals and crops and herds had made him realise the potentialities of the Empire, from an economic point of view. He had already visited Canada to open a bridge across the St. Lawrence in his mother's name. He had been young then and engrossed in the delights of dancing with his one thousand partners.[148] But the journey across the Atlantic had also given him a sense of space and distance. He had conquered an ocean in a way which could not be comprehended by his mother, who still saw the high seas from the safe decks of the *Victoria and Albert,* crossing the Solent.

The *wanderlust* was upon the Prince again in 1875 when it was suggested that he should visit India. He jumped at the prospect, but the Queen was not equally enthusiastic. She thought that the plan should be *'very carefully considered* and weighed in the Cabinet.' She looked with 'much anxiety and apprehension to so long and distant a voyage' [149] and, still thinking of foreign travel in terms of the steam packets by which she crossed the channel, she deemed it a great mistake that the heir to the throne should be away from England for so long. She might die while he was abroad, she said. She thought also that his health was not robust enough for the ceremonies which would be imposed upon him. She had her own explanations of this physical weakness; he 'unfortunately' took 'little care of himself.' The Queen still felt the old qualms about him when he was out of her sight. To her, he was still an impetuous young man, and the qualities which made other people describe him as 'adaptable' appeared to her as mere pliability. Nor had the accusations of tactlessness always been without foundation. The Prince's eagerness sometimes urged him to tell too much of the truth or to ask embarrassing questions. There was an awkward incident soon after the close of the war between Prussia and Denmark, which was never forgotten in the family. The Prince had gone with Princess Alexandra, to stay with his sister and brother-in-law in Potsdam. The Crown Prince appeared wearing a new decoration. If he had thought for a moment, the Prince of Wales must have realised that it was the fruit of the Crown Prince's part in the recent war. But he asked, and he was told that it was a reward for valour. As the 'valour' had been shown in the war against his wife's own country and as she was present, there was an awkward moment in the conversation. The Queen blamed him for this lapse, but she did not equally blame the Crown Prince. Good manners might have prevented him from wearing the medal in the circumstances.

The Indian visit had been among the Prince Consort's plans for his son's education. In the sixties, this would have been sufficient reason for the Queen's enthusiastic agreement. She had been determined enough, in 1862, in obeying Prince Albert's wish that their son should go to Egypt and to the Holy Land. The Prince Consort had been no less emphatic about the Indian visit, but the Queen was not so dependent upon his memory and guidance now. She forgot the assertion that she had made during the first months of her bereavement, that 'no human power will make me swerve from what he decided or wished!' The anniversary of Prince Albert's death was still celebrated, and the mausoleum at Frogmore was still the focus for her sad devotion. The glass from which he had drunk his last dose of medicine was still on the table beside the bed. But the Queen did not cling so unreasonably to her sorrow. She was willing now to listen to other voices.

She wrote to the Crown Princess that the Indian tour was 'quite against'[150] her desire. Irritating complications ensued. The Queen saw little need for the visit as a political gesture and said that England was 'not alarmed about India.' In the end, consent was wrung from her. But she insisted that every detail of the arrangements should be placed before her. She wrote about her son's diet and of how he should behave on Sundays; she went so far as to urge that the Prince, now aged thirty-three, should be in bed at ten o'clock each evening.[151] The Prince's position was embarrassing and there is evidence to prove Lee's statement that 'The Queen's attitude often tried his temper.'[152] The old grievance was revived and the Queen resorted to her regrettable practice of communicating with her son through her ministers. Mr. Disraeli seemed to sympathise a little, for his letters to Lady Bradford showed faint irritation over his Sovereign's wilfulness. He wrote of the Prince as 'the most amiable of mortals.' He added that he was 'a thoroughly spoilt child' who could not 'bear being bored.' 'I don't much myself,' confessed Disraeli.

The Prime Minister induced Parliament to vote sixty thousand pounds for the Prince's expenses. Some of the Prince's friends thought this barely enough and the Duke of Sutherland dubbed it 'a shabby concern....' 'If I were you, Sir, I would not take it,' the Duke said to the Prince when he met him at a party at Greenwich. The Duke added his advice that the Prince should borrow the money from some of his friends at five per cent. 'Well,' answered the Prince, 'will you lend it to me?' Mr. Disraeli told the story and said that the answer had 'shut the Duke up.' The relationship between Disraeli and the heir was not strained—it ended with a visit to Sandringham, a touching letter from the Prince, and a photograph. There was a lack of rancour in the Prince's attitude, a touch of gallantry and, here and there in his letters, signs of a strengthening will.

The accumulation of difficulties and the separation from his family darkened the Prince's departure for India so much that he wrote to Lord Granville,[158] 'I left with a heavy heart and was so depressed in spirits ... that I felt seriously inclined to return home instead of going on.' His nature was sufficiently buoyant for him to recover in Paris.

The Prince's talent for friendship increased the interest of his journey. He passed through the canal (at this time it was still owned by France and the Khedive, for Mr. Disraeli had not yet achieved his startling purchase). He renewed his acquaintance with the Khedive, noting that he was on the verge of bankruptcy. But the luxurious ruler was most hospitable and kind. Everywhere the Prince increased his knowledge; he wrote to Lord Granville about the work of the Consul-General, and he called on the widow of a French friend. He crowned his visit to Cairo by investing the Khedive's heir with the Order of the Star of India. The reports of his gaiety on board the *Serapis* disturbed the Queen. She feared that there was too much practical joking and not enough dignity, but her complaints did not disturb the success of the journey. The Prince celebrated his thirty-fourth birthday after he arrived in Bombay. Seventy Princes, encrusted with jewels, had greeted him when he arrived. On his birthday he drove among hordes of Parsees, under illuminated arches. One of them asked him, in lights, 'How is your Royal Mother?' Another said, 'Tell Mama we're happy.' His courtesy convinced the Princes and reassured the English officials who were with him. He hunted cheetahs and hogs, and shot quails, and he showed sublime tact with the disgruntled potentates. The little Gaekwar of Baroda, who was the same age as his own son, stirred him to tender appreciation of the boy's difficult position. The Indian Princes had been told about the Queen; her power had been impressed upon them at the point of the rifle. The Prince came to them as a more tangible and less alarming symbol of the English force which had quelled them. One of the officials wrote that the effect of the Prince on the Chiefs was 'miraculous.' He came home in March—the *Serapis* laden deep with tigers, leopards, elephants, ostriches and a bear—sixty-five mammals and almost a hundred birds in all. Orchids, gems, stuffs, and a fine grey Arab horse were among his treasures. The *Serapis* steamed up past Aden, where the Union Jack greeted them, and then passed Perim, where they saw the flag again. Then they came to the Suez Canal. The miracle had happened! In the meantime the Khedive's shares had been bought and the handcuffs of British control were already upon Egypt.

The Briton's child-like capacity for self-deception is revealed in an amusing incident which happened after the negotiations for the purchase of the canal shares. Lord Derby protested, no doubt with perfect sincerity, 'that nothing was further from his thoughts than the establishment of English authority in Egypt; that we merely wanted a free passage for ourselves....' He added, naïvely, 'and for the rest of the world.' [154]

These noble intentions did not prevent the British Government from sending a British statesman to enquire 'into the tangled financial situation of the country.' Here was the second tightening of the handcuffs. In time, the slow, penetrating methods of the English taught the Egyptians to neglect their overlord in Constantinople: the Lord of Two Continents and Two Oceans, the Shadow of the Most High, and the Protector of Kings. It was not long before lithographs of Queen Victoria were hung in the dingy business offices of Cairo and Alexandria.

§ II — 1876

THE QUALITIES which Mr. Gladstone brought to his politics were essentially English. The shores of the seagirt isle were the limits of his imagination. But Mr. Disraeli had travelled in the Orient, from which he drew his blood. When Mr. Gladstone thought of a mountain, he thought of Snowdon. Mr. Disraeli knew Sinai and Hermon. He had wriggled through the crowded bazaars of Cairo and Jerusalem. The edge of the world was the horizon of his imagination. Insular prosperity had been the aim of the country up to 1875, but industrial wealth and safety were not enough for the imaginative Jew and, throwing his energies into the cause of an 'imperial country,' he exploited the chances that fell to him.

He was fortunate in the time of his rule. The decay of Ottoman dominion in the hands of depraved Sultans, and the weakening of the countries of the Near East, made the Moslem races discontented over the decadence of their Caliph. The shifting ambitions of European powers and the shuffling of control between Kaffir, Boer and Briton in Africa provided problems, together with the conquest of India and the increasing importance of the southern colonies and Canada. Here were the countries of the world, thrown into the air like dice, to be caught by clever hands.

With the gifts of an oriental story-teller, Mr. Disraeli told the Queen of his dream. As Bismarck, the tempter, had whispered into the ear of the King of Prussia, relying upon royal ambition for support of his schemes, so Disraeli spoke to the Queen of power in territories of which she had never dreamed, when she was first crowned. Perhaps she was tantalised by the recollection of the King of Prussia standing in the Galerie des Glaces at Versailles and being proclaimed Emperor. Early in the New Year the Queen expressed her wish that she too should assume an Imperial title, Empress of India, to be added to the ancient name of Queen. She pressed Mr. Disraeli to incorporate the plan in a Title Bill, to be brought before the Commons at the next session. The enthralment was such that she consented to open Parliament herself, for the fourth time since the Prince Consort's death, fifteen years before. She announced the proposed assumption of the

Imperial title from the throne. There was ineffectual but loud opposition when the Bill was before both Houses. The Queen had withdrawn to Baden-Baden to visit her half-sister's grave, but the mournful journey was interrupted by telegrams, telling her of the debates. She wrote,[155] in her sitting-room at the Villa Hohenlohe, with letters from Mr. Disraeli and the Duke of Richmond beside her, '... the Duke of Somerset's language had been most ungentlemanlike and unusual in the House of Lords, disrespectful to me, and very offensive to Mr. Disraeli, insinuating that it was all a trick to get my children a higher position at the German Courts! Really too bad and too ridiculous, as it is an absolute falsehood....'

The opposition wilted; it was of no avail before the Queen's will and the Prime Minister's cleverness. The Bill passed through the Lords in April and received the royal assent. From this time, the Queen signed her name, *Victoria R. & I.,* upon all treaties and communications with foreign Sovereigns and upon the commissions for the officers in her army.

The aspect of the Titles Bill which affects this record lies in the relationship between the Queen, the Prince of Wales and Mr. Disraeli. The Prime Minister shouldered the Bill, but not without cynical comments on how much he was 'pressed ... by the Empress about her Crown,' and the 'fiery furnace' through which he went to win it for her.

Although the Prince of Wales was travelling in India, cementing the relationships which were to give reason for the assumption of the title of Empress, he was never consulted or even advised of his mother's ambition. An announcement in *The Times of India* gave him the news,

157

before he returned to England. The way in which the Queen withheld the important news from her son, who would some day assume the title himself, has suggested jealousy to some commentators. This may be unfair, but it is difficult to find any more laudable reason for keeping the announcement from him, especially as he was closely identified with Indian affairs during the time that the title was being discussed and the Bill prepared for Parliament.

The Prince was still in India when news of the Titles Bill came to him. At first he denied that India was interested in the compliment and he put it down to one of Mr. Disraeli's 'grandiose conceptions.' With more information and the realisation of his own position in regard to the title, he declared his grievance to the Prime Minister.[156]

'As the Queen's eldest son, I think I have some right to feel annoyed that the announcement of the addition to the Queen's title should have been read by me in the newspapers instead of (my) having received some intimation of the subject from the Prime Minister.'

This time he did not accept the snub so calmly. He returned from India, richer in information and knowledge, but also much strengthened in will. There were many reasons why he should feel more self-confidence now. His charm had won the day, nor was he lacking in imagination and thought when the problems of India were placed before him. He had attacked the pompousness of British officials in India, he had shown his anger over their impertinent patronage of the Indian people. 'Because a man has a black face and a different religion from our own, there is no reason why he should be treated as a brute,' he wrote. He was indignant over the 'disgraceful habit of officers speaking of the Indians as "niggers".'

He saw the great dangers of insular and ignorant English officials suddenly transhipped out of their element and allowed to assume power over subservient people. One British resident was recalled from India, through his protestations. He urged also that the power of the Viceroy should not be fettered by instructions from Downing Street. His plea was for 'the man on the spot.' The Prince's friendships with Indian Princes endured. They visited him in London and they wrote to him, appealed to him and consulted him. He became accessible and human to the Indian people and, in turn, the problems in India became comprehensible to him.

Mr. Disraeli made a mistake in the way he attempted to soothe the Prince over the Titles Bill. He suggested that he might also 'receive an addition to his titles.' This attempt at consolation only made the Prince more angry. The title implied in Mr. Disraeli's offer was *Imperial Highness.* The Prince's secretary wrote an emphatic refusal, adding that if 'it leaked out that such a suggestion had been made and refused by the Prince it would, though increasing his popularity, damage that of the Queen and her ministers.' [157] The Prince's cause became so public that one of his friends [158] gave notice of a motion of censure in the House. At this point, the heir's deference for his mother made him withdraw from the fray, especially as she 'took the blame on herself' for the way in which he had been treated. Her wish was for peace between her son and her minister and she was pleased to receive an assurance of kindliness from the Prince. But there was no humility in his statement that he would be willing to receive Mr. Disraeli 'in the kindest manner possible.' 'I have no doubt,' he concluded, 'that it was an oversight on his part not letting me know of the Royal Titles Bill, though of course I looked upon it as a slight to me, and as your eldest son also to you.'

Perhaps the rift between Queen and heir was less personal than the evidence leads us to suppose. There was a wide gap in the thought and habits of her generation and his and the stories of their differences can be found in the relations of many another mother and her son. The prominence given to the lives of Princes may cause us to forget this. The conflicts of opinion between the Queen and the Prince were the manifestation of a general condition in England. The early Victorian yoke was too much for the young of the day. It was not the Queen's yoke, but the yoke of all her generation.

Chapter Sixteen

§ 1 — 1876

IF ENGLAND, France and Germany had been the only contestants for the prizes of the last century, one chapter of history would have been simplified, for dying Turkey's possessions might have been distributed without bloodshed. But there was another rival, in the East, for Russia's ambitions had been no more than checked when she made her assault upon Turkey in the Crimean War. The trouble in 1876 was that England was still pledged to protect Turkey from invasion: to protect Mohammedans against Christians. When the Turks turned and massacred thousands of Christians in the Balkans, our position was not easy. We were morally bound to protect the people of our own faith, but in diplomacy we were bound to protect the slaughterers.

In the spring of 1876, Bulgaria, Bosnia and Herzegovina rose against their Turkish rulers. A few months afterwards, Servia and Montenegro supported them and war was declared on Turkey. The revolts were fostered by Russian agents and the undisciplined Balkan soldiers went into battle under Russian officers. Turkey was weakening: many of her dominions had already been filched from her and she was left now with Bosnia, Herzegovina, Bulgaria, Albania, Epirus, Thessaly and Macedonia. Sultan Abdul Aziz, who wore the Order of the Garter (instituted by Edward the Third, to encourage Christian prayer, honour and chivalry), was dethroned. For a few months his nephew reigned; then came Abdul Hamid, known as 'The Damned,' 'The Red Sultan' and 'The Great Assassin.'

Among the Turks who looked on at Abdul Hamid's accession was Ali Riza, a poor man, who lived in the Turkish quarter of Salonika. Five years afterwards, his wife gave birth to a son, named Mustafa, who was to weave the dream of the new Turkey in the coffee-houses of Constantinople, when he grew up. If the Red Sultan of the Yildiz Kiosk had been gifted with second sight, to see Mustafa Kemal and the new Turkey, there might have been a dead child behind the latticed windows of Ali Riza's house in Salonika.

The long reign of Abdul Hamid began; his was a miserable cause for England to support and the old promises became a strain on the British conscience. But the Russian lust for territory was equally disturbing. Two years of muddled purposes and suspicion between nations followed. Almost four hundred pages of *The Life of Disraeli* are devoted to the correspondence which was engendered by the Balkan shambles.

The Queen neglected India, her new title and her son's alleged lapses, before the stories of the Turkish atrocities in the Balkans and the reports of Russia's campaign for power. In the manner of Prince Albert, she bombarded Mr. Disraeli with helpful, shrewd memoranda. She 'writes every day and telegraphs every hour,' he said to a friend.[159] Her energy now was greater than his. The Queen was fifty-seven years old and her strength had not been affected by her bereavement as much as she imagined. She was still able to walk for miles over the moors in Scotland in weather which made her Ladies shiver and complain. Mr. Disraeli was seventy-two and he might have said, with Mr. Gladstone, that the 'senses were closing in' on him. In January he had written to Lady Bradford, 'I have just come from the Cabinet.... I have been, and am, a great sufferer.' In June he had endured so much from his gout that he had written a depressed letter to the Queen, afraid lest he would have to 'renounce the great personal happiness' [160] of serving her. There were other changes. Mr. Joseph Chamberlain had appeared in the House for the first time. The meeting between Disraeli and Chamberlain was dramatic. The violent Radical, who was some day to become old and mature, and to echo Mr. Disraeli's own Imperial language, was still young enough to show his indignation. He had said that Disraeli 'never opened his mouth without telling a falsehood.' [161] When Mr. Chamberlain first came into the House of Commons, he stood, 'carefully groomed, eyeglass in eye.' After a few minutes, Mr. Disraeli came in and sat down. He 'put up *his* glass, which he seemed to hold encircled with his forefinger, so that he might be quizzing....' The two looked at each other. When Mr. Chamberlain spoke of Mr. Disraeli, the older statesman thought his attack was one of the 'coarsest, and stupidest assaults' he could remember. 'No intellect, or sarcasm, or satire, or even invective: coarse and commonplace abuse....' [162]

Mr. Gladstone was five years younger than Mr. Disraeli, but he had also assumed the habits of an old man. He had resigned from the leadership of the Liberal Party and he had settled down to quiet study in the country, where he was sorting the thousands upon thousands of letters which had accumulated during his career. There was no hint that he would come back again as Prime Minister, as Palmerston had done in a burst of energy towards the end of his life.

Mr. Disraeli complained of his gout, but he could not

163

deny the success of this, the richest year in his career. He had made the sea-way safe between England and India and he had made his Queen an Empress. Earlier in 1876 he had confessed both his triumph and his age by accepting the Earldom of Beaconsfield, which he had refused when his wife was created a Peeress in her own right. This allowed him to act as Prime Minister from the less agitating atmosphere of the House of Lords. His last appearance in the Commons was true to the picturesque legend of his career. His final speech was upon the Bulgarian atrocities. The last words he ever spoke in the House were, 'What our duty is at this critical moment is to maintain the Empire of England.' 'He was noticed afterwards in the lobby "in a long white overcoat and dandified lavender kid gloves, leaning on his secretary's arm" and shaking hands with a good many people.'[163] When all was over his friend and colleague, Frederick Stanley, saw Disraeli shedding tears.

The beginning of the new year was celebrated at Windsor. The Queen and her Minister were both masters of graciousness. They met at dinner in the Castle on New Year's day. 'On Monday I go to Windsor to dine with the Empress of India,' he wrote. 'The Faery is so full of the great incident, and feels everything about it so keenly that she sent me a Xmas card and signed her good wishes *Victoria Regina et Imperatrix.*'[164]

There were evidences of the Queen's recovery from the morbid aspects of her grief. On December 19th she wrote in her Journal: 'Walked with Beatrice down to the mausoleum and back. She has been very busy these last days sorting old music of mine, amongst which treasures have been found. After my dreadful misfortune in '61, everything was left untouched, and I could not bear to look at what my darling one and I used to play daily together. Only within the last five or six years have I looked at my music again, and only quite lately re-opened my duet books and others. The past has seemed to rush in upon me in a strange and marvellous manner. These notes and sounds bring back memories and scenes which seemed effaced.'

On the first day of the New Year, Queen Victoria was proclaimed Kaiser-i-Hind, Empress of India, on the Plain of Delhi. Seventy ruling chiefs and Princes, and envoys from Siam, Burma, Muscat and Khelat came for the occasion. She was saluted by the Maharajah Scindia, in the name of the Indian Princes, as Shah-in-Shah Padshah, *Monarch of Monarchs.*

On January 1st, Windsor awakened to its old glory. At night the castle shone upon the hill with a thousand lights. The Queen discarded her homely black dress: she came into the room before dinner, radiant, blazing with the jewels which the Indian Princes had given her. There was much beauty, much talk and even a hint of revelry. During dinner, Beaconsfield asked the Queen if she was wearing all the jewels the Indian Princes had sent to her. She answered, 'Oh no; if you like I will have the rest brought in after dinner for you to see.' And after dinner 'a series of small portmanteaux of jewels' were brought into the room.

Nobody had ever understood her as well as Lord Beaconsfield: not even Prince Albert. He had curbed her, and however much her character had been made by her husband, there had never been chivalry, compliments, and the encouragement which the feminine side of her needed. Lord Beaconsfield had understood this so well. He had flattered her, but good had always come out of the flattery.

Prince Albert had talked to her of *duty*. Mr. Gladstone had talked of her 'extraordinary integrity of mind.' She was woman enough to be much more pleased when Lord Beaconsfield rose to his feet at the end of the dinner, breaking through etiquette by proposing the health of the Empress of India. The glasses were raised and all eyes were turned towards her. She responded with a 'pretty smiling bow, half a curtsy.'[165]

§ II — 1876–1880

As THE Queen grew older, the more balanced thoughts of middle-age came to the Prince of Wales. The journey to India seemed to tidy his mind. He wrote more convincing letters and he no longer indulged in so much of the 'chitter chatter' which had aggravated Lord Beaconsfield in the early days. Indeed, a friendship and mutual respect swept the old doubts aside and in 1880, when the Prince stayed with the Prime Minister at Hughenden, Lord Beaconsfield wrote to the Queen: 'The conversation was grave as well as gay, and H.R.H. maintained his part with felicity—even distinction.' This was no pretty compliment, cast before the Queen to please her, for Beaconsfield's letters to Lady Bradford also admitted his pleasure over his guest. The Prince had 'said some good things and told more,' he wrote.

There were other signs of the Prince's development. In July of 1878, when there was an uproar because England was meddling with French influence in the Mediterranean and in Egypt, the Prince talked with Léon Gambetta in Paris. With the candid pursuit of facts which was his characteristic, the Prince arranged to lunch with him, but the British Ambassador was not asked to join the party.

Gambetta 'spoke strongly in favour of an alliance between France and England,' a subject dear to the Prince's heart. Afterwards the British Ambassador reported to Lord Salisbury that he had heard 'from all quarters' that Gambetta was extremely pleased with the interview. The Ambassador was assured, he said, that the Prince of Wales acquitted himself with great skill.

With such letters of commendation arriving at the Foreign Office, the relationship between the Prince and the Government changed and his views were taken more seriously. A tangible sign of this growing respect was given in a letter from Lord Salisbury written [166] after the interview with Gambetta in Paris.

'I trust your Royal Highness will not think I am guilty of an intrusion if I venture, on the score of my official position, to thank your Royal Highness very earnestly for what you have done in Paris. The crisis has been one of no little delicacy, and if the leaders of the French opinion had definitely turned against us, a disagreeable and even hazardous condition of estrangement between the two countries might have grown up, which would have been very much to be regretted. Your Royal Highness's influence over Monsieur Gambetta, and the skill with which that influence has been exerted, have averted a danger, which was not inconsiderable.'

It was admitted that the Prince's sagacity had postponed the friction between France and England, threatened by the changes of influence in the Mediterranean and in Egypt.

The Prince's eager interest in human beings—a quality which his father had not understood and therefore deplored—was above prejudice and opinion. Delane of *The Times,* who had so often derided the Court, was his guest at Marlborough House, and Sir Charles Dilke, who had attacked monarchy in the Commons, became his friend. Joseph Chamberlain, the Radical leader, who brought the provincial point of view into politics as it had never been brought before, sunk all prejudices when he met the Prince at Birmingham in 1874. They liked each other immediately, realising that a man can be human in spite of his politics. The simple truth was that the Prince met people with the intention of discovering the best in them. Criticism might come afterwards, but it was never the basis of his approach.

§ III — 1876-1877

THE STRENGTHENED understanding between Lord Beaconsfield and the Prince was soothing to the Queen. All three met in common anxiety and sympathy over the atrocities in the Balkans. They never knew which way the 'monstrous' Bismarck was going to turn next, and they were equally perplexed by the gap between the peaceful protestations of the Tsar and the warlike mien of his soldiers. The Queen wrote,[167] 'it is clear England *cannot fight for* the Turks, but she also cannot fight against them.' This anomalous state of mind might have been as perplexing to Bismarck as his own vagaries of decision were disturbing to the English Government. But appreciation of the other man's point of view is sometimes fatal in diplomacy.

The apparent timidity of Lord Beaconsfield's Government and their failure to act against either the Russians or the Turks stirred the veteran quiet of Mr. Gladstone's retreat at Hawarden. He was working on his notes for *Future Retribution*. These notes are still among his papers, with a docket attached to them. On it he wrote 'I was called away to write on Bulgaria.' This was in August of 1876. The pages of his diary show with what physical pain he wrote the pamphlet which was to protest against the failure of the Government to act. Between August 28th and September 4th, Gladstone worked upon his manuscript. One day he was forced to stay in bed until four o'clock because of his lumbago pains. Another day he read *St. Thomas Aquinas on the Soul,* and he went to church twice on Sunday. Between the periods of pain and writing he read *Waverley,* 'as a treat.' In these seven days of mixed suffering and contemplation, he produced the pamphlet, *The Bulgarian Horrors and the Question of the East,* which 'spread like fire.' Forty thousand copies were sold in a few days.

The fierce sincerity of his attack made Gladstone the leader of Liberal thought again, but his high purpose was wasted on the Queen and on Lord Beaconsfield. To them Mr. Gladstone had turned the atrocities into a party question and he was using them as a Liberal spring-board from which to dive back into power. When the British Government refused to subscribe to the Berlin Memorandum, signed by Germany, Austria, Russia, France and Italy, and designed to impose certain reforms on the Turks, Gladstone saw in this a sign of the Jew's own hand. His dive into history was not as apt as Lord Beaconsfield's would have been. Mr. Gladstone drew a long bow in suggesting that the Government policy grew out of 'Dizzy's crypto—Judaism.' 'The Jews of the east *bitterly* hate the Christians...'[168] he wrote.

The results of the Great War have changed the fortunes of the countries of the Levant so drastically that the forces behind the Eastern question of the seventies belong only to the history book. They have either changed so much as to be unrecognisable or they are so dead that they are one with the ruins of Baalbek and Jerash. They are of importance in this story only in so far as they affected the relationship of the Queen, the Prince, Lord Beaconsfield and Mr. Gladstone. The Balkan atrocities awakened Mr. Gladstone from his torpor and the trappings of old age were thrown aside for the campaign which led, in time, to the Liberal victory in 1880. He stood under the dripping rainclouds at Blackheath and painted a theatrical picture of the iniquities of the Turks. His was the voice of Christendom—he believed this and the people seemed to believe it too. He talked of 'the flood-gates of lust' and 'the dire refinements of cruelty.' He attacked, with humourless, passionate invective. Perhaps it was not only because of the Turk that the people listened to him. The time for a political change was almost at hand.

On April 21st, 1877, Russian soldiers crossed the Turkish frontier. There was no doubt now of Russia's intentions. What had been talked of as a purely moral problem in our diplomacy now became cold, material anxiety over the safety of Egypt, where the new harbour of Alexandria had been built with British capital. England had wavered over the moral issue for many months, but, with the Russians already across the Turkish frontier, the British Government demanded and received the promise of Russia that the countries and waterways which affected British interests should be respected. Upon this pledge we agreed to remain neutral. This was not enough for Mr. Gladstone. In May he proposed resolutions which would have bound England to join Russia against the Turks. Two hundred and twenty-three voters went with him, but three hundred and fifty-four 'declined to embarrass the Government.'

In the middle of July the Russians crossed the Balkans —it seem as if they would surge south and occupy Constantinople. Their progress was checked by Osman Pasha: for five months he held Plevna against them. But on December 10th Plevna fell and there seemed to be nothing between the Russian soldiers and Constantinople One must read the Queen's letters to Lord Beaconsfield, written during the months of the Turko-Russian war, to realise what a positive part she played in the government of the country and the framing of policy during this time. The letters did not cling so tenaciously to the personal pronoun as in the sixties. They showed an increasing breadth of judgment. Their characteristics, compared with other documents of the time, are her calm and foresight, and her refusal to be hoodwinked by Russia's alleged Christian crusade against the Mussulmans. When one has read the letters, covering many pages, one recalls Prince Albert's memoranda written during the Crimean War, tracing some of the qualities of his judgment in them, his freedom from pettiness and excitement.

The dissensions in Parliament, the confused loyalties of party against party and statesman against statesman, provided an acid test for the growing abilities of the Prince of Wales. He had already convinced Gambetta, Beaconsfield and Salisbury of his talents. At last his mother had made the gesture for which he had waited for so many years. In June she had drawn him a little closer to her confidence by asking Lord Beaconsfield to keep him informed 'of the plans and proceedings of Russia and of the extreme danger of being deceived by them.' Twenty days afterwards she quoted her son's opinion in a letter to her Prime Minister. Her old fear, when he went abroad, had been lest he might talk too much. When he went to

Berlin in February of 1878, she was willing that he should
have a private interview with Bismarck. The questions
which Bismarck asked him show that the Chancellor
cared for the Prince's opinion. Beaconsfield was also generous in his judgment of the heir. On one occasion he said
that the Prince's opinions on foreign affairs were more to
be trusted than the 'feeble and formal diplomacy' of English Ambassadors to foreign courts. On July 13th, the
Queen went all the way from Windsor to London to
attend her son's party in the gardens of Marlborough
House. They walked about together and they had tea, 'in
a beautiful Indian tent.' When she arrived back at Windsor again, the Queen wrote a long description of the garden party and she said that it had been 'very successful.'
There was a subtle proof of the change in her feeling for
her son when the Queen went to see H.M.S. *Thunderer,*
in the Solent. She went to the turret and she was shown
a torpedo. She looked into the engine room, and although
she found the ladders 'rather steep,' she had not forgotten
her *sea legs*. In the evening there was a dinner party at
Osborne and among the guests was Lord Charles Beresford. He had been the chief instigator of the frolics at
Marlborough House and the inventor of the practical
jokes which had imperilled the dignity of her son's journey to India. Now she thought him 'very funny,' 'beam-
ing with fun and a trifle cracky, but clever, and a good
officer.' This was not the only sign of the mellowness
which seemed to come to her. One traces the little evidences which shine out of the story of the year: the courage which made it possible for her to look over the old
music, the duet books which she had shared with her
husband. A trifling sign of fortitude, perhaps, but important in a woman who was steeped in sentimental feelings

about inanimate objects. Then one recalls the dinner on New Year's Day when the great halls of Windsor were alive again; and the first signs of trust in her son which came in June. It seemed that, towards the end of Beaconsfield's brilliant rule of the Commons, she emerged from the.darkness and gave to affairs something of the sustenance they were to lose with his ultimate eclipse. It has been said that women become like the men for whom they have affection. The Queen had assumed the conscientious virtues of the Prince Consort when he died in 1861. Now, on the eve of losing Beaconsfield as a minister, she seemed to be infused by his restraint, his calm judgment. The change is as apparent in her letters of the eighties as the change of 1861 is apparent in the letters which the Queen wrote after Prince Albert's death. *She* whispered the words of caution now and *she* sounded the trumpets of courage when Beaconsfield was beset by the violent abuse of Mr. Gladstone and his supporters. When he was to speak at the Mansion House, she wrote, 'Try and avoid saying *anything positive,* nothing that could let people make a handle of it for agitation.'[169] 'Be firm, and act as *you intended,*' she wrote in July. Two days before he had come up to her, at the Prince's garden party, and he had said, 'The crisis has begun and I shall need all your Majesty's support.' He may have written with his tongue in his cheek in the early days, but now she sustained him, in the time when he was ill and tired. On Midsummer Day he had opened the Artisans' and Labourers' buildings near Battersea Park, wearing some of the lilies which she had 'so graciously, and so gracefully presented to him' when he had been to see her at Windsor the day before. In December she threw precedent to the winds and drove over to Hughenden to lunch with him.

Chapter Seventeen

§ 1 — 1877

WHEN PLEVNA fell in December, the British Cabinet
stirred in its cocoon. The vision of the triumphant Russians marching on to Constantinople, and the alarm lest
British interests in the Mediterranean should be molested,
at last awakened the members of the Government. They
began to realise Russia's 'duplicity and skill in deception.'
The phrase had been used by the Queen almost a year
before. The Cabinet was hastily summoned on December
14th. Lord Beaconsfield closed his hand firmly. He had
made his plans, but he shared them with none but the
Queen. Their partnership was complete and powerful.
Beaconsfield urged three measures upon the members of
the Cabinet. In view of the Russian advance he wished
that Parliament should be summoned immediately. He
asked for a considerable increase in the country's defence
forces and that the Queen should be advised to intercede
between Russia and Turkey.

Lord Beaconsfield said that there was 'dead silence'
when he finished speaking. Lord John Manners supported
the measures, 'with much energy and ability,' but the
Foreign Secretary held back. Lord Derby had been the
most pacific of the Ministers all along, and he still seemed
to feel that 'any active interference in Eastern affairs by
England was to be deprecated.' Lord Salisbury and Lord
Carnarvon were equally loth to make this compromising
move in Turkey's favour. In this unsettled state, and with

no prospect of decision, the Cabinet adjourned for three days.

In the brief interim of the week-end, the Queen made her great gesture of confidence in her Minister: a gesture which grew out of courage as well as affection and trust. She drove over from Windsor and lunched with Beaconsfield at Hughenden. This was the first time she had paid such a compliment to a Minister since 1841: she had been little more than a girl then, and the Minister had been Lord Melbourne.

Once assured of what she deemed to be right, it mattered little to the Queen that Mr. Gladstone was still thundering through the provinces, holding his audiences under a spell with his talk of the perfidy of the Turks and the wickedness of the Government. She was willing to lose her crown rather than condone the action of the Russians. The Queen contemplated the unrest in the provinces with a clear conscience. When *Othello* was played in Liverpool and the words,

> News, friends; our wars are done; the Turks are drown'd,

were spoken, the audience rose and interrupted the performance with their cheering.[170] They did not seem to comprehend the possible disasters to British power in the Mediterranean. The spell of Mr. Gladstone's oratory gave the people of the provinces a light upon their simple reactions to the story of Turkish devilry. The meretricious arts of oratory awakened Liberalism again: the political change which was to sweep Beaconsfield and his Government out of power in 1880 had already begun, under Mr. Gladstone's popular wand.

The Queen was undaunted. While the members of the Cabinet were languishing in their week-end of contemplation before the meeting on Monday, the Queen displayed her will and her favour. She went to Hughenden with Princess Beatrice, through 'cheering crowds and beflagged streets,' to call upon her Minister. They lunched simply and afterwards the little Queen walked with the old and stooping Beaconsfield on the terrace, where Lady Beaconsfield had planted geraniums in the Florentine vases. The Queen planted a tree in the garden to celebrate the day. She admired the swans and she accepted Beaconsfield's Trentanova statue as a memorial of her happy experience. She traveled back to Windsor late on Saturday afternoon.

The next Cabinet meeting was on the Monday: a stormy affair, with neither confidence nor decision. Half the Cabinet, especially Lord Salisbury, Lord Derby and Lord Carnarvon, were arrayed against Beaconsfield. When the machinery of government failed him, he assumed the trappings of the actor. If the members of the Cabinet distrusted his purpose and judgment and if support were withheld from him, he said that he would resign. The members of the Cabinet paused before his challenge and they gained one more day in which to meditate. News of the Prime Minister's threat reached Windsor. The Queen did not pause to consider its full meaning; she wrote hastily. In no circumstances would she 'accept Lord Beaconsfield's resignation....' He wrote to her next day, pointing out that even if he did resign, it was within the Queen's power to entrust him 'with the formation of a new ministry.' [171]

The Cabinet slept upon their differences, and they came to the meeting next morning a little chastened and calmed. The Prime Minister won the day as far as the Government was concerned. The Queen had told him to be '*very* firm and decided ... and not to give way to any-one, even if Lord Derby should wish to resign. ...' It was her strength which supported him now. She had prom-ised him that the other Ministers would 'surely yield,' if he would be decided, supported as he would be and had been, *all along,* by herself. Lord Derby climbed down at the threat of his chief's resignation. He wrote a note to Lord Beaconsfield and he came to see him an hour before the Cabinet meeting. He would be happy, he said, if they could see their way 'out of this mess.' 'We all want to keep together: and no one in the Cabinet will feel as I shall if circumstances separate me from my old friend and teacher in public life.' [172]

Lord Salisbury too seemed to be drawn more closely to his leader. At last the three measures were accepted. The defence forces were to be increased, Parliament was to be summoned, and the Queen was to be advised to mediate between the two countries in the hope of arresting the destructive advance of the Russian army. England at last declared her will, but damage had already been done to her name in Europe. The dilatoriness and indecision cre-ated an impression of weakness among statesmen on the Continent. The German Crown Princess wrote to the Queen of the popular talk: that England was 'quite pow-erless, has no army, a fleet that is of no use ... has no statesman and cares for nothing more than making money.' The Crown Princess said that she longed 'for one good roar of the British Lion from the housetops, and for the *thunder* of a British broadside!'

For the moment, Beaconsfield had won. 'The great struggle is over, and I have triumphed,' he wrote [173] to Lady Bradford. With the Queen, he accepted the hard won battles as 'another proof' of what might be done when the Sovereign and the Minister acted together. He added, as reminders of their political union, 'Witness the Public Worship Act. Witness your Majesty's Imperial Crown....' [174]

But Lord Beaconsfield was tired. The confusion was so great that it seemed like 'the end of the world' to him. Lord Morley tells us that, during these months of Beaconsfield's anxiety, 'great parties of tourists from the north and midland towns began to make it a fashion to go on high pilgrimage' to Mr. Gladstone's house in the country. There, 'besides a fine park they saw the most interesting man in the country, and had a good chance of hearing an eloquent speech, or watching a tree fall under the stroke of his vigorous arm.' [175] There was something akin in an oak and a Tory. The Liberal veteran was preparing for 1878, which he afterwards described as 'a tumultous year' in his life.

§ II — 1878

LORD BEACONSFIELD's patching up of peace in the Cabinet was no more enduring than the Turkish stemming of the Russian army. After Plevna, Sofia fell and the Russians came nearer to the coveted shores of the Bosphorus. In January of the new year the Russians entered Adrianople, and before the month was ended they stood on the beautiful coast of the sea of Marmora, triumphant.

When the Cabinet met on January 23rd the fleet was ordered to Constantinople, and the Chancellor of the Exchequer was directed to give notice in the Commons of a vote of credit for six million pounds. At last England was to arm herself against the threat of Russian dominion in the Mediterranean. Lord Derby and Lord Carnarvon resigned after the Cabinet decided to send the fleet to the Dardanelles. Lord Salisbury remained on the side of his leader, in company with the majority of the ministers. The imagination of the Commons was also stirred by the menace to British interests in the Near East, and when the financial vote came before the House, the Liberal opposition floundered and died. Complication followed complication—of little interest now, except to show how the figures in this story played their part definitely and with persistently war-like declaration against Russia. But it was not until the Russians saw the blue waters of Marmora, not until they were almost within sight of the palaces of Abdul Hamid on the shores of the Bosphorus, that the Government stirred with anything like vigour. Late in January, Lord Napier of Magdala was appointed to command any military expedition which might be needed. Thus, at last, Britain was awake upon land as well as sea.

On March 3rd the intimidated Turks signed the treaty of San Stefano. It was a pernicious document; the death warrant of Turkey and the last gasp in her sordid and ignoble decline. But the treaty allowed for more than Turkish humiliation: there was promise of the aggrandisement of Russia which was still more menacing to British interests than the nearness of the Russian soldiers to Constantinople. The terms of the treaty were kept secret at first. When they became known, they seemed to be so preposterous in the eyes of Britain that Lord Beaconsfield at last displayed the ruthless decision to which the Queen had been urging him for almost a year. The confidence between them was perhaps more constructively powerful than between any Sovereign and Prime Minister in England's history. It can be said that neither of them failed the other, in any important issue, during the close relationship of ten years. Once she chided him, when she felt that he had been 'unable to fulfil his engagement to her.' But the letter of complaint, written from Osborne in February, was accompanied by some camellias, 'grown in the open air,' and some primroses, his most beloved flower. The misunderstanding passed. Beaconsfield's letter to the Queen,[176] in response to her rebuke, was charming, calm, and wholly fair to his colleagues. It set matters to right, and at the end, he wrote, 'Lord Beaconsfield is deeply touched by your Majesty's gracious kindness in deigning to send him flowers from your Majesty's home. Truly he can say they are "more precious than rubies"; coming, as they do, and at such a moment, from a Sovereign whom he adores. . . .'

In March, when Prince Leopold's illness added to the Queen's dejection, Lord Beaconsfield wrote, 'anxious and unhappy,' about the pressure which was put upon her. He said with sincerity that, from 'the bottom of his heart,' he wished that he could be the Queen's secretary. He would 'willingly relinquish his present exalted post' to soothe her and to lessen the weight of the troubles and anxieties which beset her. It 'would not only be an honour; it would be happiness of the greatest.'[177] Their affection was deep with all the calm quality vouchsafed to people when they are old. Living near to the Queen and knowing the secrets of her purposes, weighing the steadfastness of her character against the occasional errors in judgment had created sincere, grateful affection in the lonely Minister. He had promised 'devotion' in the letter which he had written when he first came to her as her Prime Minister in 1868. At that time the devotion had been given with the wise smile of the diplomat. In 1878, it was given with all his heart.

When the Cabinet met in March, Beaconsfield cajoled
the still recalcitrant Ministry into calling out the Reserve
and sanctioning the transport of seven thousand native
troops from India to Malta. Here was the move which
would intimidate the Russians; with all their bravado,
they did not wish war with England. The Lords accepted
the measure without demur and the Commons passed it
with a healthy majority of 121. But Lord Derby fell by
the way. He had resigned in January when the British fleet
was ordered to Constantinople but had come back as
Foreign Secretary again. He resigned once more, at the
renewed brandishing of the English sword. This last
action covered him with Royal blame and disfavour.
Princess Alice had written to her mother from Darmstadt of the opinion in Europe. She said that Lord Derby
shook the confidence of 'all the world' in England's policy by his vacillation and indecision.[178] When Lord
Derby's resignation was announced the Crown Princess
wrote in high delight, because one could 'hold up one's
head again.'[179] The Queen was more gentle. She knew
his 'health to be bad,' and she wrote of 'poor Lord Derby's
extraordinary state,' but she felt that he *must* go.'
· Lord Salisbury assumed Lord Derby's place as Foreign
Secretary and he straightway infused the foreign policy
with life and confidence. His first strong action was the
drafting and publication of a despatch declaring the diplomatic position of Britain to the powers. He was aided by
Lord Beaconsfield. Lord Salisbury demanded that the
iniquitous Treaty of San Stefano should be submitted to
the judgment of the European powers and he expedited
the bringing of the Indian troops to the troubled Mediterranean. They arrived in Malta in May, but they went no
farther into the fray. When the Emperor of Russia

equivocated over the proposed changes to the San Stefano Treaty Salisbury took matters into his own hands. He arranged a convention with Sultan Abdul Hamid which bound us to protect the depleted dominions of Turkey, on the understanding that Cyprus was occupied by Britain as a base. This he followed up with a convention between Britain and Austria, allowing her to occupy Bosnia and Herzegovina, with the promise that she would support the British view upon Bulgarian affairs. Russia assented to this strong-handed tidying up of the muddle. She consented to have these clauses put forward in the framing of the treaty which was considered and agreed upon by the Powers at the Berlin Congress, in June and July of 1878.

§ III — 1878

RECOGNITION OF the talents of the Prince of Wales increased during the agitating negotiations of 1877 and 1878. Both Lord Salisbury and Lord Beaconsfield seemed to be convinced that it would not be a mistake to allow the heir a little more knowledge of the inner workings of the Government. Lord Beaconsfield called the Prince Albert Edward, *Prince Hal*. The nickname was apt. One turns to Prince Hal's lines in *Henry IV*,

> If all the year were playing holidays,
> To sport would be as tedious as to work,

to find reason behind Beaconsfield's choice. The Prince was learning to work as well as play. More, the Prime Minister believed that Prince Albert Edward would also be a great Sovereign when he came to the throne. Nor did the Queen withdraw the modicum of confidence which she had extended to her son when he came back from India. Indeed, her faith in him slowly grew: she referred to his opinions in her letters to Ministers and she answered his expressions of opinion with grave consideration.

The violent letter which the Queen wrote to Lord Beaconsfield in January of 1878 might be mentioned again. She had been distressed at the 'low tone' which the country was inclined to hold. Perhaps there was a touch of bitter prophecy in the way she harped upon 'the low, sordid love of gain' which seemed to possess her people. She saw the high road to arrogance and moral ruin in the riches with which the country was blessed. The tardiness of the Cabinet to act boldly against Russia was a sign to her: a sign of the moral decay which threatened. 'Oh, if the Queen were a man,' she wrote to Lord Beaconsfield,[180] 'she would like to go and give those Russians...such a beating!' When she added that she felt she could not 'remain the Sovereign of a country' that was 'letting itself down to kiss the feet of the great Barbarians,' she said that upon this matter, 'Her son felt more strongly than herself even.'

She discussed most questions with him now: none more candidly than the important conference of the powers in Berlin which was to apportion the spoils of the war. On May 28th, the Prince wrote to his mother. He had been talking with Corry, the Prime Minister's trusted secretary. The Prince had said that 'Lord Beaconsfield was the only man who could go....' However clever Lord Salisbury was, the fiasco which had rewarded his attempts at the Conference in Constantinople[181] made it plain that 'he really would not do.' The Prince continued in his letter, 'I understand that President Bismarck particularly begs that there should be no *ad referendum*.

'Under these circumstances, it strikes me more forcibly than ever that the Prime Minister is not only *the* right man to represent us at the Congress but the *only* man who can go, as he will show Russia and the other Powers that we were really in earnest. . . . If a Congress takes place, it must be the *last* one on the Eastern question—which must be finally settled and I trust for ever. . . . Now, do let me implore you to urge Lord Beaconsfield to go. . . . It struck me that if you wrote a mem. which was to be laid before the Cabinet—in which you expressed your positive desire that Lord Beaconsfield should go—the matter would then be settled. . . . Of course this letter is only intended for you, and for nobody else's eyes. Excuse my having written on the subject, but it is one in which I take such interest, that I cannot help doing so.'

Neither the proposed Congress nor the Prince's plan appealed to the Queen immediately. If the Congress were to have been held at Brussels, The Hague, or Paris, she might have consented. She wrote to her son, '. . . you know that Lord Beaconsfield is seventy-two and a half, is far from strong, and that he *is* the firm and wise lead and hand that rules the government, and who is my great support and comfort, for you cannot think how kind he is to me, how attached! His health and life are of *immense value* to me and the country, and should on no account be risked. . . .'

The Queen relented and Beaconsfield went with Lord Salisbury to represent Britain at the Congress. He travelled slowly, pausing during the journey of four days so that he should arrive 'quite fresh.' He went with dejected views of what might be the outcome. 'In all his troubles and perplexities,' he wrote to the Queen, 'he will think of his

Sovereign Lady, and that thought will sustain and inspire him.'

§ IV

LORD BEACONSFIELD arrived in Berlin about eight o'clock in the evening, and after he had dined he waited upon Prince Bismarck. He had not seen the Chancellor for fifteen years. Beaconsfield was himself an older man: he was bent, and his eyes seemed tired and lustreless when he was in repose. Bismarck, too, had grown massive and a little tired. The giant of six-foot-two, the 'tall, pallid man, with a wasplike waist,' of fifteen years ago, was now 'extremely stout.' Beaconsfield described him to the Queen. His face was ruddy and he was growing a silvery beard. The Prince of Wales, who was also drawn into these confidences, echoed the wish of many a man when he wrote to the Prime Minister, 'How I should have liked to have seen him and you together!'

The first serious interview between Bismarck and Beaconsfield lasted for an hour and a half. The second talk which they had alone was a 'monologue; rambling, amusing egotistical autobiography.'[182] Beaconsfield did not guess the object of the second interview, but Odo Russell had warned him that it was probably to ascertain how 'squeezeable' he was. In view of this, Beaconsfield would 'not open on any point.'

The Chancellor said of Beaconsfield, *'Der alte Jude, das ist der Mann!'* The implication was true, for Beaconsfield slowly drew the interest and the emotions of the Congress about himself. For most of the time Bismarck played second fiddle to the Jew with his subtle talents, his restraint, and the beauty and force of his English. When he sat next to Bismarck at dinner he listened to Rabelaisian monologues: 'endless revelations of things he ought not to mention.' Lord Beaconsfield's letters to the Queen and to the Prince of Wales, during this anxious but amusing month, show how much he revelled in the splendour and in the talks with the great men of Europe. But he complained again and again of his tiredness. Of evening parties, he said, 'I begin to die at ten o'clock and should like to be buried before midnight.' One night at dinner Bismarck threw care to the winds, and he assured Beaconsfield that he ought 'never to trust Princes or courtiers.' His illness, he assured him, was not from the French war, but because of the 'horrible conduct of his Sovereign.' Indeed, he went on in 'such a vein' that Beaconsfield at last bethought himself of the Faery at Windsor and told Bismarck that he served one who 'was the soul of candour and justice,' one who was loved by her Ministers.

The business of the Congress wore on. England had already declared the terms which would safeguard her interests in the Near East. Russia struggled against the treaty, but in the end she surrendered. Beaconsfield played one actor's trick, when it seemed that Russia might falter and the Congress fall to pieces. He ordered a special train to be in readiness, to carry Lord Salisbury and himself back to Calais. If he had boarded the train, the only result could have been war between Russia and England. Bismarck was alarmed for he was more mighty than subtle in his diplomacy. He hurried off to Beaconsfield's hotel for still another informal parley. As in most conferences, the vital business was done in the intervals between sessions.

'Is this really the ultimatum of England?' asked Bismarck.

'Yes, my Prince, it is,' Beaconsfield replied.[183]

'Where do you dine to-night?' was the next question. 'I wish you could dine with me.'

Beaconsfield ate at Bismarck's house in response to the invitation. It is fascinating and yet tantalising to grope among the phrases which record the meetings between these two giants, opposed in diplomacy, drawn together by mutual recognition of greatness, often exiled from common men by reason of their courage and their vision, yet prevented on these occasions from the wholly candid talks which they could have enjoyed. The sly, cynical humour in Lord Beaconsfield's letters almost makes one forget the grim purpose of the Congress. There are engaging descriptions of Berlin society, shrewd sketches of the people who sat next to him and of the last dinner before the surrender of Russia. Bismarck did not talk of politics at the table: he merely 'ate and drank a great deal.' Afterwards, when Princess Bismarck and her daughters retired, the two men smoked vigorously. Beaconsfield vowed that the smoking had given 'the last blow to his shattered constitution,' but he felt it to be necessary. For an hour and a half they talked. That night, before he went to bed, Beaconsfield received the news of Russia's acceptance of the Treaty. In the morning he was able to telegraph to the Queen, 'Russia surrenders, and accepts the English scheme for the European frontier of the Empire, and its military and political rule by the Sultan.' The Queen's answer came back, across Europe: 'It is all due to your energy and firmness.'

It was said that Beaconsfield and Salisbury had achieved more at the Congress table, for their country, than the Generals had achieved on the battlefields of the Crimea.

The Prime Minister came home, this time travelling with Lord Salisbury, with whom he generously associated himself in the victory. They returned to the welcome London gives to heroes. But Beaconsfield was tired. The endless receptions and the attacks of gout had broken him. There was honour—'peace with honour,' for what it was worth to an old man,

> ... when victories are vain,
> When those who conquer do not win,
> Nor those receive the gain.

He was suffering all the disappointment which follows when, in age, the dreams of boyhood come true. There had been amusement: the joy of talking and the stories of whole editions of his novels being bought up by the people of Berlin. But he came home to an empty house and to the bitter exile of greatness.

In the cooler years that followed, critics questioned the wisdom of the Treaty of Berlin, but they could not belittle Beaconsfield's personal achievement. Londoners crowded into the streets: they sang and they cheered as he drove past. He came to his house and there he found a letter waiting for him, and flowers, from Windsor. When he went to Osborne, after a brief rest, the Queen found him 'in excellent spirits.' She gave him the Garter, but this was not enough. 'Would he not accept a Marquisate, or Dukedom *in addition?*' He refused the added honours. Everybody was delighted, it seemed, except Mr. Gladstone. The Queen told Beaconsfield that Gladstone was 'frantic,' but this only added a touch of fun to the victory. In Berlin, Bismarck contemplated the only three photographs in his private room. They were, he said, his *Sovereign,* his *wife* and his *friend.*

Chapter Eighteen

1877

PRINCESS ALEXANDRA's part in the Edwardian story cannot be indicated through incident so much as by studying the quiet influence which she bestowed upon her family and upon all who came near her. Her gentleness and compassion were so unassuming that she never appeared in a spectacular role. But she was loved, especially by the mass of people upon whom she smiled when she drove through the streets. Her smile and her kindliness awakened a popularity enjoyed by no other Princess of her day. Princess Alexandra had an especial talent for sympathy with the poor and needy.

We have already recalled the scene of her childhood, when her imagination was touched by the stories told to her by Hans Andersen, who was a popular guest at the Danish Court. Her nature was reflected in her simple wish, expressed at that time: all that she had asked was that she should be loved. Her wish was granted by the British people.

Someone who knew the Princess well has said that she never forgot her husband's early tenderness and loyalty to her, during the war between Prussia and her own country. This was the nucleus of a devotion which sustained her through many difficulties which came as the years rolled on. Sometimes her sense of fun brushed her shyness aside. She once chaffed Lord Rosebery about his supposed radical tendencies, suggesting that instead of being a peer

189

he might be content to remain a simple 'Primrose.' The war left her with one bitterness: she never forgave the Hohenzollerns for the mischief they had done to Denmark. We read, in the reminiscences of the de Reszkes, of how she would say, 'half jokingly, half seriously,' 'Now you're not going to Germany, are you, to sing for that horrid man?' The butt of her dislike was the Emperor. The de Reszkes, to whom she was devoted, obeyed her wish and they never sang in Bayreuth, despite Cosima Wagner's pleading.

During the months when the Queen's feelings for the Prussian cause had estranged her from her daughter-in-law, the picture of the calm, beautiful Princess, who came with her books of devotion, in 1862, had been a little dimmed. The Queen had seen in the Princess the reason why her son was drawn away from Prussian sympathy. But this grievance had passed. Their affection had been strengthened during the anxious weeks of the illness of the Prince of Wales. While the Queen had been sitting behind the screen in her son's room at Sandringham, or moving about the silent house, she had seen the shy, tender qualities in the Princess developing into womanly sympathy, when she was faced with the threat of death. One letter can be taken from those written by the Princess to the Queen to show how this relationship was strengthened as years passed. The Queen could never find full play for her interests in talking to her daughter-in-law. Politics and worldly power were not comprehensible to her. But there was happy trust which is revealed in a letter written to the Queen in December of 1878. 'Many, many thanks for your affectionate letter,' wrote the Princess. 'I feel really quite ashamed of so much praise as I don't deserve a quarter of it, though one thing at least is

Her Royal Highness
THE PRINCESS ALEXANDRA OF DENMARK
January 1st 1863

His Royal Highness
THE PRINCE OF WALES
January 1st 1863

true—how entirely I return your affection, which I value above all things... the little brooch is too pretty, and is doubly precious in my eyes from your having picked up the stone yourself.'

The brooch had been a birthday gift. The Princess had spent a 'quiet day' with her husband, who had 'quite overloaded' her with lovely presents.

All who knew the Princess were entranced, and if her limited education in Denmark sometimes forbade her full interest in intricate problems of State, she gave tenderness from her heart, which was as important to her friends and to the education of her children as any scholastic theories might have been.

The awful responsibility of educating an heir to the throne belongs to the government as much as to the parents. Queen Victoria realised this responsibility and, from the beginning, she tried to supervise the instruction of her grandchildren. She was pleased that the chosen tutor, the Rev. J. N. Dalton, was a 'fearless, honest man.' The Prince of Wales was sometimes nervous of his mother's plans. He had already told her that for their 'education, proper discipline and undisturbed studies, they must leave home.' This was one of the problems which confronted him upon his return from India, although it was not until May of 1877 that his sons joined a training ship for instruction. The Prince and the Queen did not always see eye to eye over the plans. Perhaps it was unfortunate that they talked these matters over at Windsor, where Prince Albert Edward had suffered so much under his father's curriculum. Sitting with his mother in the room at Windsor, he could look out of the window towards the playing fields of Eton which had haunted him so much when he was young. He had never been allowed to play, and on the rare occasions when a few carefully chosen boys had been allowed to take tea with him, his father had always been present, to dampen any attempts at fun or mischief.

Loyalty to his mother prevented the Prince of Wales from discussing this wistful fear lest the mistake of his own education should be repeated. But he once unbent a little to one of the Queen's Ladies-in-Waiting. She had been to luncheon with the Prince and the Princess at Marlborough House and afterwards she wrote [184] of the good behaviour of Prince George and his elder brother. 'No noise or fuss of directions about them. I congratulated their poor father—he said he thought it very happy not to have to be always at them.' Then he added, '*We* were perhaps a little too much spoken to and at, at least we thought we could never do anything right, anyhow.'

The Prince's two sons were always in awe of his authority but the curbing reins he put upon them were never unduly tight. When the young Princes were allowed to extend their experience, on board the training ship *Britannia,* they showed as much human and healthy naughtiness as did their less exalted contemporaries. There is one irrelevant but enchanting story which gives us a picture of Prince George as a boy. One day he was taken with his brother to Westminster, where Dean Stanley had been asked to show them the treasures of the Abbey. Nobody could make the memorials of Westminster come to life . again as Dean Stanley did, with his vivid historical sense. In spite of the charms of the Dean's stories, Prince George wandered away by himself. At last he was found in a dim little side chapel. He had scrambled on top of Queen Elizabeth's tomb, and, looking down at the effigy, he was saying, 'What an ugly old woman!'

Prince George was twelve when he became the youngest cadet on board the *Britannia*. He was conscientious: the flame of duty, which was to be the guiding force of his reign, was already alive in him. It was an inheritance from his Coburg grandfather. Æsthetic tastes and devotion to scholarship did not go with the inherited conscientiousness, but, when he was a boy, there were already signs of the similarity in character. The signs were to increase as the years passed. But, in leisure, he was as spirited and impish as his contemporaries. On one occasion, a couple of marline-spikes found their way into the bed of an officer. A certain cadet was suspected. Then Prince George admitted that he was the culprit and he faced his punishment. His leave was stopped for one week.

From the *Britannia,* Prince George and his brother went to the *Bacchante* in which they toured the world. There was no hint yet that Prince George would become heir to the throne, through his brother's death. He was therefore educated as a second son, with the consequent difference in aims and responsibilities. A sailor's life suited him: he was a man's man, and his character and humour and tastes were of the mould that thrives in a wardroom or an officers' mess. In the *Bacchante* the Princes travelled as far as Australia and New Zealand. In Australia they descended a gold mine; they aimed with boomerangs and they ate minced kangaroo. In New Zealand they shook hands with dusky Maori chieftains who had fought against their Grandmother's soldiers. Prince George was at home on both land and sea. He wrote in his Journal, 'After dinner much amusement, trying to sit on an empty corked bottle, on the deck, at the same time holding a candle in each hand, one of which was lighted, the other to be lighted from it, without rolling over.'

While he was in Australian waters, Prince George left the *Bacchante* to stay with an Australian hostess. She made a charming gesture which showed him that graciousness was to flourish, as well as corn and wool, in the primitive countries of his Grandmother's Empire. When he went down for his breakfast, he found a wreath of rosebuds about his plate. They were, he was told, 'for Sunday morning and in memory of England.'

Chapter Nineteen

1878–1880

IF THE energies and talents which Lord Beaconsfield devoted to the Eastern problem had been spared for the building up of the Empire, the history of India and Africa might offer less dark pages. When he was a fledgling in politics, Beaconsfield had imagined an Imperial Parliament and an Empire bound together, not all upon the beautiful but uncertain foundations of loyalty and sentiment, but with the strengthening elements of trade and co-operation in Government. He had talked of the Empire conferences which might have prevented evils instead of merely correcting them, if they had been held in the last century instead of this. But Englishmen were pre-occupied with affairs nearer home. The Eastern question, the malefaction of the Irish, the cynical, bombastic campaign of Bismarck, and the electoral and social reforms kept the British Government busy. They had enough to think about and frown over from the men they already knew, without caring very much for Zulus, Hindus and Maoris.

The tumult over the Berlin Congress had barely died when a fresh danger threatened Britain's peace. The Russians had not confined their ambitions to conquest over Turkey. Peter the Great was said, in his will, to have charged Russia to march through Central Asia, Persia and Afghanistan and make India her own. The Russians had remembered the will of the Father of the Fatherland. They had been disappointed in their thrust through the

Balkans, into Turkey, but there was still Peter's way to
follow. In July of 1878, Russian troops passed through
Turkestan to the borders of Afghanistan. Here they
paused, perilously near to the Indian border. A Russian
mission followed and a convention was signed with the
Amir of Afghanistan. His country was a corridor now,
between Russian influence and British territory. When
Britain proposed that the Amir should also receive a
British mission, to counteract the Russian influences, he
was so elated by his friendship with Russia that he not
only refused to receive the members of the British mission, but ordered his soldiers to arrest their advance, at
the entrance to the Khyber Pass. After this monstrous
impertinence the British Governmen sent the Amir an
ultimatum. This he ignored. He was as clever as a bag of
monkeys in dealing with his Oriental equals, but he was
perplexed by this assault from the powers of Europe. He
was dazed, with a bomb in each hand. On November
21st the British forces advanced through the passes, and,
while Gladstone and his supporters wailed again against
the Tory lust for war, General Roberts routed the Afghans
at Peiwar Kotal. Another division held the Khyber Pass,
a third occupied Pishin, and, early in the New Year,
reached Kandahar. The Amir found that, of the two
bombs, the British one went off first. He retreated, begging the Emperor of Russia to aid him. The plea was
ignored, and the Amir withered and died in the ignominy of exile. His son succeeded as Amir, and at first he
seemed to welcome the British mission and the control
which was forced upon him. But the British were still
children in dealing with the undercurrents of intrigue in
the East. Six weeks after the members of the mission
were established in Kabul, Afghanese soldiers massacred

them in the Residency. The Amir did not raise a finger in their defence. Again General Roberts led his soldiers, this time through the Kurran Pass, to Kabul and to victory. The Amir fled to General Roberts' camp and he was sent to India.

The next eruption was more interesting to the Prince of Wales. At the end of 1876 the Prince's friend, Sir Bartle Frere, was appointed Governor of the Cape of Good Hope and High Commissioner for South Africa. His duty was to promote federation between the African States, but when his steamer arrived at Cape Town, early in 1877, he came upon so many disruptions and plots that peaceful federation became a mockery. In September he sent a despatch to England in which he said that he feared war with the Zulus was imminent. There were only six thousand of H.M.'s forces in the country, and he asked for two more battalions of infantry. The threat of war with the Zulus was not all. Three months after his arrival, the Boer Republic of the Transvaal was annexed to the British Crown. The sinister forces which met in the South African War of 1899–1902 were already at work. Boer, Briton and Kaffir were to struggle through many bloody conflicts before South Africa was to enjoy peace. But the magnitude of these forces was not understood in Downing Street, in 1878. The first Kaffir rebels were defeated in June and the Boers of the Transvaal seemed to be calmed by Sir Bartle's assurances.

The Prince of Wales wrote to Sir Bartle Frere continually during the unrest in Africa. Nor did he allow friendship to be satisfied with mere sympathy, for he was in continual touch with the Prime Minister on Frere's behalf. The Prince did not allow his loyalty to 'good, excellent Sir Bartle' to fade.

The great King Cetewayo was the defiant black Napoleon of the Zulus. He was a nephew of Dingaan and
Chaka, and Chaka had been the creator of Zulu warfare.
Cetewayo was not a dim-minded savage, blundering in
wrath against his enemies. He had an old feud with the
Boers for the possession of the land between the Buffalo
and Pongola Rivers, and when the British Government
annexed the Transvaal they inherited this feud with the
territory. Cetewayo planned a bigger war. It was not the
end of his dreams—that the stretch of country between
the rivers should be his. He saw the dark tide of millions
of black people, rising to expel the white man from Africa
for ever. It was against this formidable dream that Sir
Bartle Frere had to make his plans. Cetewayo had made a
raid into Natal. Frere sent him an ultimatum, demanding
reparations, but the challenge was ignored. Without
authority from the Cabinet, Frere then ordered Lord
Chelmsford, who commanded the British troops in Natal,
to march against the defiant Cetewayo. This was on January 11th, 1879, and on the 22nd eight hundred white soldiers and almost five hundred natives were slaughtered
by Cetewayo's Zulus, at Isandhlwana. There is a touch of
irony in the study of dates about this time. While this
ghastly massacre was afoot, to the horror of Westminster
and the humiliation of Frere and Chelmsford, there was
a letter for Frere on the high seas from the Prince of
Wales, in which he wrote, 'You have, indeed, not got a
bed of roses.' [185] Reinforcements were sent out to the Cape,
but also a despatch which censured Frere for exceeding
his instructions. Again we have proofs of the Prince's
loyalty to his friends. Indeed, it seems that sometimes caution suffered through these expressions of affection and
trust. The Prince wrote to Lady Frere, assuring her that

he had 'never ceased exonerating Lord Chelmsford from the blame' of Isandhlwana, and that he 'sincerely and earnestly' hoped that her husband 'would not think of resigning.'[186] A few days later he repeated his assurances to Frere, this time in a letter written direct to his friend. 'You may be assured that my thoughts are continually with you . . . I only earnestly hope that you will stick to your post, and not think of resigning . . .'

The Prince's enthusiasm and confidence were not shared by many people in England. The mass of them damned Chelmsford and Frere for the slaughter of Isandhlwana.

But Frere and Chelmsford were on the other side of the world. The Cabinet was at hand, ready for its full burden of blame. Lord Beaconsfield drooped under the weight. The Cabinet was divided, prestige in Europe was weakened and Beaconsfield's personal hold over the country suffered one more strain. 'Prince Hal is sanguine—nay, sure—that Bartle F. and Chelmsford will come out triumphant,' he wrote.[187] 'I wish I shared his convictions . . .'

Again it was the Queen who roused Beaconsfield with encouragement. '. . . Show a bold front to the world,' she urged him. But she dwelt upon the need for preparedness. At every moment of danger in her reign she had pleaded for the increase of her army. The lesson was again pressed home by the calamity of Isandhlwana. She told Lord Beaconsfield he 'must not be downhearted for a moment,' but she saw in the appalling news 'a lesson *never* to reduce our forces . . . with our enormous Empire, we must always be prepared for such contingencies . . .'

She was gracious to him, even as she scolded. Primroses arrived from Osborne, tied into little bunches. The gardener had been told to send them every week. The Queen received in return a birthday letter, more heavily laden with humility and flattery than any her Minister had sent her before. He talked of the 'strangeness of his destiny,' which allowed him to be the 'servant of one so great.' He hoped that the 'bright shadow of the coming hours' would 'illumine her with their happiness, sustain her in her state and touch with an enchanting ray the hallowed influences of her hearth.'

There were moments in which the Queen was frigidly sane. In the intervals of calm and prosperity she was willing to languish beneath her Ministers' compliments. But, in time of anxiety, she was not deluded. The Cabinet decided that Frere was no longer capable of coping with the South African complications and they wished to send Sir Garnet Wolseley to govern Natal and the Transvaal, thus relegating Sir Bartle Frere to the limited sphere of the Cape Colony. Perhaps Beaconsfield's subtlety was on the wane: perhaps he misjudged his Sovereign at times, for the fulsome birthday letter was inopportune. The day after she received it, she wrote a letter which is still another example of the calm which the Queen could muster in a time of crisis. She saw the South African question not merely as a local affair between Boers, Britons and Zulus; nor was it a problem to be smoothed away hastily by the Cabinet. Her detachment helped her to place the question before Beaconsfield perhaps more clearly than he saw it himself. She defended Frere and she deprecated the plan to send out a superior officer to take over his control of Natal and the Transvaal. She wrote:

'... Whatever fault may have been committed in declaring (perhaps) too hastily, war, Sir B. Frere seems to have succeeded, by his personal influence, in conciliating those important portions of the Colonies, who were considered to be disaffected. To reward his efforts therefore by sending out an officer with the powers pro-

posed, instead of encouraging him, will be a public mark of want
of confidence—at a moment of great difficulty—which will have a
most disastrous effect both at home and abroad; and will make it
almost impossible for any public man to serve his country if on
the 1st misfortune occurring he is to be thrown over!'

In this paragraph, the Queen laid down a principle
which might have saved many a misfortune if it had been
made law in Whitehall. The next paragraph of her letter
to Beaconsfield reveals the fullness of her experience and
the historical sense which caused her to see all contemporary problems in relation to her memory of forty years
of government.

'...the Queen most strongly protests against the use of private
information, than which nothing more injurious to discipline and
good government can exist. This was one of the causes of our
suffering in the Crimea and led to every sort of evil. No Commander or Governor can stand against or submit to that; and the
Queen can only attribute this to the inexperience of public life in
some of his [the Prime Minister's] colleagues.'

Her letter concluded with a plan less drastic than the
one proposed by the Cabinet. '...send somebody out with
messages to Sir B. Frere and Lord Chelmsford,' she wrote,
'to explain exactly what the Govt. wish and what they
object to. But do not upset everything—which will be the
case if an officer, whoever he may be, is sent out with the
powers proposed.' The Queen said that she would sanction the proposal if her 'warnings' were disregarded, but
she would not *approve* of it. The Cabinet proceeded in
spite of her agitation, and Wolseley sailed for Africa.

Sir Garnet Wolseley arrived in Africa in the midst of a
renewed battle between Lord Chelmsford's soldiers and
the Zulus. In this conflict Chelmsford led his men more

gloriously, and Wolseley had little to do in the time that followed except to tidy up the shambles of war and re-organise the country into the forms of peace. On July 4th Chelmsford's soldiers devastated Cetewayo's army before the Zulu King's own kraal.

On September 3rd Lord Chelmsford arrived at Balmoral with a Zulu shield for Queen Victoria. It had been taken out of Cetewayo's own Shield House at Ulindi and, like a knight of old, Chelmsford brought his trophy home to his Queen. She wrote in her Journal of the shield, 'made of oxen hide, stiffened and prepared in a peculiar manner.' It was white, with a little black, and it had belonged to the regiment of unmarried men. 'Formerly they always used to carry these large shields. . . . But Cetewayo, finding them very inconvenient in fighting with fire-arms, had them reduced to about one-third of their size.' The Zulu shield was added to the Queen's collection of trophies from her growing Empire.

Queen Victoria made a characteristic gesture of consolation to Sir Bartle Frere: she sent him a copy of the new volume of the Prince Consort's life, inscribed by her own hand. When he was obliged to resign, after the Liberal victory of 1880, the Prince of Wales gave him another proof of friendship by inviting Sir Bartle to be his guest in Scotland.

Lord Beaconsfield pursued his Imperial vision in spite of the difficulties which beset him. He appointed Lord Lorne to be Governor-General of Canada. Lord Lorne's wife was Princess Louise, the beautiful and witty daughter of the Queen. This appointment of a semi-royal peer to a dominion was significant. It showed that Beaconsfield saw the countries of the Empire, not as poor second cousins, but as sons and daughters of the parent England.

He made one shrewd comment to the Queen in the midst of the wrestle and bother with Zulus and Afghans. He wrote, 'It is wise that the fountain of honour should flow freely in the colonies.' Beaconsfield knew, from his experience of men, that honours would be doubly valued by the colonists if they were conferred direct by the Crown.

There were little flashes of compensation in the distress over Afghanistan and Natal. In November Beaconsfield went to Sandringham, where 'Prince Hal was very gracious, agreeable, and in high feather; and very proud of having four Knights of the Garter at dinner.'[188] And there were occasional wisps of news from Europe which showed that Beaconsfield's triumph in Berlin had not been forgotten. Bismarck wrote two or three friendly letters and Lord Odo Russell wrote to Beaconsfield's secretary on November 23rd to say that it was 'most remarkable and refreshing to see how the Oriental policy of H.M.G. in, and since, the Congress, has elevated England in the eyes of the Continent.'

Chapter Twenty

§ 1 — 1879-1880

THE PRINCE OF WALES had been able to play the part of a friend in the Zulu War, confining his influence to the cause of Sir Bartle Frere. But he assumed something of the influence of a statesman when Egypt came into the arena in the early part of 1879. The Prince had invented the phrase *Entente Cordiale* in conversation with the French Ambassador in London. The phrase had been most happy. The Ambassador had repeated it in a letter to Paris. The Prince's dream of an *Entente Cordiale* was shaken when the Khedive of Egypt, wallowing in debt and extravagance, tried to free himself of French and British control. He dismissed his responsible Minister, together with the French and English Ministers who had been elected to check his squandering and his muddles of administration.

If Bismarck had not been so late in joining the other European Powers in their desire for Colonial expansion, the history of the past sixty years would be still more complicated than it is. But Germany was not a competitor for the spoils which attracted Beaconsfield. Nor was Russia any longer a frightening adversary, with the story of the Crimea and the Treaty of Berlin to curb her ambitions. But France was inoculated with the same virus as Britain. She had been deprived of Alsace and Lorraine, so she cast her eyes elsewhere—about the Mediterranean with especial longing for Egypt, through which the great

Napoleon had led his soldiers. Both France and England were bound to Egypt by the ties of old conquests. Nelson's victory of the Nile gave England a background for her more material and tangible interest in the Suez Canal. Egypt was to be the first obstacle in the Prince's plans for an *Entente Cordiale*. The Khedive's rebellion against French and British control was a jolt to Anglo-French relationships and the Prince of Wales, remembering his many friends in Paris and the hopes he had of peace between the two countries, wrote anxiously to the Prime Minister. Beaconsfield answered gloomily, but the Prince hoped that the 'difficult and troublesome' question would be solved if Britain would act 'in concert with the French Government.' [189] 'Can we depose the Khedive?' he asked. Thus the Prince suggested the obvious and only way of dealing with the perverse Khedive Ismail. With the support of the Sultan, Abdul Hamid, who was still titular Overlord of the Egyptians, France and England joined in deposing the ruler. The young Prince Tewfik, whom the Prince had decorated with the Order of the Star of India a few years before, was chosen as Khedive in his father's place. The new Khedive was permitted to govern Egypt under the supervision of French and English officials: a more drastic control than that imposed upon his father. The English official who was chosen to tighten the handcuffs upon young Tewfik was Sir Evelyn Baring, afterwards Lord Cromer. He was destined to wrestle with the problems of the country for thirty years. The enthroning of the new Khedive and the appointment of Sir Evelyn Baring calmed the Prince. Perhaps he was too optimistic on this as on other occasions. The Anglo-French control worked peacefully for only three years. When French influence was finally withdrawn from Egypt, in 1883, a new

Government was in power in England. Sir Charles Dilke, disliked by the Queen, but nevertheless a good friend of the Prince, was Foreign Under-Secretary, and he encouraged the Prince in his attempts at diplomacy as he had never been encouraged before.

§ II — 1879–1880

Towards the end of November Mr. Gladstone began his Midlothian 'pilgrimage of passion.' With the 'black art' of oratory, perhaps richer in him than in any other of his time, he travelled over the country like an evangelist possessed. The strange tides of public sympathy and allegiance to leaders can never be explained. They change and they turn by no known laws and with little semblance of reason. The great, intense figure of Mr. Gladstone seemed to dominate every audience. The people came in thousands, from as far away as the Hebrides, to hear him. The fierceness of his speeches, the talk of *freedom,* of *justice,* and of *humanity* cast a spell over Carlisle, Hawick, Edinburgh and Glasgow. The hills in some places were white with snow and bitter winds chilled the streets of the towns. Gladstone went on, from place to place, like a prophet.

At Hughenden, Beaconsfield was fingering the souvenirs of his long, long life. He did not heed a word of what Gladstone said: nor did he read a word of what he wrote. He had also been near Hawick once, to see Sir Walter Scott. That was many years ago, when he was the young, little known Benjamin Disraeli, eager and undaunted. Now he was old, tired, and solitary. Not even power could lessen the pathos and tragedy of his loneliness. In September, when he had displeased the Queen

206

because he did not wish to receive Lord Chelmsford on his return from Natal, he had written a pathetic letter to Lady Ely. 'I love the Queen—perhaps the only person in this world left to me that I do love ... it worries me and disquiets me, when there is a cloud between us ...'

On November 26th Beaconsfield went to see his Sovereign. 'What nerve! What muscle! What energy!' he wrote to Lady Bradford, describing the Queen. He was, he said, 'very deficient in all three.' He had not read 'a single line' of the 'row' in Gladstone's campaign. It was 'wearisome rhetoric' and 'a waste of powder and shot.'

But Gladstone was speaking in a language the people understood. They listened to his beautiful voice:

> Remember that the sanctity of life in the hill villages of Afghanistan among the winter snows, is as inviolable in the eye of Almighty God as can be your own. Remember that He who has united you as human beings in the same flesh and blood, has bound you by the law of mutual love; that mutual love is not limited by the shores of this island, is not limited by the boundaries of Christian civilisation....

Lord Morley tells us that by these speeches, 'Men were recalled to moral forces that they had forgotten.'

§ III — 1879

THERE WERE many who were not cowed by Gladstone's oratory. It was easy for some people to imagine that his performances were pure acting, as had been said of the performances of Lord Beaconsfield. But they were actors of different schools. Beaconsfield was of the French school, with technique as its basis. Once when he wished to answer a statement in the House, he held up what seemed to be a note, from which he read and quoted. He crumpled it in his hand at the right moment and threw it away. Somebody picked it up afterwards, and found that it was a blank slip of paper. Gladstone was of the violent, heroic school and some were not impressed by him. The oratory left them cold. It is said that when Parnell paid his only visit to Hawarden he sat next to Gladstone's daughter at dinner. As an aid to conversation, she asked him whom he considered to be the greatest actor he had ever seen.

'Without doubt, your father,' was his answer.

The Queen did not allow her feelings to overwhelm her reason. She was fully conscious of the perils which lay in the Liberal campaign. The stories of Gladstone's victories were told to her and she was obliged to contemplate a weakening Conservative cause. In June of 1879 Beaconsfield was a prisoner, moving in pain from his bed to his sofa. When the Queen summoned him, he could not go, 'or even move.'[190] He was weak and could scarcely write to his beloved friends. In August he complained to Lady Bradford of the Lord Mayor's banquet. He could 'eat nothing.' He had to get up 'with a confused brain and exhausted body' to make his speech. In September he urged the Queen to realise the advantages there would be in having a younger Minister who could 'hasten to her at critical moments!' This, he confessed, he could not do.

For five days the Queen watched these miserable signs of the end of what had been her happiest years since Prince Albert's death. Gladstone's high-falutin phrases were ringing through the provinces. Gladstone was well and strong. The danger was obvious and the Queen expressed her fears and her will in a letter which she wrote to Lady Ely on September 1st. She wished that Sir Henry

Ponsonby could *'get at some of the Opposition,'* as Prince Albert's Secretary and Stockmar had once done: they had given discreet, whispered warnings to the Opposition of what they might expect from the Queen if they came into power. She was a constitutional monarch, subject to the dictates of Parliament. But when she set down her views of the situation, she wrote like a grand despot of a less enlightened régime. She wished the principal people of the Opposition to know that there were *'certain* things' to which she would *never* consent:

1. Any lowering of the position of this country by letting Russia have her way in the East, or by letting down our Empire in India and in the Colonies. This *was* done under Mr. Gladstone, quite *contrary* to Lord Palmerston's *policy,* which, whatever faults he had, *was always* for *keeping up England,* which of late years had *quite* gone down, so that we were *despised abroad.*
2. That I would never give way about *the Scotch Church,* which is the real and true stronghold of Protestantism.

These are points which I *never* could *allow* to be *trifled with,* and I could have *no* confidence in any men who attempted this. Our position in India, and in the Colonies, *must* be *upheld.* I wish to *trust my* Government whoever it is, but they should be *well aware* beforehand I never could if they intended to *try* and *undo* what has been done.

In the same way I never could take Mr. Gladstone or Mr. Lowe as my Minister again, for I never COULD have the slightest *particle* of confidence in Mr. Gladstone *after* his violent, mischievous, and dangerous conduct for the past three years, nor could I take the *latter* after the very offensive language he used three years ago against *me.*

. . . I never *could* take Sir C. Dilke as a *Minister.*

The depression deepened. Four days later Beaconsfield wrote again: the state of affairs was 'not free from peril,' but he hoped that events would show that his Faery was 'arbitress of Europe.'

Early in February of 1880 the Queen opened Parliament for the last time with Lord Beaconsfield as her Prime Minister. He had pleaded with her to appear, since this would perhaps be the end of his Ministry. The Queen faced the ordeal which she always compared to an *execution,* and she answered him from Osborne: this time she would make the *sacrifice.* The session opened in the wake of disasters almost as poignant as the threat of Beaconsfield's defeat in the coming elections. His Ministry had fought through four wars and four wretched harvests. There was gloom among the people: trade was feeble, there were poverty and unemployment, and the Irish were hungry.

A few weeks before the opening of Parliament the Commissioner of Police for the Metropolis had been to see the Prime Minister. He had told Beaconsfield that he was confident of the Queen's security and of the welcome the people would give her. They had been touched by her messages of sympathy. But he felt that the royal procession should be 'as splendid as might be convenient.' There was nothing which the great body of the people more appreciated than this spectacle. He suggested that there might be a good muster of the household troops, not for the Queen's *security,* but because the 'splendour of Royalty' delighted the people.[191]

At the end of March Queen Victoria went to Darmstadt. Her daughter, Princess Alice, had died in December of 1878, and the Queen wished all the more to be present at the Confirmation of her grand-daughters. From Darmstadt the Queen went to Baden-Baden. It was there, on April 2nd, that she received the *terrible* telegram which told her of the Liberal victory at the elections and of the inevitable defeat of her Minister.

At first the Queen closed her heart against all advice and reason. She would have 'nothing to do with Mr. Gladstone,' whose conduct, since 1876, had been 'one series of violent, passionate invective against and abuse of Lord Beaconsfield.' She said that Mr. Gladstone *caused* the Russian war.[192]

For the first time in the Queen's reign her sons took their part as advisers in the formation of her Government. In the turbulent changes of 1868 and 1874 the Prince of Wales had been abroad and unable to be more than an onlooker. Now he threw himself into the discussion with foresight which had come to him as the fruit of his experience and travel. Lord Beaconsfield had described him, only a few months before, as 'one who has seen everything and knows everybody.' This was almost true. The Prince knew men like Dilke and his friend Gambetta: he had entertained and acknowledged such men as Delane and Chamberlain whom his mother did not like. While the Queen clung to the old régime, desperately afraid of the political upheaval which menaced her peace of mind, her sons seemed to be able to gauge public feeling and to understand the mysterious changes of the political game. The Duke of Connaught, then married and living at Bagshot Park, wrote to his mother on April 11th gently suggesting the state of mind which was forced upon her, when her bitterness was conquered. 'I know how strongly you feel against the line that the Liberals have taken up these last three years. . . . It is indeed very hard for you to bear, dearest Mama, but I know how nobly you can sacrifice your own feelings at the call of duty. I can't understand what is to be done with Mr. Gladstone if he is not to be in the new Ministry; won't he be a terrible thorn in their side out of office?'

The Queen was willing to send for Lord Hartington, as official leader of the Opposition. If he failed to form a Government, she was willing to send for Lord Granville in his place—but never Mr. Gladstone. The Prince of Wales wrote letters almost every day to his mother's secretary, and he communicated with Lord Hartington and Lord Granville.

There was one unfortunate influence near to the Queen. Her youngest son, Prince Leopold, was as violent in his dislike of Mr. Gladstone as was his mother, and he encouraged her antipathy. The Prince of Wales openly acknowledged this disadvantage. His secretary wrote to Lord Granville,[193] 'The Prince of Wales feels sure that if the Queen would only look upon Mr. Gladstone as a friend instead of as the enemy of Her Majesty and the Royal Family, which Prince Leopold deliberately delights in persuading her he is, she will find him all she could wish.' Both Lord Granville and Lord Hartington agreed, and urged that Mr. Gladstone was the only man who could form a Government.

The Prince of Wales said that 'nothing could be nicer' than the way in which Mr. Gladstone was speaking of the Queen during this unfortunate time of indecision. He had said 'how much he felt for her in the difficult position she was placed in' and that he would do all he could to 'meet the Queen's wishes and be conciliatory in every possible way.' The Prince ended his letter to his mother's secretary, 'I am strongly of the opinion that the Queen should send for Mr. Gladstone. Far better that she should take the initiative than that it should be forced upon her.'

The Queen's stubbornness went hand in hand with wonderful frankness. When she sent for Lord Hartington, she talked to him of Mr. Gladstone's 'violence and bitterness.' She thought that he had passed the 'ordinary bounds of opposition,' and she said that she had no confidence in him. Lord Hartington asked her if he might repeat any part of the frank conversation to Mr. Gladstone. The Queen said that he might, for she would 'say the same to Mr. Gladstone himself, if she saw him.' Again the young Victoria ruled England; the girl who had called the Duke of Wellington a rebel and refused to allow her husband in the room when she was interviewing her Ministers. A flash of the impetuosity of the forties came into the scene. But it passed. The grim allegiance to her constitutional responsibilities prevailed, and when Mr. Gladstone came to her she received him with 'perfect courtesy.' Gladstone acknowledged this in his diary for the day. It was the courtesy, he said, 'from which she never deviates.'

When they had discussed the formation of the Ministry, the Queen said to him, 'I must be frank with you, Mr. Gladstone.' She recalled the Midlothian speeches which had caused her concern and pain. Gladstone replied that he considered all violence and bitterness 'to belong to the *past.*' He did not deny that he had used 'very strong language.' [194]

When one turns from the Queen's record of the interview to the pages of Mr. Gladstone's diary, there is an additional remark. Gladstone wrote:

With regard to the freedom of language I had admitted, she said with some good-natured archness, 'But you will have to bear the consequences,' to which I entirely assented. She seemed to me, if I may so say, 'natural under effort.' All things considered, I was much pleased. I ended by kissing Her Majesty's hand. [195]

Chapter Twenty-One

§1 — 1880

Mr. GLADSTONE's new Parliament met at the end of April, with gloomy prospects for the Queen. She had been obliged to accept the *very advanced Radicals,* Sir Charles Dilke and Joseph Chamberlain, in important offices. Lord Granville had assured her, through her secretary, that the Radicals were not as truculent as she feared. He thought the Government to be 'like bread sauce—made up of two substantial elements.' 'The few pepper corns are very obvious,' he said, 'and perhaps give a little flavour but do not affect the character of the food.' [196] No solace of this kind could make it easy for the Queen to accept Sir Charles Dilke, after his impertinent comments about her finances in the Commons. He had been unfeeling enough to ask for an enquiry into the Civil List, a few weeks after her dreadful ordeal over the illness of her son. Mr. Gladstone had promised her that, in the minor role of Under-Secretary for Foreign Affairs, Dilke would not be brought into contact with her. Also there had been humility after the defeat of his Civil List motion in the House—he had been very young and foolish then. Providing that she should not be obliged to meet Dilke, the Queen consented to his appointment, but she shrewdly tied his hands by asking for a letter from him, admitting his error and promising his good behaviour in the future. When the letter arrived she made a copy before returning it to Lord Granville.

214

Mr. Gladstone also tried to calm the Queen in regard to Mr. Chamberlain, the Unitarian who was to be President of the Board of Trade. Gladstone thought she would like him. Mr. Chamberlain was 'very pleasing and refined in feelings and manner,' he told her, and he had never spoken against her or against her family.[197]

Both the Queen and Mr. Gladstone were older and the calm of age and wisdom softened the first interview when he went to see her at Windsor on April 28th. She found him *courteous throughout*, grateful for the way in which she received his proposals and repeatedly asking whether he did not weary her.[198]

The Queen began the five years of Gladstone's administration with attempts at friendliness. They often talked together without disagreement over the legislation when it affected life in England. But Mr. Gladstone had no interest in foreign affairs, a subject in which the Queen revelled. Mr. Gladstone looked at the country through the wrong end of the telescope. Because of this limitation, the honour and dignity of England, so vigorously upheld by the Queen and Beaconsfield in their dealings with Germany, Russia, France, Africa, India, Egypt and Afghanistan, were allowed to droop through the blunders of the new Government. Gladstone was unable to see that the problems of the Empire could not be treated as moral issues, divorced from the everyday weaknesses of human nature. 'I do believe that the Almighty has employed me for His purposes,' was the tenor of his thought and speeches.

There were few signs of tranquillity in the Government, despite the talents and character of men like Lord Hartington, Lord Granville and Mr. Chamberlain. Some

215

of Gladstone's old friends were disgruntled because they were excluded from the Cabinet, and the atheist member for Northampton vulgarised the early proceedings by refusing to take the oath of allegiance which obliged him to say, 'So help me God.'

The speech which Mr. Gladstone made in the House upon the Oaths question was memorable and sincere. But its theme revealed Gladstone's affiliation with the Divine rather than his kinship with the infirmities of man. He could thrash the money-changers in the temple, but only with his tongue. Indeed, they profited through his high-minded preoccupations and they carried on their business with increased zeal.

There was no longer as much force in Gladstone's hands as in his voice. Beaconsfield had ruled the Cabinet with a ceremoniousness which Lord Rosebery once described as 'majestic.' Mr. Gladstone had also been *majestic,* during his Midlothian campaign, when his speeches had been full of promises. But the story was different when he achieved the responsibilities of power. He attempted to fulfil his promises, but the changes from Beaconsfield's foreign policy were attempted with little precision. Britain's hold on Afghanistan was weakened, for Mr. Gladstone's Government did not see any reason for holding Kandahar, in spite of Russia's ambition for a foothold in the countries so perilously near the Indian border. In Constantinople the Turks tried to wriggle out of the promises they had made in the Treaty of Berlin. Relations with the Porte became so strained that the Queen was afraid that we were coming 'nearer and nearer to war.' She displayed a little more vision than the Cabinet by pointing out the dangers of arousing Turkey. The Turks had it in their power, she wrote, to rouse the

Mussulmans in India against us. She feared that this was not sufficiently considered by the Government.

There was weakness too in the conduct of affairs in Africa—weakness which led to the disaster of Majuba in the following year. Sir Bartle Frere, against whom so much of the Liberal spleen had been directed, was not recalled for some time. South Africa was tormented again by the savage jealousies between Briton, Boer and Zulu. Confederation seemed to be impossible and the Transvaal Boers once more tried their strength in favour of independence from British rule. The Basutos also rebelled, encouraging other tribes to follow. All were subdued, but the peace which resulted was no more than an interlude.

There was every reason why Britain should cling to the Transvaal. Sir Garnet Wolseley had written of the country in the previous year as rich in minerals. Gold had already been found and there was little doubt that larger and still more valuable fields would be discovered. Wolseley had been clever in seeing the solution of the Boer problem in the minerals. The gold mines would bring thousands of British people to the Transvaal, he said, reducing the disgruntled Boers to a minority. Mr. Gladstone did not see the promise of prosperity in Wolseley's report, and he regretted the cost and trouble of retaining the country. He confessed his own bewilderment when he said, 'I have always regarded the South African question as the one great unsolved and perhaps insoluble problem of our colonial system.' [199]

Few soldiers or politicians have denied Gladstone's responsibility for the failure to pacify the races in South Africa. When Beaconsfield was in power, the Liberals had attacked the militant policy of Sir Bartle Frere, and Gladstone had pleaded for magnanimity in dealing with

Afghanese, Boers and Zulus. But when the reins were in his hands, the magnanimity proved to be nothing but weakness as far as South Africa was concerned. There were not enough British soldiers in the country to intimidate the Boers or to substantiate the boast Wolseley had made to them ... that 'The Vaal River would flow backwards through the Drakensberg sooner than the British would be withdrawn from the Transvaal.' [200]

The Queen and the Prince of Wales watched the weakened military forces in Africa with anxiety which was justified in February of 1881, when the Boers devastated the Natal army and killed its commander, in the battle of Majuba Hill. Mr. Gladstone was forced to change his theme. Instead of his wish to yield to the demand for Boer independence, he was obliged to strengthen our defences. General Roberts sailed for Africa with reinforce-forcements, British honour was patched up and peace was arranged. But Britain had been punished for her weakness: she was now *obliged* to sanction the independence of the Boers under the suzerainty of Great Britain.

§ 11 — 1880

THE QUEEN asked much of Mr. Gladstone in expecting him to govern her Empire without her trust and her encouragement. The inveterate nature of her prejudice was the big mistake of the last twenty years of her reign. In all other questions she became more leinent. Gentleness, and escape from the more morbid forms of her sorrow, drew her nearer to her people and she was loved and acclaimed again, wherever she appeared and whenever her name was mentioned. She became the symbol of her great century and the mother of her great Empire. But she clung tenaciously to her old antipathy. The memory of Gladstone, struggling against this frustration, honourably, wistfully at times, never detracting a tittle of his loyalty and esteem, must stir the imagination of even those to whom Liberalism is anathema: and of those to whom Gladstone appears as a disquieting figure.

The Queen had not always disliked him. At the time of the Prince Consort's death, when her grief isolated her from her people, Gladstone had been among the most tender to her. Of all her Ministers he 'had entered most into her feelings.' She had thought his conduct in 1861 to be 'beautiful, noble, touching to the very last degree.' Mr. Gladstone had been equally impressed by the 'firm texture and elasticity of her mind and her marked dignity and strength of character.' He had been 'astonished at her humility.'

In 1880, the Queen's happy recollection of Gladstone was dead. She ignored her Constitutional promises (with excuses perhaps, when we remember her loneliness), and she wrote to Lord Beaconsfield,[201] saying that she *never* wrote to Gladstone 'except on formal *official matters,*' and that she looked always to Beaconsfield 'for ultimate help.' In July[202] Gladstone wrote in his diary that the Queen was 'as ever perfect in her courtesy,' but, as to confidence, she held him now 'at arms length.' The wisdom of Solomon and the patience of Job could not have combined to succeed against such frustration.

All through the year the Queen wrote letters of protest, mostly to Lord Granville: in August the extreme Radicals aroused her. She was alarmed at the way they were cajoled by the Government and she thought that the moderate members should court the support of the *moderate* Whigs instead of the *extreme* Party. She talked of the policy which struck at the *'root and existence* of the Constitutional Monarchy.' She wrote: [203]

'The Queen herself can *never* have *any confidence* in the men who encourage *reform* for the *sake of alteration and pulling down what exists* and what is *essential* to the *stability* of a Constitutional Monarchy. A *Democratic Monarchy* ... she will not *consent to belonging to. Others* must be found *if* that is to be, and she *thinks* we are on a dangerous and doubtful slope which may become too rapid for us to stop, when it is too late.

'The Queen is all for *improvement* and *moderate reform* of *abuses,* but not merely for *alteration's and reform's sake,* and *not* ... because the *present* "House of Commons is pledged to *Administrative Reform."* ... The Queen thinks, from what Mrs. Gladstone and *his* private Secretaries write, that Mr. G. will require *very long rest.'*

In September [204] the Queen wrote again. The indignities of the proceedings in the Commons, the vacillation and the personal abuse depressed her when she read the accounts each day. She assured Lord Granville that the House of Commons was becoming 'like one of the Assemblies in a Republic ... the way in which the present House of Commons is allowed to *dictate* and *arrogate* to itself the *power* of the *executive,* disregarding both *the House of Lords and the Crown,* OUGHT to be *firmly* and *strongly resisted....'*

The Queen's only consolation was in the occasional visits of Lord Beaconsfield. He drove over from Hughenden three times between the day of his fall and the end of the year, to stay with her. He came first in May and found her dismal over the troubles of the country. But the clouds were dispelled by dinner time and, sitting next to him, she said, 'I feel so happy that I think what has happened is only a horrid dream.' He had not bothered to tell her then that he was working on *Endymion,* his last book. Week after week he had been alone at Hughenden, sometimes walking out with a stick, looking 'very ill,' sometimes pausing to write to her, 'Madam, and most beloved Sovereign,' sometimes opening the letters she sent back to him, signed, 'Ever your affectionate and grateful friend.' She could not withhold a thrust at their common enemy, now and then. Mr. Gladstone's language was 'the cause of all evil,' she wrote.

Endymion was finished in October and on the 28th Beaconsfield wrote to tell the Queen of his venture. He prayed that he should be allowed to send a copy to her, 'who is the Sovereign not only of my person, but of my heart.'

Chapter Twenty-Two

§1 — 1880–1881

WHEN MR. GLADSTONE was to speak at the Lord Mayor's banquet in November, the Queen wrote [205] to him, 'extremely anxious' that there should be the utmost caution on the part of all the speakers, *especially of himself.* A word too much in the after-dinner speeches might do 'irreparable mischief.' She warned him to be most careful about Ireland and to leave no doubt in the minds of the listeners 'as to their determination to maintain the law and to put down the terrible spirit of lawlessness and violence...' A month afterwards, she wrote, '...the more one does for the Irish the more unruly and ungrateful they seem to be.' [206]

The plight of Ireland during the autumn of 1880 was too terrible for reason: the Irish were so melancholy that they could not be grateful. Poverty had bred lawlessness which it was impossible to control and in Galway there was a policeman for every forty-seven adult males and a soldier for every ninety-seven. [207] The pulse of the organised revolt was the Land League, formed to wrest the agricultural areas from the English-Protestant landlords. In September, Lord Mountmorres was murdered by the malcontents in Galway.

Terror wrung the unhappy people after this and, under the leadership of Parnell, the tenants boycotted the land-owners, refusing to pay rent and intimidating servants and labourers, so that they dared not work for those landlords who evicted their tenants. Lord Beaconsfield's gloomy prophecy proved to be true. Something 'worse even than famine and pestilence' had come to the accursed country.

For almost two years, Ireland was demoralised by intrigue and crime. Men were murdered in their homes, farm-buildings were burned down and cattle were mutilated. These attempts at ruining the landlords at last urged the British Government to legislate. The Bill for the Protection of Persons and Property and the Irish Land Bill were placed before the Commons. The Land Bill was based on the three F's—Fixity of tenure, Fair rents, and Free sale. (Beaconsfield suggested for the three F's, three *fiddlesticks,* believing landed tenure to be one of the reasons for Britain's greatness.) These bills suffered more set-backs and criticism than any in Ireland's history. When the Protection of Persons and Property Bill was before the House, Parnell led the extreme Nationalist Members in a campaign of obstruction so violent that Mr. Gladstone was obliged to move an Urgency Resolution to outwit them. Parnell's followers defied the Speaker, and were finally removed from the House in ignominy by the Sergeant-at-Arms. Lord Beaconsfield watched the plight of his old enemy: he made his last gesture of fidelity to his Sovereign by advising his followers to support the Government in the struggle against Parnell's ugly behaviour. When the Protection of Persons and Property Bill was passed, Parliament turned to the more formidable Irish Land Act of 1881. It was born in great pain. The combat of tongues in the House was almost as deplorable as the stories of lawlessness in Ireland. The Duke of Argyll, a devout believer in landed tenure, resigned from the office of Lord Privy Seal as a protest against the Bill. On the same day, Mr. Gladstone was obliged to report a 'scandalous breach of confidence' [208] to the Queen. The provisions of the Land Bill had leaked out and had been published in the *Standard* newspaper. The Cabinet was to be summoned to search into the causes of the treachery. One miserable event piled itself upon the other. In June the troops and constabulary in Ireland were ordered to fire upon the people in case of necessity. The Queen was *glad*—the Irish would no longer have 'a false impression of our power and intentions.' Then the Lords made amendments to the Bill which aroused Mr. Gladstone to what the Queen called his 'high-handed dictator style.' [209] A compromise was reached and the Bill, which was calculated to defeat the machinations of the Land League, became law on August 22nd.

Law did not beget reason or peace. Almost two months after the passing of the Land Act, Parnell was arrested and imprisoned in Kilmainham. The 'unscrupulous enemy of the State' appealed to the Irish tenants, on the eve of his incarceration, to pay no rents and to continue their defiance of the law.

No new plan was attempted for the control and pacifying of Ireland before April of 1882, when Lord Spencer, a man of character and experience, was appointed Viceroy. It seemed then that the law might prevail, especially as Parnell compromised and said that if he were released from prison he would help to quell crime and destruction. All hopes were dashed to the ground on the day of the Viceroy's arrival in Dublin. The Chief Secretary and the permanent Under-Secretary were stabbed to death as they were walking home through Phœnix Park. There were more murders in June, and in August a whole family was massacred at Maamtrasna. In this case the criminals were hunted down and hanged. One horror followed another in Mr. Gladstone's Armageddon. The story of the distressful country had no end in his time, nor has it in our own. One reiterates the dismal and appalling incidents only to impress upon the reader the weight of Mr. Gladstone's burden. From this we may find an excuse for his neglect of foreign affairs, for it is not easy, when one's house is on fire, to be wholly cognisant of events in distant places.

The Queen turned to her son for advice and support more readily after Lord Beaconsfield was defeated. The Prince's friendships with some of the Radicals did not please her, but they opened the way to a field of influence which would otherwise have been closed. There is one letter which proves the extent of her increasing faith in her son, written from Balmoral during one of the darkest times in the political upheaval over the Irish Land Bill. The Queen wrote: [210]

'Dearest Bertie,—The state of affairs—this dreadful Radical Government which contains many thinly-veiled *Republicans*— and the way in which they have truckled to the Home Rulers— as well as the utter disregard for all my opinions which after 45 years of experience ought to be considered, all make me very miserable, and disgust me with the hard, ungrateful task I have to go through and weigh on my health and spirits. You as my eldest son, and so intimate as you are with Lord Hartington, *might* and *should* I think speak strongly to him, *reminding* him *how* HE *asked you to tell me in* '80 *that if I took Mr. Gladstone I should certainly* NOT *have to take these violent and dangerous Radicals,* instead of which, *two* days after I had *most unwillingly* taken this most dangerous man, *all* the *worst men* who had no respect for Kings and Princes or any of the *landmarks* of the Constitution *were put into the Government in spite of me.* The mischief Mr. Gladstone does is *incalculable;* instead of *stemming* the current and downward course of Radicalism, which he could do *perfectly,* he *heads and encourages it* and alienates all the true Whigs and moderate Liberals from him. Patriotism is nowhere in their ranks. How differently do the leaders of Opposition in the House behave to the disgraceful way in which in times of great difficulty the *Liberal Opposition* opposed Lord Beaconsfield and tried to injure him! You and all of you should *speak* to *those* who *might and ought,* to act *differently* to what they do! Lord Granville behaves miserably; he is the only one *I know well* and he never *even answers* my remarks!! Your devoted Mama, V.R. & I.'

§ 11 — 1881

ON MARCH 15th Lord Beaconsfield spoke in the House of Lords for the last time. Next day he wrote his last letter to Lady Bradford, no more than a *hurried line,* telling her all about the Prince of Wales who had just come back after two weeks on the Continent. 'I am very unwell,' he wrote at the end of the letter, 'and go about as little as I can....'

People who saw Beaconsfield at this time said that he had lost his old spirit and that he seemed very aged. He sighed for the spring, but March and April came, still cold and bitter and refusing to yield the colour for which he waited. He confessed himself ill to his friends, and when Dilke went to see him on March 27th he was lying on a couch, breathing with difficulty. But his mind was playful still and not above a pleasant, spiteful thrust at that verbose Mr. Gladstone. On March 28th Beaconsfield wrote his last letter to Queen Victoria, ashamed, he said, 'to address your Majesty not only from my room, but even my bed.... At present I am prostrate, though devoted.—B.'

There were spurts of playful cynicism during the melancholy days which preceded the end. Once he was able to read the bulletin, which stated that 'Lord Beaconsfield's strength is still maintained.' He remarked, 'I presume the physicians are conscious of that. It is more than I am.'

On the last day of the month Beaconsfield corrected the proof of his final speech in the House of Lords, for *Hansard*. Still relishing a gesture, he said, 'I will not go down to posterity talking bad grammar.' These pungent little comments were made in London, not at Hughenden, where he would have wished to die. His room was gay with the hyacinths and daffodils which had been sent to him from the banks at Windsor: and the ever fragrant primroses, the flowers of his gallantry. On April 5th the Queen sent him more primroses from the castle slopes: the slopes upon which eight hundred years of English history had left their mark: the slopes upon which every King had walked since the Conqueror. They were primroses from a place which must have been agreeable to a man who had never ceased to be romantic in all the seventy-seven years of his life.

When it was feared that he was dying the Queen had asked if she might see him. Every day there had been a message, and the flowers in his room were never allowed to seem faded. When she asked again if she might come, it is said that the weak, tired face turned and that Beaconsfield said, 'No, it is better not. She will only want me to take a message to Albert!' The perverse strain of his humour remained strong, even when his body was half dead. From the ironical little jokes, he turned to the last, magnificent avowal of his greatness: he said, 'I had rather live, but I am not afraid to die.'

On April 19th Benjamin Disraeli died, 'without suffering, quite calmly, as if in sleep.' The two or three men who were beside his bed, who had known him and loved him, leaned over and kissed his forehead.

Four days afterwards Lord Rowton wrote to the Queen. He had 'looked on that dear face for the last time,' he said. 'There lies, and will ever lie, close to that faithful heart the photograph of the Queen *he* loved.'

§ III — 1881

AT THE beginning of the new year the Queen wrote the humble note which has already been quoted. She felt *sadly deficient ... over sensitive and irritable.* She deplored that when she was *annoyed and hurt,* her temper was *uncontrollable.* She had ended the day's entry in her diary, which she kept so diligently, 'I will daily pray for God's help to improve.'

On the same day the Queen wrote a kindly letter to Mr. Gladstone. The appalling menaces from Ireland made her forget Turkey and Africa and Afghanistan. She wrote: [212]

'The Queen thanks Mr. Gladstone for his two most important letters ... She thanks him for his good wishes and prays that the heavy clouds, which now surround the political horizon and her Empire, may by God's blessing be dispelled, and that Mr. Gladstone may be guided by Him to do what is right and just.'

The members of her Government soon devised a breach which put a strain on the Queen's New Year resolutions. When the draft for her speech for the opening of Parliament arrived for her to sanction, it was 'very wrong.' [214] The announcement of the withdrawal of defence forces from Kandahar ... the position for which her soldiers had fought so valiantly in Afghanistan . . . was included in the Speech, without her having heard a word about it before. On the same day the members of her Council attended at Osborne for a meeting. There followed a comedy in which one sees how easily the Queen defeated her Ministers in a difficult situation. She wrote in her Journal:

'Directly after breakfast I telegraphed to Mr. Gladstone to have the Speech altered. . . . All was ready for my Council, and I was waiting, when Sir H. Ponsonby came to say that the Ministers, Lord Spencer and Sir Wm. Harcourt, declared they would wait till Mr. Gladstone's answer came. In vain I assured them (through Sir H. Ponsonby) that I would approve the Speech, leaving out that paragraph; they insisted on waiting . . . 3 o'clock passed, and still no answer came, but it at length did so at half past 3. It was not favourable, saying that the matter had been agreed upon yesterday.

'So I had my Memorandum given to the Ministers, and settled to hold my Council at once. After waiting 10 minutes in the drawing-room, Sir H. Ponsonby came in, saying the Ministers objected to the word "disapproval," which rather amused me. Called in Leopold, and after some difficulty, suggested altering "disapproval" to "much regrets." This seemed to settle the matter, but 20 minutes elapsed before Sir H. Ponsonby again returned, saying they objected to the last part, in which I asked for an assurance. So I said, Very well, I would not send the Memorandum through them, but straight to Mr. Gladstone, and would hold the Council. Dreadfully put out, they at length came in, after 4, including Lord Sydney. The business was hurriedly gone through, and the Speech approved. I spoke to no one, and the Ministers nearly tumbled over each other going out. . . .'

The incident permits a glimpse of the Queen's courage. She was not dispirited—merely *amused* by the Ministers' attempt at intimidation. The fullness of this courage, which was the basis of her character, bursts upon one, leaving one in awe, in an incident of the spring of 1882.

The Queen was then sixty-three years old. She wrote in her Journal:

'2nd March, 1882.—At 4.30 left Buckingham Palace for Windsor. Just as we were driving off from the station there, the people, or rather the Eton boys, cheered, and at the same time there was the sound of what I thought was an explosion from the engine, but in another moment I saw people rushing about and a man being violently hustled, people rushing down the street. I then realised that it was a shot, which must have been meant for me, though I was not sure, and Beatrice said nothing. . . .

'Took tea with Beatrice, and telegraphed to all my children and near relations. Brown came in to say that the revolver had been found loaded, and one chamber discharged. Superintendent Hayes, of the Police here, seized the man, who was wretchedly dressed, and had a very bad countenance. . . . He is well spoken and evidently an educated man. . . . An Eton boy had rushed up, and beaten him with an umbrella. Great excitement prevails. Nothing can exceed dearest Beatrice's courage and calmness, for she saw the whole thing, the man take aim, and fire straight into the carriage, but she never said a word, observing that I was not frightened. . . . Was really not shaken or frightened. . . .

'3rd Mar.—I slept as well as usual, and never once thought of what had occurred. . . . Brown brought the revolver for me to see. It could be fired off in rapid succession with the greatest facility, quite small but with six chambers. I saw the bullets. Was much relieved to hear that the missing one was found. . . . Walked with Beatrice down to Mausoleum, and here I knelt by my beloved one's tomb and offered up prayers of thanksgiving for my preservation to God our Heavenly Father. . . .'

§ IV — 1881–1882

IN 1879, when Great Britain and France elected Ministers to work hand in hand as advisers to the Khedive of Egypt, the Prince of Wales had looked upon the Dual Control as an expression of Anglo-French friendship: a guarantee of his beloved *Entente Cordiale*. The merchants of Egypt prospered during the European control, but there were other Egyptians to whom the signs of French and British power were unwelcome. Arabi Bey, a passionate Nationalist and a *fellah* with a deep-rooted feeling for the soil, spread his disturbing doctrines among the Egyptian soldiers. They revolted against the Khedive, under the spell of Arabi's leadership, in January of 1881. It was more than a struggle between the Egyptian and the Khedive: it was against Turkey, England and France—a crusade to establish themselves as masters of their own earth. Unfortunately for their laudable ideal, much of the earth of Egypt was already pledged to the bondholders of Europe.

While the Queen was treating Sir Charles Dilke as a disloyal interloper, the Prince gave the Foreign Under-Secretary his friendship, receiving trust and encouragement in return. Dilke even agreed to his interviewing the French Prime Minister, early in 1881, when a commercial treaty between the two countries was being considered. The suggestion had come from the Prince, and Dilke had treated him as a professional diplomat, sending him off to Paris with a paper of 'instructions.' [215] Here was usefulness at last. Dilke acknowledged the success of his intervention and Gambetta said that the Prince had made 'some impression' on the Premier. He told a friend that it was 'no waste of time' to talk with the Prince, 'even over a merry supper at the Café Anglais.' [216] Here were the interests and opportunities which delighted him. He went so far in his friendliness as to approve of the proposal to construct a channel tunnel between the two countries.[217]

The Prince had been so severely snubbed when he showed an interest in Ireland in the sixties that he seemed to develop an inhibition in regard to the country. He spoke and wrote little during the painful shaping of the Land Bill and the reign of terror in Ireland. But the jealousies and struggles for power in the Mediterranean interested him vastly, especially when they formed a depressing cloud over the *Entente.* In April, the French, who were already established in Algeria, invaded Tunis and humiliated and frightened the Bey into accepting terms which made the country little more than a protectorate of France. The apparent failure of the Dual Control in Egypt, and the annexation of Tunis, made the Queen pause in her doleful letter-writing about Ireland to warn the Ministers. A friend had told her that the French talked of Egypt as 'an *ultimate* object.' She hoped that England's apparent acquiescence over the annexation of Tunis would not lead France and Europe to believe that Britain would equally tolerate her taking Egypt. She wrote to Lord Granville, 'Egypt can be in *no other* hands but ours if it is to be taken from Turkey or rather from the Khedive.' [218]

The crisis in Egypt came at a fortunate time for the Prince of Wales. His friend Gambetta had been elected Premier of France and on the eve of his accession, Gambetta, the Prince and Dilke had eaten *dejeuner* together at the Moulin Rouge restaurant in Paris.[219] Lee tells us that 'Political confidences were freely exchanged.' Gambetta reigned for only sixty days, but in that time he was able to substantiate the Prince's faith in him. Arabi Bey followed up the revolt of the army by trying to set up a nationalist dictatorship in Egypt. Gambetta showed no signs of the French treachery which the Queen suspected, nor of any attempt to advance the interests of France against England. He prepared a note in the name of both

France and Britain promising to protect the Khedive's Government against all forms of attack. Both countries followed up the moral effect of the note by sending a naval squadron to Alexandria.

The warships went side by side, in the spirit of the *Entente,* but there the fraternity ended. Arabi's cry, *Egypt for the Egyptians,* was droned in the bazaars of the city. Arabi had forced his way to dictatorship, and Tewfik, the Khedive, was playing the innocuous part of William the First to Arabi's Bismarck.

From May until July the warships waited off the low-lying coast of Alexandria. Arabi was made of arrogant stuff: the sight of the squadrons in the bay and the threats of French and English attack did not frighten him. On June 11th, pillage and massacre devastated Alexandria, and a number of French and English people were murdered. Still the warships waited, while Arabi was building new defences on the harbour front. In July, the French warships withdrew at a call from their Government. France was too conscious of Bismarck's menacing shadow to engage in promiscuous fracas abroad. The British warships were left alone to bombard Alexandria and to subdue Arabi. When the harbour fortifications had been destroyed, the bluejackets plunged into the fetid bazaars of the town and slowly impressed upon Arabi's adherents that the cry was to be *Egypt for the English.* The Alexandrians succumbed. On land, Sir Garnet Wolseley, with Prince Arthur among his officers, defeated Arabi's army at Tel-el-Kebir.

Queen Victoria read the stories of her sailors and soldiers with the ecstasy she had felt in 1854. She had followed her warships when they were setting out for the Crimea, waving her handkerchief as she stood on the deck

of her little ship, until long after the fleet had melted into
the distance. Prince Albert had been with her in 1854,
but in 1882 she was alone. Yet she had crossed Southampton Water to see the troopship of the 4th Dragoon Guards
before it sailed. She had followed the *Olympus* and the
Grecian out into the broad water, giving them a parting
cheer.

In September the Queen was waiting at Balmoral,
where she had watched Prince Albert lighting the bonfire
for Sebastopol, also in September, almost thirty years before. News of the victory at Tel-el-Kebir came to her,
news of the courage of her Irish soldiers, of her son's
unflinching bravery under fire, and of the capture of
Cairo. Arabi was a prisoner in the hands of the British
and the power of the Khedive was restored. The French
warships were hugging their home ports. M. Tissot [220] told
somebody that 'the loss of French influence in Africa by
the running away of the squadron from Alexandria . . .
will not be recovered for years.'

The anxiety caused by Sudanese rising and the death of
Gordon hung over the future, but the British were already
masters of Egypt and the Prince's *Entente Cordiale* suffered a blow which depressed him, especially when his
friend Gambetta died in Paris at the end of the year.

Prince Arthur came home, and among his trophies was
a fine Turkish carpet from Arabi's tent. It was spread
in the quadrangle of Windsor Castle and the Queen stood
upon it while she pinned the medals on the breasts of her
soldiers.

The politicians and their fatal tardiness did not matter
in a scene like this. They were despicable and irritating
in the face of war. *She* comprehended the sensations of
soldiers. The blood of a hundred Kings, Plantagenets,

234

Stuarts and Guelphs, was in her. The Queen's men fought for *her,* not for the puny-minded, compromising politicians of Westminster. It was *her* head, not that of Gladstone or Dilke or Granville, which was on the Queen's shilling. No politicians could understand, as she did, the emotions of the hero who had *boasted,* when he was hit, 'I am the first Life Guardsman who has been wounded since Waterloo.' [221]

On the wings of the victory of her army, the Queen assumed the grandeur of monarchy. Two communications, one a telegram and the other a letter, tell all that can be known of the Queen's emotions in this heroic time. Arabi had been handed over to the Khedive for punishment and he had been dismissed with the lenient sentence of exile in Ceylon. Lord Dufferin thought it a moment for a gesture in diplomacy. He wrote to Lord Granville:

'It would be a good thing if the Government, and still better her Majesty, would send a personal message to the Khedive congratulating him on the magnanimity and good sense he has shown in the Arabi affair.

'It would give him courage to face his womankind, who are frantic.' [222]

The Queen's answer was as sharp as the sword of one of her soldiers:

'The Queen *cannot possibly* send the message of approbation to the Khedive for his "magnanimity" to Arabi, as she *so highly disapproves* of the weakness which actuated it. It is for the British Government, who are solely responsible for this act—which was *forced* upon the Khedive, and the *Queen must ever* think very unwisely—to send him this message.

'The "womankind" show a right feeling in being "frantic".' [223]

§ v — 1883

THE AFFECTIONS of nations are as unreasonable and fickle as those of individuals. The comradeship between France and England, so eagerly planned in the Prince's talks with Gambetta over the dinner-table in Paris, did not withstand the shock of the Egyptian affair in 1882. There was confusion in the motives of both countries. The Queen had been 'terrible in constant resolution,' when she learned that the French had occupied Tunis, and that their ultimate goal was Egypt. She was equally indignant when their warships fled from the bay of Alexandria, leaving the British to subdue the Egyptians alone. Her naïve remark to Lord Granville [224] when the French began the conquest of Madagascar, is amusing, since it was written on the heels of our conquest of Egypt and five weeks before New Guinea was occupied in the Queen's name. She wrote, 'Are we to let the French go on taking what they like with impunity? First Tunis and now Madagascar? ...'

The motives of the French were also confused. They had not helped in the bombardment of Alexandria, yet they were livid when they saw the English enjoying the spoils for which they had fought. The only statesman who was not perplexed was Bismarck. He rubbed his hands with glee over the rift in the *Entente*.

The Prince of Wales had now come to enjoy the dual role of play-boy and diplomat in Paris, but in 1883 he found that the French no longer smiled so gallantly at the mention of his name. He was the ambassador of the English, who now held Egypt in the hollow of their hand. Here was one reason for anger and jealousy. Also, he was a *princely* ambassador, and the royal appellation had suddenly become distasteful again in Paris. This was a political whim, born in a sudden, anti-royalist agitation, when the Chamber of Deputies passed a Bill [225] for the expulsion of all the Bourbons and Bonaparts. His beloved Paris rejected the Prince for the first time, and, out of loyalty to his royalist friends, he upset the fashionable programme of his year by canceling his visit to France in the spring. This was on the advice of the Ambassador. The unreasonable change in the feeling of the French caused the Prince to examine his own enthusiasms more calmly. He doubted France, and he came to think more kindly of Germany, for the first time since the invasion of Schleswig-Holstein in 1863.

In September of 1883, the German Crown Prince was in London, and the Prince of Wales revealed the faint change in his affections by telling his brother-in-law that 'a strong desire was growing in the English political world, irrespective of Party "to establish a more intimate relationship with Germany".' [226] The Prince substantiated this view by a number of gracious actions. He twice went to Germany, he attended the gay celebrations of his sister's silver wedding and he gave his nephew a costume of Royal Stewart tartan, with 'all the accoutrements of the Highland dress.' Prince William was so pleased to be able to dance at the silver wedding in a kilt that he insisted on being photographed. He revealed his vanity in the way he distributed the photographs to his friends. He revealed also the reason why the friendly approaches of the Prince of Wales were to be nipped in the bud. Beneath each photograph of himself as a Scotsman, he wrote in English, 'I bide my time.'

The pathetic young Prince was already on the way to

237

disaster. His mother had prayed that he might grow up in the image of the Prince Consort, but every quality of Prince William's inheritance was contaminated by his nature. He had taste, but it was faintly vulgar. He had talents, but there was a tinge of the meretricious in his music, his pictures and his conversation. Just as Bismarck's mighty will lifted Germany to fearful eminence, so the treacherous qualities in Prince William were to lead her to humiliation. Not until he had suffered dethronement and exile did he wear the aura of dignity which is the right of Princes. When it did come, at Doorn, it was greatly due to the compassion men feel for a faded actor.

Prince William could not hide his hatred for England, and for his uncle. He was a braggart and he could not resist the satisfaction of saying and writing what he felt. His ambitions were already shaped: when he was twenty-five years old he admitted that he wished to inveigle the Tsar into a plot to crush Great Britain. In 1884, Prince William went to stay with the Tsar and 'he won the ear of his imperial host by enthusiastically pledging himself to do all he could to aid Russia in her quarrels with England.' [227]

When he returned to Berlin, Prince William began a correspondence with the Tsar: letters full of lying gossip, intended to inflame Russia. In 1884, after the Prince of Wales had been in Berlin, Prince William wrote:

'The visit of the Prince of Wales has yielded and is still bringing extraordinary fruit, which will continue to multiply under the hands of my mother and the Queen of England. But these English have accidently forgotten that *I* exist! And I swear to You, my dear cousin, that anything I can do for You and Your country I will do, and I swear that I will keep my word! But only it will take a long time and will have to be done very slowly.' [228]

In March of the following year, when the Prince was again expected in Berlin, Prince William wrote once more to the Tsar:

'We shall see the Prince of Wales here in a few days. I am not at all delighted by this unexpected apparition, because—excuse me, he is Your brother-in-law—owing to his false and intriguing nature he will undoubtedly attempt in one way or another to push the Bulgarian business [against Russian interests]—may Allah send them to Hell, as the Turk would say!—or to do a little political plotting behind the scenes with the ladies.' [229]

One sentence in Prince William's letter, referring to the British expedition against the Sudanese, reveals all that can be known of his feeling for England at this time. He wrote: 'May the Mahdi chuck them all into the Nile.' [230]

Chapter Twenty-Three

1883

THE QUEEN left London once more and sought the quiet of Osborne. The Court settled to the most simple habits and entertainments when they were thus away from the hurly-burly of the metropolis. For an hour or more each morning the Queen would sit at her desk: there were despatch boxes from Whitehall, or a Minister who had hurried down from London the night before. Her desk was covered with family photographs. The inkstand was a silver boat, with two winged boys and two mortal boys in silver, pushing the craft along a rough silver beach. The pen wiper was a gold cock's head with a red cloth comb upon his crown. By this time, every possession of the Queen told its little story.

At Windsor her four rooms contained almost two hundred and fifty pictures. Each was the window through which she looked at some cherished memory. One showed the Queen as a nun, standing with clasped hands before a vision of Prince Albert. Others were of the Rosenau, of Prince Albert and Duke Ernst in velvet doublets slashed with satin—of Princess Beatrice, a baby of ten months, sprawling on a white cushion. There was one picture after another: every dead friend was remembered. She was more than sixty years old now and two generations of friends had already died about her. Her memory stretched back to the days of the gibbet. Sometimes, at Windsor, she would rise from her chair and walk about the room.

Her servants often found her thus, fingering the souvenirs of sixty years, among them a silver teapot which she had used when she was a child at Kensington Palace. Upon the tables there were water-colour sketches of the Rosenau, where she had walked beside the stream with Albert. Memory after memory, drifting through her tired brain, as she moved from picture to picture until she came at last to the window from which she could see the green roof of the mausoleum above the trees at Frogmore.

The most personal and loved of the objects were carried everywhere with her—from Windsor to Osborne, where the rooms in which *he* had worked were awakened from their slumbers beneath dust sheets. There was more leisure here. Old letters were read, old friends recalled. But the business of government was not forgotten. When she came to the throne, Carlyle had written, 'Poor little Queen, she is at an age when a girl can hardly be trusted to choose a bonnet for herself: yet a task has been laid upon her from which an archangel might shrink.' One day the Queen read this to one of her Ladies and she smiled. 'Don't you think that is very amusing?' she said. Now she ruled half the world. When she opened an atlas the red ink of her possessions seemed to make the pages burn, as evidence of her glory. She was Queen of the Empire upon which the sun never set. Greater than Alexander, the Romans or the Greeks. Greater than Elizabeth. Livingstone had named the mightiest waterfall in Africa after her. The biggest lake in Africa was Victoria Nyanza and a State in Australia bore her name. The main streets in remote colonial towns, mere lines of higgledy-piggledy shanties, were Victoria Streets; the Maoris had made a statue of her in one of their villages; Canadian woodmen sculptured her out of snow in a clearing they had made in the backwoods and they planted a fluttering Union Jack in her snow hand. Victoria, Victoria! Faraway Universities were built in her name and she was prayed for in a hundred tongues.

When she drove through the streets of London, the old resentment was forgotten. The people were silent as she drove past, because they knew that she wished them to be. Her wish was so respected that when a visitor from America cried 'Hurrah! Hurah!' as the Queen drove by, she was buffeted and jeered at for daring to offend the quiet of her progress. The Queen was not stately to look upon, but the spirit within her plump body gave her a dignity which was inviolable.

At Osborne, simplicity touched every hour.

> For thou hast dignified Home-life
> As daughter, mother, friend and wife.
> And round the brow of England's Queen
> A fair domestic wreath is seen.

The pretty verse of the poet was true. She loved her release from splendour. Once in Scotland, when she was eating haggis, in a small house, she had written, 'I thought how dear Albert would have liked it all. He always said things tasted better in small houses.'

This simplicity ruled her to the end.

Sometimes at Osborne, her neighbours came to see her, with as little fuss as if she were the squire's wife. One afternoon 'the great Poet Tennyson' came and stayed for almost an hour. It was 'most interesting.' He had grown very old, and his eyesight was failing. He was 'very shaky on his legs,' but 'very kind.' Tennyson too had been a rebel in his day; a bombastic Titan when aroused. But

OSBORNE HOUSE

Her Majesty's Marine Villa, Isle of Wight

the restraint of age had come to both of them: they talked of the past. Tennyson had been born in 1809—in the reign of George the Third. 'He spoke of the many friends he had lost, and what it would be if he did not feel and know that there was another world where there would be no parting.' He talked of his horror of unbelievers and philosophers.

There was so much for them to say. They had lived from the age of craftsmanship into the age of machines. Inventors were already working on the strange devices which were to photograph the actual movements of the Queen at her Jubilee, and to record Tennyson's voice upon a cylinder so that his great, booming song should go down to posterity:

> I said to the rose, 'The brief night goes
> In babble and revel and wine.
> O young lord-lover, what sighs are those,
> For one that will never be thine?'

Tennyson was in a sad mood when he had recalled so many days and so many friends. He turned to the Queen and said, 'I am afraid I think the world is darkened; but I dare say it will be brighter again.'

Then they talked of *In Memoriam,* which had always been a *comfort* to the Queen. He told her of the 'shameful letters of abuse' which had been written to him about it. She thought it 'incredible.'

When the Queen took leave of the old poet, she thanked him for his kindness. 'I ... said how much I appreciated it, for I had gone through much....' Tennyson answered, 'You are so alone on that terrible height. I have only a year or two more to live, but I am happy to do anything for you I can.'

So they said good-bye. But he was not quite right in saying she was 'so alone.' There were many compensations now. Her son had changed so. And she had changed!

Only a few weeks before the Prince had celebrated his forty-second birthday. The Queen wrote in her Journal, of his being 'warm-hearted' and 'kind.' She added, in the secret pages in which she wrote so many, many things, '... he is always a very good son to me.'

The scenes at Osborne, in the quiet hour after dinner, might have belonged to any home. She would sit as far away as possible from the beechwood fire, listening perhaps to a duet being played by Princess Beatrice and one of the Ladies. Her Ladies and Gentlemen were growing older, just as she was. The vexing anxiety of ambition was past for most of them and they lived in the calm and secure avenues of their memories. Sometimes a younger guest would come, like an energetic finger stirring a bowl of potpourri, awakening the little Court to life again. One who came often to them would play and sing. There were the sprightly tunes of Mr. Sullivan, so different from the ballads of *their* day. Sometimes the Queen would send for him to play for her in her own sitting-room. Or she would sing herself, when there were none but her own daughters in the room.

Once, when she was almost sixty-five, she paused by the music stand and picked up a copy of *H.M.S. Pinafore* which had been so fashionable in 1874. She placed it on the piano, and then she sang:

'I'm called Little Buttercup—dear Little Buttercup,
Though I could never tell why,
But still I'm called Buttercup, poor Little Buttercup,
Sweet Little Buttercup I!

'... Then buy of your Buttercup—dear Little Buttercup,
    Sailors should never be shy,
So buy of your Buttercup—poor Little Buttercup,
    Come, of your Buttercup buy!'

The Queen finished her song without one faltering note. She turned to somebody in the room and said, 'Yes, it is all over now. But, I *used* to be able to sing quite well. Once Mr. Mendelssohn listened to me, when I sang with the Prince. He said that we used to sing very nicely together. But, it is all over now.'

Chapter Twenty-Four

§ 1 — 1883

THERE WERE enough tragedies left over from the previous year to keep the Government busy in 1883. Mr. Gladstone showed the first signs of breaking down with the weight of Ireland, Egypt, Africa, India and France: almost the load of Atlas on his shoulders. Nor were his personal relations with the Queen likely to lessen his burden. In December there had been an interview with her [231] on 'most difficult ground.' He wrote in his diary, '... aided by her beautiful manners, we got over it better than would be expected.'

The store of strength from the years of tree felling at Hawarden had petered out. Mr. Gladstone was inclined to take to his bed 'on less provocation than most people,' [232] but this time he was so ill that he had to abandon his proposed journey to Midlothian. The Queen was sympathetic, but she did not fail to make capital out of his breakdown. She recalled the first Midlothian speeches with a shudder, and she wrote to her Minister on January 5th, expressing her 'earnest hope' that he would be 'very guarded in his language' when he was in Scotland. Immense importance would be attached to *every* word falling from him. She had heard that he was not strong: was it not 'rather venturesome' for him to go, in cold January, to cold Scotland, with the opening of Parliament so near? [233]

A doleful letter came back from Mr. Gladstone: his

246

doctor had forbidden the journey, so the danger was removed. The Queen was very sorry: she insisted that he should be *really quiet* and not occupy himself at *all* with affairs, and not write long letters. There was no end to the generous thrusts. 'Would he not now, for his health, accept a Peerage?' [234]

Mr. Gladstone did not accept the honour: he marshalled his shattered strength and, after five weeks of lotus eating at Cannes, he returned to England and faced the fourth year of his Parliament. The Queen was glad he took the offer of the Peerage 'so well.' [235]

Ireland, South Africa and Egypt were still the heaviest burdens. A number of executions in Dublin did not deter the Irish in their crazy tactics. They blew up part of the Local Government Board Office in Whitehall, and in January a gasworks, in Glasgow. In the same month they tried to blow up an aqueduct, and in March they dared to plant explosives in the office of *The Times*. In the sixties, the Queen's heart might have been softened by this last escapade.

In South Africa, Britons, Boers and Zulus paused for breath after the Basuto risings and the bloody fiasco of Majuba Hill. Cetewayo, who had been brought to England and foolishly dressed in a frock coat and top hat for presentation to the Queen at Osborne, was back in Africa and hatching new plots against his kind, but not against the British. He had heard the drone of London's traffic and he had seen the grey warships on the Solent. He had seen the amazing little woman who had sat so still when he bowed before her. She had said that he was a brave man. Cetewayo had learned his lesson.

§ 11— 1883–1884

THE NEW horror which broke upon the Government was in the Southern Provinces of Egypt where the Sudanese rallied about a mystic who incited them to refuse British rule. The Mahdi, or prophet, claimed divine inspiration, and, like Mohammed, he believed that God's business should be done with a sword. His soldiers spread to the shores of the Red Sea and they threatened the entrance to the Suez Canal. While Britain was trying to soothe the Egyptians in the north, she was obliged to send troops into the Sudan. The gendarmerie who formed the first expedition were defeated. A brigade of the British Army then went south from Cairo and routed the Sudanese at El Teb, in February of 1884. But Mr. Gladstone's Cabinet had learned very little from the massacre of the British mission by the Afghans, or from Majuba Hill. Sir Gerald Graham, who commanded the British troops, was ordered to withdraw and return to Cairo. The order was in keeping with the bloodless, unimaginative policy which finally led to the murder of General Gordon.

While members of the Cabinet sat back with their thinking caps drawn over their eyes, loyal Egyptian garrisons were isolated in Sudanese territory in peril of their lives. Again the Queen and the Prince of Wales were of one mind. 'We must make a demonstration of strength,' the Queen wrote. The loyalty of both mother and son was pledged to the soldiers and the apathy of the Government left them aghast. General Gordon was sent out to the Sudan—as mediator, to arrange for the withdrawal of the garrisons to Egypt. With all his knowledge of the Sudan and his personal powers, Gordon failed, and in April of 1884, news reached England that he was besieged at

Khartoum. May, June and July passed. Mr. Gladstone, who had cried out so sententiously about 'the sanctity of life in the hill villages of Afghanistan,' when he had an election to win in 1879, and of *Almighty God* who had united the electors of Midlothian with those same Afghan barbarians, 'by the law of mutual love,' allowed Gordon to wait for three months before a relief expedition set out, under Lord Wolseley, to approach Khartoum by the Nile route.

When the Duke of Connaught joined Wolseley's expedition to Egypt in 1882, the Prince of Wales had pleaded to be allowed to serve with him. He repeated his request when Lord Wolseley was preparing for his expedition in 1884. Again neither the Queen nor the Ministers would allow him to face the hazards of active service.

Wolseley and the Prince wrote to each other through the stages of the expedition. Wolseley was forcing his way up the tortuous river, to Korti, and then over the Bayuda desert to Khartoum. The Prince was in London, deploring the delay, for which the Government was 'alone responsible.'[236] He hankered after active service. He kicked against the traces of domesticity and hoped that, for the sake of his friends who were with Wolseley, and who had not been in a battle, there would be fighting—'... perhaps I ought not to say so,' he added. The Prince's opinions had not been ignored in the planning of the expedition. On his advice, Lord Charles Beresford had gone with Wolseley as A.D.C. to the Commander-in-Chief. At one point on the Nile passage to Khartoum, Lord Charles had been 'the only person who really had his wits about him.'[237] The Prince was interested in every detail of the expedition. the work of the Camel Corps and the personal service of each officer. The once regretted interest for people, instead of things, became a great merit in time of war. When the Prince was lured up the Nile in 1862, in search of temples, he had been bored. He had wished only to shoot crocodiles and to leave the fallen down stones to crumble back into the desert to which they belonged. But now the Nile was a river of life and adventure to him.

On January 22nd the Prince wrote to Wolseley, 'Most sincerely do I trust that you will get safely to Khartoum ... and find Gordon safe and sound. But what will you do with him when he is released? And what will you do after occupying Khartoum? That is the question. I sincerely hope that we are not going to hurry away and leave the Sudan in the state you have found it. Not being a member of H.M.'s Govt., I can give no opinion on the subject. . . .'

The Prince's hopes were dashed to the ground when news of the failure of Lord Wolseley's expedition arrived on January 28th. When he reached the country about Khartoum Wolseley found that it had been attacked by the Mahdi's followers two days before. After eleven months of waiting—waiting for the rescuers who had, in turn, waited for the order of the Government—Gordon had been murdered.

The name of the devout, spontaneous hero of Khartoum has never been allowed to rest by critics and biographers. The Prince of Wales chose practical ways of proving his devotion to Gordon's memory. When Henry Morton Stanley set out for the Sudan to find Emin Pasha, who had been Gordon's lieutenant, the Prince asked him to Sandringham and wrote to him continually during his expedition. Stanley found Emin Pasha, but he had no wish to return to England. So Stanley came home alone. He had been encouraged all the way by the Prince of Wales's letters, and when he discovered a new lake, he celebrated his devotion by naming it Albert Edward Nyanza. The Prince attended the memorial service for Gordon in St. Paul's, and he fostered the Gordon Boys' Homes. He presided at a dinner where five thousand pounds were raised to help the foundation and even when he came to the throne, he followed the work of the homes with personal interest. The devotion was typical of the single-minded way in which the Prince persisted in any cause to which he had pledged himself, all through his life.

The politicians won in the end. Neither the Queen, the Prince nor the generals could stimulate the Cabinet to hold the Sudan. The dishonourable affair of Gordon's death was allowed to wait for eleven years before Kitchener, who had taken part in the Nile expedition in 1884, made his splendid conquest in 1889.

§ III — 1883

Two NEW forces came into the history of colonising in 1883. Prince Bismarck did not wish the obedient millions of his formidable empire to dream of lands beyond the Mediterranean. He was willing that England should be mistress of the seas and that his Germany should be master of the land, which was Europe. While he played France against England over power in North Africa, and Russia against England for the spoils of the Levant, he was able to realise his *Politik* in Europe and to bind the once divergent States together in national aims, law and trade.

251

Bismarck was not romantic. There was one aspect of the colonising vogue which he had not taken into account—the romantic quest which drew many of the younger Britons to the fertile coast-lands of Australia, the veld of Africa and the rich foot-hills of the Rockies. There was no romance for the young Germans in the grim struggle with France and Austria, on their own ground. They had seen the new maps of the world with British and French colonies marked in brilliant colours. Literature was enlivened by the stories of courage in countries where mountains and animals and trees and the climate, and even the colour of the inhabitants, were different from anything known in Europe. Bismarck ignored the desire for adventure which was satisfied in strange lands. Young Germans read of Clive, of Livingstone and of Gordon, and they were brought up on the story of *Robinson Crusoe*. Impelled by envy and the thrill of expedition and conquest, the German people also wished for overseas possessions. In 1884 Bismarck waved a wand. (It seems that he did little more when we recall the struggles through which Britain's dominions were amassed.) Mr. Buckle [238] reduces a chapter of history to one sentence when he says that Bismarck set to work to give the Germans the colonies they wished for, 'mostly in territories adjacent to British Colonies, with a promptitude, masterfulness, and duplicity which easily overmatched the dilatoriness, considerateness, and good faith of Lord Granville and Lord Derby.'

§ IV — 1884

BISMARCK ANNEXED the north coast of New Guinea, and in South-West Africa he took possession of the bay of

Angra Pequena and the poor country behind it. To the north he took 'The Cameroons' with the jungles, yielding timber and ivory, and the land into which the Germans introduced cocoa and other fruits and crops.

These ventures stirred a second, unexpected force in colonisation. Great Britain was obliged to realise that her colonies had come of age, and that they had wills of their own.

The Australians, Canadians and New Zealanders lost much of their English sophistication in the new countries. The rigours of colonial life forced them to live without class distinctions, and a healthy vulgarity grew up in place of the subdued spirit which they had left behind them, in the farm-houses of Sussex or the drab slums of Glasgow. The colonists were finding the independence and the courage which made it possible for them to come home again in 1914 and fight for their monarch, with the lusty courage of the Tudors.

Loyalty in the colonists was simplified when they lived so far away from meddling politicians. Boundary riders in Queensland might not know whether 'Dizzy' or Gladstone was in power, but they did know who was Queen of England. They did not consider the will of the Cabinet or of the policy of the Foreign Office early in 1883, when the European powers were snatching colonies all over the world. North of the Peninsula of Queensland was New Guinea—the eastern half waiting to be annexed by the first power which came along. Without reference to any authority but their own anxiety and loyalty, the Queenslanders had annexed the mainland of New Guinea, adding a fine feudal touch to their bravado by claiming the island 'in the Queen's name.' The British Government, in

which Lord Derby was the sedate but lethargic Colonial
minister, snubbed the heroic gesture of the Australians by
abandoning the island, on the ground that no purpose was
served in the annexation.

Chapter Twenty-Five

1884

DURING THE two Parliamentary sessions of 1884, even the civilities disappeared from the letters exchanged between Queen Victoria and Mr. Gladstone. The delay over the rescue of the garrisons in the Sudan and then the unwillingness to save Gordon in Khartoum had killed the Queen's last hopes in her Government. Personal animosity was not the basis of her fear now. She believed that the 'weakness and vacillation' of Mr. Gladstone's Government had lowered Britain's prestige among the nations. This was true. The German newspapers forgot the dignified figure of Beaconsfield at the Berlin Congress. To the distress of the Crown Princess they published 'rude and impertinent' articles which echoed Bismarck's contempt for Gladstone. The Prime Minister was not alone in the Queen's gallery of Liberal scapegoats. She had 'no confidence in Lord Granville' [239] who had seemed a steadfast friend in 1880. In 1884, she thought him 'weak as water,' and she feared that Lord Derby's influence was harmful.

The personal sorrow of Prince Leopold's death deepened the Queen's unhappiness in March, but she fought against the bereavement with courage. The demoralisation of the Cabinet called for persistent censure, in letters from herself and in votes from the Opposition. The weakened reputation of Great Britain among the countries of Europe was emphasised in criticism of the terms arranged for the British occupation of Egypt. Gladstone was willing to yield to the wish of the Powers that the British should withdraw from Egypt after five years. The Queen thought the attempt to intimidate the British Government to be an impertinence. '. . . Why are we to be bullied and frightened by other Powers?' she wrote.[240] 'The Queen feels *much* aggrieved and *annoyed*. She was never listened to, or her advice followed, and *all* she foretold *invariably* happened, and what she *urged* was *done* when *too late!* It is dreadful for her to see how we are going downhill, and to be unable to prevent the humiliation of this country.'[241]

Nearer home was the dissension over the Franchise Bill. In his own memorandum, Mr. Gladstone said that the Bill would add to the present aggregate constituency of the United Kingdom, taken at 3,000,000, . . . 2,000,000, nearly twice as much as was added since 1867, and more than four times as much as was added in 1832. Mr. Gladstone's plans for modified franchise were an added cause for hostility, this time, in the main, between the Lords and the Commons. The Peers were attacked and belittled by Mr. Chamberlain and his Radical friends for rejecting the Bill during the first session. Here the foundations of the Constitution were undermined. The Queen said that she yielded 'to no one' in true Liberal feeling, but she would never tolerate the wild attacks and the daring attempts at flouting the authority of the Lords. According to Mr. Gladstone's observations, she wrote, 'there ought to be a Radical House of Lords.' 'The Monarchy would be utterly untenable were there *no balance* of power left, no *restraining power.*'

The speeches of the inflamed Radicals drove the Queen to fury. '. . . Mr. Gladstone has great power over his Cabinet,' she wrote to the Prime Minister, 'and he should exert it for the benefit of peace. . . .' His reply was almost rude. He had neither *time* nor *eyesight* 'to make himself acquainted by careful perusal with all the speeches of his colleagues.' [242] From peevishness, the Queen's letters changed to anger; from anger to candid accusation of his failure. Gladstone defended himself once more. He had '*no general* jurisdiction over the speeches' of his colleagues 'and *no right* to prescribe their tone and colour.' The Queen did not agree. She said that the 'Prime Minister *has* and *ought to have* that power.' [243]

The sense of failure which was hanging over the Government slowly permeated the country. The chariot of political favour began to turn, and Gladstone felt the reins of influence and power slipping from his hands as definitely as he had felt them falling into his hands when he was thundering through Midlothian on his Liberal crusade in 1879. The Prince of Wales did not withdraw his friendly devotion to Gladstone, but he deplored the decadence of the Ministry, and his letters to Lord Wolseley and his friends show how he resented the agitation over the Franchise Bill, the agonies of Ireland and the attacks upon the House of Lords.

When Parliament met again at the close of the year, the rickety career of the Franchise Bill ended in compromise. The Opposition leaders conferred with Mr. Gladstone and they agreed to support the Bill, providing a Redistribution Bill was also passed. The pages of Queen Victoria's correspondence during the months of these worrying negotiations between Liberals, Conservatives and Peers, reveal the full measure of her political influence. In a crisis, she still ruled the country. Her dogged insistence, her direct appeal to Lord Salisbury, and her patience, drew the contestants together and forced them into reconciliation. She urged the policy of 'country before party' upon them and proved her power to enforce constructive legislation to be more effective than the divergent interests of two political parties and the House of Lords. There was no doubt of her success in bringing the opposed statesmen together and all of them paid tributes to her sagacity. Mr. Gladstone thanked the Queen for her 'wise, gracious, and steady exercise of influence.' Lord Salisbury expressed his 'humble and earnest gratitude for her powerful intervention.' '...Your Majesty must feel proud,' wrote Lord Granville.[244] '...I certainly am,' the Queen wrote in her Journal.

The Lords passed the Franchise Bill on December 6th. The Prince of Wales was pleased to tell Lord Wolseley that 'Parliament is up and we shall be able to go to our homes and digest our Christmas dinners in peace and comfort.'[245] The Prince was reconciled to Gladstone, although he had little patience with the delays and dissensions which marred his control of the Cabinet. This personal regard induced Gladstone's friends to press a delicate service upon the Prince.

The rift between the Queen and her Minister would never now be bridged. His friends thought that Gladstone would perhaps retire with the bedraggled laurels of his Franchise Bill. They asked the Prince to intercede with the Queen on Mr. Gladstone's behalf and induce her to give him the most coveted honour in her keeping—the Garter. She had guarded the tradition of the Order all through her reign, as far as English Knights were concerned. She had striven against bestowing the Garter upon the Sultan of Turkey because he did not conform to the principles laid down in the foundation by Edward the Third. It would not be easy to soften her heart towards the fierce Liberal veteran, but Granville told the Prince that he might be able to speak the right words at the right moment.

The Prince trod carefully. It would be useless for him to approach his mother at Windsor or at Osborne. Better, he said, to wait until they were in the solacing atmosphere of Balmoral, where the Queen always felt that she was released from the bitterness and agitation of business with ministers. His mother was, the Prince said, 'always in a better way,' when she was at Balmoral, and she might yield to persuasion.

The Queen went to Scotland in September. In November when the 'dear place' was 'bright with snow on the highest hills,' the Prince spoke to his mother of Gladstone, but without success. 'He found her unresponsive and confessed that he had chosen an inopportune time.' The Franchise legislation was not completed then, and the Prince suggested to Lord Granville that it would be better to wait until the Bill was passed. Even then, the Queen refused to invest Gladstone with the Order, which had been founded in honour of prayer and chivalry. The Queen did not approve of the tenor of Mr. Gladstone's prayers nor did she count him chivalrous. She offered her minister an Earldom when he retired in 1885, but Mr. Gladstone refused the honour, at the same time expressing his 'profound and lasting gratitude' for her 'generous, most generous letter.' [246]

Chapter Twenty-Six

§ 1 — 1884–1885

THE QUEEN usually went to Osborne for Christmas. In 1884, despite the memory of the Franchise Bill, the holiday season on her beloved island gave her pleasure. As compensation for the failure of the politicians, she seemed to gather increased affection about her, from her family and from her people. The talk of abdication had died long ago and the reports of the old discontent were yellowing in the bound files of the newspapers. The Queen came to represent security to the mass of people. Trade had suffered to show them that they must not worship industry. Governments had fallen to prove that statesmen were frail and dependent upon the favours of the electors at polling time. The powers of Europe had been alternately friends and foes, and there were the stories of Afghanistan, Majuba Hill, and Khartoum to shake confidence in British colonisation and military supremacy. In all this medley of events, the Sovereign represented the continuity of English life.

The names written on the Queen's Christmas greetings had revealed the extent of her influence and power. One of her sons was married to a daughter of the Tsar of Russia, and her heir was married to a Princess of Denmark whose brother was King of Greece. The Queen's cousin was King of the Belgians, and her daughter was Crown Princess of Prussia. The rulers of lesser states claimed kinship with her. Her third son had fought with the army in Egypt, and her daughter, Princess Louise, had been châtelaine at Government House in Canada. Her youngest daughter, whose charm and fidelity had been tested through twenty-five years of the Queen's widowhood, was engaged to Prince Henry of Battenberg. There were many causes for happiness, in spite of the ogre in Downing Street. The Queen watched her eldest son with increasing satisfaction. He had penetrated into a hundred spheres of usefulness, not by the road of scholarship as Prince Albert would have wished, but by ways which were related to experience of people and life. They were the ways the Queen might have chosen if the discipline of her married life had not made it possible for her to turn against the pleasures for which her heart had craved when she was in her teens. Once when she was quite old, one of her Ladies induced her to listen while she read a novel aloud. The Queen *never* read novels, and her daily relaxation was always in the more solid realms of biography and history. But there was a new novel by Marion Crawford with scenes set in the gardens of somebody she knew quite well in Sicily. Perhaps, the Lady suggested, this would excuse them for putting aside Dean Stanley's life, in four volumes, for a day or two. The Queen was like a child over Marion Crawford's story. When she drove in the afternoon, she would say to her Lady, 'I am excited to arrive home, so that we can get on with it. I wonder what happens next?'

When the novel was finished, the Lady suggested that perhaps they might read another. There was another romance, set in Rome! Perhaps! But the Queen tightened her self-imposed control. 'No, not two novels running!' So they continued reading Dean Stanley's life, in four volumes. The Prince of Wales would have made no effort to resist the second novel. The lives of mother and son were far apart, but they were not alone in this estrangement. Most other mothers of the Queen's generation were the same, eschewing the pleasures into which the Prince's friends threw themselves so wholeheartedly. The early Victorians had been brought up on discipline: no fires in their bedrooms, no shawls for walking through the icy corridors. At Balmoral the Ladies used to shiver in their low-necked dresses in the evening, with a small fire in the grate, and the chairs drawn away into the cold shadows of the drawing-room. Once the Queen went into one of the Ladies' bedrooms and found a fire lighted. There were reproaches for the offender. The Ladies who attended the Queen in her later life remembered the fortitude of service at Balmoral long after the Queen died. Although the Queen was punctual for public occasions she had little sense of time within her palace, and the simple dinner would often be half an hour late. Through long experience of the cold passages one of the Ladies used to carry a small Shakespeare in her pocket, so that she could improve her mind and divert it from the draughts and delay, while she was waiting. When they went into dinner, about half-past nine, they were allowed only a limited time to eat. A Spartan atmosphere hung over the Queen's repast: soup, fish, cold roast beef and, almost every night, a big pear.

But there was a respite now and then. During the Prince's rare visits, the Queen would often forget her rigid discipline. Sometimes a door would be opened and mother and son would be discovered sitting upon a sofa, rocking with laughter. There were more than forty years for them to talk about and the Queen's memory linked the dismal twenties with the prosperous eighties. Time, the great healer, is kindly about memories. He allows the wounds and irritations to disappear. Humour proportionately grows and enriches the lives of people when they are old, so that their memories are a store of pleasure and fun rather than of lost tempers and resentment. Christmas of 1884 passed pleasantly at Osborne, and, in the New Year, the Queen enjoyed three weeks of quiet before Westminster or Whitehall disturbed her again.

News of the progress of the Sudanese expedition was sent to the Queen all through January. Late in the month she telegraphed a message to Lord Wolseley, after the battle of Abu Klea. Lord Hartington bristled in the War Office, and he wrote a letter to Sir Henry Ponsonby, asking if it was the Queen's 'desire to adopt the same course on other, similar occasions which might occur.'[247] He added, 'I cannot help thinking that it would on the whole be most convenient that any message from the Queen should be sent through the Secretary of State.'

The peace of Osborne was shattered. The Queen, with all justice, thought Lord Hartington's letter *very officious and impertinent in tone.*[248] She added, in her letter to her secretary, 'The Queen *has* the right to telegraph congratulations and enquiries to *any* one, and won't stand dictation. She *won't* be a machine. But the Liberals always wish to make her *feel* THAT, and she *won't accept it.*'

The party at Osborne scattered after the holidays. With Lord Hartington's uncouth letter in her hand, the Queen looked up from the pleasant scene of her family and her court to contemplate Westminster again.

The electors slowly came to share the Queen's anxiety over Mr. Gladstone's pacifism. It seemed to be futile for him to roar in Midlothian without biting in Ireland, South Africa or Egypt. The disasters of Majuba Hill and

Khartoum, the weakening of Britain's hold in Afghanistan, and the murder and incendiarism in Ireland accumulated in the public mind and, when the Queen left Osborne for Windsor in February, there was already ominous talk of the fall of the Government. The defeat was hastened when the Irish members joined the Conservatives in voting against the Government's plan to increase the tax on beer. Late in May the Queen travelled from Windsor Castle to Balmoral. On June 9th, she received a telegram from Mr. Gladstone. In the face of the defeat in the House, he wished to resign.

§ 11 — 1885

WHEN PRINCE BISMARCK spoke in the Reichstag early in March he lost his patience with Gladstone's wavering foreign policy and stated, in a moment of vehemence, that the 'loquacious futility of Downing Street rendered negotiation with it intolerable.'[249] Bismarck trembled for Britain's prosperity and good name when the country was in the hands of a vacillating Liberal Government. The English political machine had always stirred the Chancellor's envy. When his own professional politicians exasperated him he sighed for the class of English gentleman who served his country for his country's sake. To Bismarck, the perfect example of the English type was Lord Salisbury, whom he had met and respected during the Berlin Congress in 1879.

Bismarck was delighted and full of congratulations in June of 1885, when news came to him of Lord Salisbury's journey to Balmoral. The Queen had summoned the great Foreign Secretary two days after she had received the letter from Mr. Gladstone, telling her that her 'serv-

ants, assembled in Cabinet,' felt that they 'had no alternative but humbly and dutifully to render...their
resignation.' [250]

The 'Chance,' which is 'incessantly modifying, the
whole course' of politics, centred the hopes of the Queen
and the country upon Lord Salisbury, and, on June 23rd
the Queen was awakened at eight o'clock in the morning, at Windsor, to sign the letter which was to bring him
to the Castle to kiss hands. He was to come at four o'clock
in the afternoon. The Queen wrote in her Journal, 'What
a relief.' [251]

§ III

THE EXPERIMENT of Conservative Government, under
Lord Salisbury, lasted only seven months. The Liberals
swept back again under Mr. Gladstone, at the end of the
year. But the interlude of rest from the party which she
disliked, and the Ministers whom she distrusted, threw
light upon the Queen's changing character, especially in
relation to her son. The Prince, personally interested in
the Government because his friend Lord Randolph
Churchill was to be Secretary for India, went down to
Windsor for the Council on June 24th. What would have
been viewed by his mother as an intrusion ten years before was now welcomed as a friendly and affectionate
act. The Queen wrote, 'Bertie kindly came to be with
me during the Council, and lunched with us....Bertie
left again, having kindly spent the whole afternoon at
Windsor, which was the greatest help to me.' [252]

On July 4th, Lord Randolph Churchill dined at Windsor. For some time, especially during the misfortune of a
divorce in his family, the Queen had disliked him. She
had regretted her son's friendship with Lord Randolph

as much as she had regretted his intimacy with Sir Charles Dilke (who was also to fall by the way through a divorce action). In 1885 the Queen was more willing to throw her prejudices aside and to accept Lord Randolph on his own merits. She had warmed to the frivolous Lord Charles Beresford, and now she willingly saw merits in Churchill. 'He is very quiet and has an extraordinary likeness to darling Leopold which quite startled me.... Lord Randolph talked sensibly,' she wrote.[258]

Lord Salisbury was Bismarck's ideal of a great British statesman: an aristocrat, with no axes to grind. He was above corruption, cultivated but not pedantic; he combined intellectual powers with his talents in foreign diplomacy, and over all, there was a shyness and vagueness, giving him touches of eccentricity which made him attractive as well as imposing. The Queen had liked him for many years. He had been Lord Beaconsfield's friend: so many of the pleasant letters from her best loved Minister had been written from Hatfield, when Beaconsfield had been staying with his Foreign Secretary. The Queen knew that Beaconsfield had shared many ideas with Salisbury, and she was willing to trust in his judgment and to believe in his friendship. He was the heir to Beaconsfield's policy.

When Lord Salisbury had dined on an evening early in 1875, the Queen had thought him 'particularly agreeable and gentle.' She would not believe, meeting him thus, that he could be so 'severe and sarcastic in debate.' The many occasions on which they met during the Beaconsfield Ministry had always pleased and reassured her, especially after the Berlin Congress, when Salisbury shared the honours of the diplomatic victory with Lord Beaconsfield. The Prince of Wales had not always been as con-

fident as his mother. He had been too willing to blame
Lord Salisbury for the failure of the Conference in Constantinople, when Britain made an effort to tidy up the
Eastern question, before the Congress in Berlin. When
Salisbury came into power again, the Prince yielded to
better judgment. He recognised the Minister's staunch
character, his genius in foreign affairs, and his immacu-
late ethics. They became good friends and the Prince
was as much entranced by the humorous aspects of Salisbury's personality as he was reassured by his talents.
Salisbury's vagueness about people was a source of perpetual fun to his friends. It was said that an apparently
harmless maniac once joined him in his carriage, when
he was driving to Hatfield from the railway station. Lord
Salisbury was willing to believe that he was an expected
guest, and they travelled to Hatfield without mishap.
Only the skill of a servant ridded the house of the
wretched man before anything untoward happened. Salisbury could remember nobody's face. Once when he was
talking to the Prince of Wales, the Prince showed him
some photographs of himself. Lord Salisbury looked at
one of the photographs with apparent interest and then
said, 'Poor Buller.'

These little vagaries in a great mind pleased the Queen.
She liked the human aspects of her Ministers, and by
June she had been bored by the impersonal letters and the
cold, deferential manner of Gladstone for long enough.

The short spell of Conservative Government allowed
few experiments in legislation or policy. But there were
signs, unfortunately erased again at the end of the year,
of a fulfilment of Salisbury's earlier dictum. Many years
before he had written:

'A nation may uphold its honour without being quixotic, but no reputation can survive a display of quixotism which falters at the sight of a drawn sword.'

In these words Lord Salisbury prophesied the tenor of his own foreign policy, pursued in later years. But the brief seven months of power in 1885 gave him limited scope for display of force or attempt at reconciliation abroad, although the policy he laid down in Egypt determined 'the course of Egyptian history for more than a generation.' [254] Ireland was soothed during the Conservative spell by the withdrawing of the Crimes Act and, true to character, Paddy neither fired nor murdered as much when political crimes were declared to be less without the law than before.

A revolution in Roumelia, where the inhabitants swore allegiance to Prince Alexander and their union with Bulgaria, gave Lord Salisbury one of the foreign tangles which he delighted in unravelling. But the dissension passed, and, just as his calming and powerful influence was establishing England's name again in the respect of Europe, the harassing campaign for the November elections came upon the Government.

Mr. Gladstone's followers had not pursued peace and reconciliation during their respite from power. They had divided: Lord Hartington had gathered the Whigs about him, and Mr. Chamberlain was leading the Radicals. The General Election was spread over November and December, and as the results dribbled into the Queen's hands, she watched the rise and fall of the Conservative figures anxiously. On December 3rd, she was 'much distressed' by the returns. She sensed the revival of her Liberal enemy, and she wrote to Lord Salisbury of the '*absolute* NECESSITY of having strong and able and safe men to conduct the government of the Empire, such as is the case in Lord Salisbury's hands. She therefore looks to *him* to help and advise her in this critical juncture.'

'Things must and cannot return to what they were, for it would be UTTER ruin to the country and Europe.... We want a strong coalition and to this end every nerve must be strained.... The Queen appeals to Lord Salisbury's devotion to her person and Throne and asks him not to desert her, which she is sure *he* and many others will not.' [255]

§ IV — 1886

ONE OF the incongruities of British Government has always been the exaggerated importance of Ireland in times of political crisis. The tenure of many a Government and the fame of many a politician has depended, not on how well the thirty million people of Great Britain have been governed, but on how skilfully some five million people in Ireland have been policed. Again in 1886, Ireland was the fulcrum upon which the scales of political power were balanced. In their political speeches Lord Salisbury and his followers were more or less silent upon the Irish question; but Mr. Gladstone spoke ominously, with the full knowledge that when the elections were over, the leader who successfully wooed the affections of Parnell and his followers would win the day.

Two hundred and fifty Conservative members, three hundred and thirty-four Liberal members, and Mr. Parnell's eighty-six Nationalists gathered in the Commons for the opening of the new session. The Queen manifested her Conservative affections by opening Parliament—for the last time in her life. She was horrified at the impending decision and clung to the hopes of Salisbury's success to the last moment. Five days after the opening of Parliament, Lord Salisbury's Government was out-voted, and the Queen was obliged to send for Mr. Gladstone, and to accept his troth once more as her Minister. There was one ray of hope in the dismal return to the old régime. Lord Granville was removed from her intimate political circle by being appointed Colonial Secretary. He could no longer squander Britain's good name in Europe with his anæmic control of the Foreign Office. In his place came Lord Rosebery 'on the preliminary understanding ...that the policy of his immediate predecessor should not be changed.'[256] The imposition of this condition was a tribute to the Queen's sagacity, but, more than this, a revelation of her power and influence in the political fluctuations of her long reign. Her despair lay in the loss of Lord Salisbury. In seven months he had given her a glimpse of the security she used to feel with Lord Beaconsfield in the seventies. There were no sly impertinences in Salisbury's letters; no tricks with despatches explained away afterwards, when it was too late. In brief, Lord Salisbury was a gentleman, in the broader, ethical sense of the word. With him she had felt the 'blessing of having a Prime Minister in whom she could *thoroughly* confide, and whose opinion was always given in so kind and wise a manner.' It had been a 'pleasure and a comfort' for her to receive him and to read his letters. In her last letter, written on the day when he gave up the seals and became no more than her distant friend at Hatfield, the Queen rang the old, sad note of loneliness. She wrote:

'The Queen does not trust herself to dwell on parting with Lord Salisbury. It would quite upset her—for the loss to her is so great, and she is so alone.'[257]

Chapter Twenty-Seven

§ 1 — 1886

WHEN LORD SALISBURY'S first, short time as Prime Minister ended, the Queen wrote him a letter in which she expressed her 'admiration.' She hoped that it would be a 'very short time' before she saw *him* 'in office' again. Eight months of stormy administration were the extent of her sentence of Liberal Government: they centred about Mr. Gladstone's passionate campaign for Home Rule for Ireland.

Mr. Gladstone was encouraged when he went to Osborne, for this third term as Prime Minister. He had written in his diary of his hope that his Ministry would last for 'a brief time only.' The Queen shared his wish, but she seemed to swallow her resentment during the first audience. Mr. Gladstone wrote, 'I am bound to say that at Osborne in the course of a long conversation, the Queen was frank and free, and showed none of the "armed neutrality," which as far as I know has been the best definition of her attitude in the more recent years towards a liberal minister.' The Queen's 'armed neutrality' did not withstand the conflict for very long.

When Mr. Gladstone announced his plan to grant the Irish their own government some of his followers fell away from him: Lord Derby, Lord Northbrook, Mr. Goschen and Mr. Bright were among the first. Mr. Gladstone had been strengthened by a rest at Hawarden. His attacks upon the trees in the park, in his seventy-sixth year, sent him back to the fray in London with his celebrated vigour. When Sir William Harcourt warned him of the possible disintegration of his party over the Irish Home Rule Bill, Mr. Gladstone was not deterred. He was prepared to 'go forward without either Hartington or Chamberlain.'

Mr. Gladstone introduced his Bill to an excited House on April 8th. When he recalled the dynamic speech, lasting about three and half hours, he wrote, 'Voice and strength and freedom were granted to me in a degree beyond what I could have hoped. But many a prayer had gone up for me, and not I believe in vain.'[258] All the prayers were not for Mr. Gladstone.

The failure of the Bill did not detract from the drama which surrounded the long days of debate. Too many pepole feared the betrayal of the loyalists of Ulster to accept the Bill as a solution of the long, ghastly story of Ireland's discontent. But the fair day of April was no less exciting, nor was London less thrilled by the event, because of the shadow of failure which hung over Mr. Gladstone's magnificent fiasco. The streets and wide places about the Commons were crowded from early in the morning. Within the House, princes and statesmen, plenipotentiaries, prelates and journalists waited for the veteran.

When Mr. Gladstone rose to speak the members listened to the deep, beautiful voice unfolding the promises of the Bill, in heroic phrases.

Again the Members listened in silence, under the dangerous spell of Mr. Gladstone's oratory:

'Ireland stands at your bar expectant, hopeful, almost suppliant. Her words are the words of truth and soberness. She asks a blessed oblivion of the past, and in that oblivion our interest is deeper even than hers. . . .'

The debates, the criticisms and the abuse followed: and then Lord Salisbury's savage exposure of the weakness in the Bill, and the haranguing in the newspapers. The atmosphere became 'thick and hot with political passion.' Mr. Gladstone was like a mighty man beating his hands against a storm.

The division among his followers was not his only cross. England divided itself upon the issue, and hostesses censored their lists of guests according to their attitude to the Irish question. The veneer of politeness was deeply scratched by the vicious controversy, and when Mr. Gladstone wished to celebrate a royal birthday with a dinner party feeling was so bitter that he was 'seriously perplexed.' He wrote to Lord Granville, 'Hardly any peers of the higher ranks will be available, and not many of the lower. . . . Lastly, it has become customary for the Prince of Wales to dine with me on that day, and he brings his eldest son now that the young Prince is of age. But his position would be very awkward, if he comes and witnesses a great nakedness of the land.'

At Windsor the Queen wrestled with one of the most violent crises in her reign. Her distrust of the Irish may have been softened since the early mishaps of the sixties, which closed her heart against the murdering insurgents. But there were no subtleties of conviction in view of Mr. Gladstone's scandalous proposal. She contemplated the Home Rule Bill with horror. No conversation at Windsor or Osborne could pass without reference to the dire plot of Mr. Gladstone. He was ruining the country. No letter could be posted which did not refer, in some way, to the

impending disaster. Even when she wrote to Lord Tennyson, while his son was dying, she could not resist a
sentence of complaint. 'I cannot in this letter allude to
politics, but I know what your feelings must be.' There
came back the answer she wanted. The Poet Laureate
wrote, 'Since your Majesty touches upon the disastrous
policy of the day I may say that I wish I may be in my
own grave, beyond sight and hearing, when an English
army fires upon the loyalists of Ulster.' [259]

The anxiety passed in the summer. On June 9th one
of Lord Salisbury's sons was waiting at the Hatfield telegraph office for the news of the division which had been
held at one o'clock in the morning. Telephones were not
then used in private houses. It is said that when the news
came, at three o'clock in the morning, this loyal young
Cecil ran up the hill towards the park gates, making such
a bedlam of shouting and cheering over the Liberal fall
that the village sleepers were awakened. Lord Salisbury
had been waiting in his room all night for the news of
Mr. Gladstone's failure.

§ II — 1886

IN JUNE the political parties again paraded their talents in
an election, and Mr. Gladstone went back to the scenes
of his triumph in Midlothian. His diary contains more
talk of God and Divine intervention than of the Irish or
of the rickety state of the Liberals. 'The whole a scene
of triumph,' he wrote on June 22nd. 'God help us, His
poor creatures.' On June 28th, he spoke in Hengler's
Circus. 'Few buildings give so noble a presentation of an
audience. Once more my voice held out in a marvellous

manner. I went in bitterness, in the heat of my spirit, but the hand of the Lord was upon me.'

Unfortunately Mr. Gladstone was obliged to depend upon human votes as well as Divine co-operation, and when the results of the election were declared in July the opponents of Mr. Gladstone's Irish policy exceeded its friends by a majority of one hundred and ten.

Again the venerable defeated leader went to the Queen with his seals. A strain of sadness runs through Mr. Gladstone's record of the conversation—his 'closing audience,' he wrote, and probably his 'last word with the Sovereign after fifty-five years of political life, and a good quarter of a century's service rendered to her in office.'

'The Queen was in good spirits; her manners altogether pleasant. She made me sit at once. Asked after my wife as we began, and sent a kind message to her as we ended. About me personally, I think, her single remark was that I should require some rest. I remember that on a closing audience in 1874 she said she felt sure I might be reckoned upon to support the Throne. She did not say anything of the sort to-day. Her mind and opinions have since that day been seriously warped, and I respect her for the scrupulous avoidance of anything which could have seemed to indicate a desire on her part to claim anything in common with me.' [260]

The Queen could afford to be 'altogether pleasant.' Eight days before, she had written to her new Prime Minister, 'Lord Salisbury knows *what confidence* she reposes in him.' [261]

Chapter Twenty-Eight

§ 1 — 1886

LORD SALISBURY waited on the Queen at Osborne on July 24th, and when they were sitting together, planning the Cabinet which was to bring her a long spell of security and contentment, she observed that Salisbury looked 're-markably well.' Mr. Gladstone, who had looked 'ill and haggard' when she saw him in May, was safely withdrawn from the arena. The tired veteran sought rest in Bavaria, in September, in 'an out-of-the-way place, peaceful and silent.' His host tried to divert his mind from the ruins of the Irish Home Rule Bill in the direction of some 'little French comedies.' One day Mr. Gladstone walked seven miles across the hill by the Tegernsee.

There were fewer ripples on the political sea. The Queen was disturbed because the Prince's friend, Lord Randolph Churchill, 'so mad and odd,' and who said 'some strange things,'[262] to her when he dined, was to be Chancellor of the Exchequer and Leader of the House. This she 'did not like.' But Lord Randolph was to resign before the new Government was more than five months old, and if there were other alarms Lord Salisbury did his best to shield her from them.

The Queen encouraged her Minister. 'Lord Salisbury will succeed,' she wrote. 'Lord Beaconsfield raised up the position of Great Britain, from '74 to '80, in a marvellous manner. Mr. Gladstone and Lord Granville pulled it down during the five years of their mischievous and fatal

276

misrule, but already in seven months, Lord Salisbury raised our position again.'[263]

The reactions in Europe from the change of Government were immediate. Prince Bismarck shared the Queen's opinion, and spoke in Berlin of his confidence in Salisbury as he had so many times since they met in 1879. Once Sir Edward Malet was distressed by the news that his wife was ill while on a visit to her parents in England. He was anxious lest contemporary affairs might suffer in his absence from the Embassy in Berlin, and he admitted his fears to Prince Bismarck. The Chancellor assured him that he need feel no anxiety in absenting himself so long as Lord Salisbury was at the Foreign Office.[264]

Lord Salisbury did not act as Foreign Secretary during the first few months of the new Government: the office was given to Lord Iddleleigh. But Lord Salisbury exercised the control over foreign policy which slowly raised England's reputation among the powers. A test of the will of the new Cabinet came in August when the Balkans staged another theatrical scene, inspired by Russia's agents. Russia was not demoralised by the clauses of the Treaty of Berlin. She still dreamed of Constantinople, as of old, and if she was not to be allowed to surge over the Balkans to the shores of the Bosphorus, she would at least keep the little countries in a state of unrest. The Balkan States were over-run by Russian Spies and agents. There were few men in the troubled countries who had not got their price. Bribery and treachery burst into flower in August. Prince Alexander of Bulgaria, brother-in-law of Princess Beatrice, was kidnapped 'by night in his palace.' In the manner of the many theatrical pieces inspired by the Balkans, the unhappy Prince was forced by threats of death to sign his abdication. The troops he had led to victory against Serbia turned upon him, and he was carried down the Danube and handed over to a Russian gendarme. This plot of the 'Russian fields' gave the first months of Lord Salisbury's Ministry the material and impetus they needed. Floods of moral indignation poured from Windsor and from Whitehall. The 'bad and wicked' Emperor, so unhappily tied to the Queen's family by marriage, stirred her to defend the wretched Prince. She saw in the plot still another 'stepping stone' by which the Russians wished to usurp power in the Balkans and advance to Constantinople.

Prince Alexander returned to Sofia and, at first, there were hopes of his triumph, but there were attempts to upset his train and a plot to murder him in the Cathedral. His officers had been 'debauched by foreign gold' [265] and Russian influence had corrupted his officials beyond recall. He was obliged to resign his throne and leave the government of his country in the hands of a Regency. From the bedlam of his Balkan court he travelled to Windsor. The tales of his capture and his escape amazed the usually complacent ladies in the Castle. The Queen wrote, 'It seemed like a dream to see Sandro sitting quietly *amongst* us, after his having gone through such unspeakable dangers and horrors. . . . It was intensely interesting to hear him speak of his terrible experiences, but his poor face looked so sad while doing so.' [266]

Commiseration with Prince Alexander was suddenly displaced by another alarm over Bulgarian affairs. Prince Ferdinand of Coburg was proposed for the crown of Bulgaria. When this talented youth was chosen to be Prince of Bulgaria in 1887 the Queen greeted the first announcement with grave fears. She thought him 'totally

278

unfit—delicate, eccentric, and effeminate.' She talked of the 'absurd pretension of this foolish young cousin of mine,' but she could not thwart the plan. The fantastic scholar was elected Prince of Bulgaria in July, and twenty-one years afterwards he was proclaimed King.

§ II — 1886

EXCEPT FOR her alarm over Prince Alexander's fall in Bulgaria, the Queen showed signs of confidence in the letters which she wrote between the months of August and November. Her Journal also reveals a calmer spirit. Every night Princess Beatrice came to her, between ten and eleven o'clock, to write down her mother's recollections of the day. The signs of age were upon the Queen. Her eyes were tired and she could no longer walk with the old sprightly air: the poise which gave such beauty to her movements when she was young. When she opened Parliament in 1886, Prince 'Eddy' had been obliged to help her up the steps 'quite nicely,' and Princess Beatrice, who stood on her right hand all through the gruelling ceremony, helped her down again when all was over. Some months afterwards the Queen wrote, 'Feel very tired and exhausted, being really much overdone, and fell asleep in my chair, after tea—a very rare thing for me.' [267]

The Queen wrote more naturally of the Prince of Wales in the pages of her Journal. Ten years before, she had dreaded having him, or anybody, standing near to her on a public occasion. No one was to take Albert's place. But this antipathy had passed, and when she opened the Colonial and Indian Exhibition in May the Prince had walked beside her, past the groups of Aus-

279

tralians, New Zealanders, Canadians and South Africans, Lascars and Parsees. She had found the walk among the displays of her Empire 'very long and fatiguing.' [268] But 'Bertie' had kindly helped her 'up and down the steps' whenever they came to any. There had been a great ceremony in the Albert Hall, and the talent of the day had been summoned, as Prince Albert would have wished. There was an ode written by Lord Tennyson, music composed by Sir Arthur Sullivan, and Albani had sung a solo. 'Bertie' read a very long address to which the Queen read an answer. The name of father and son were linked together. Late at night, before she went to bed in Buckingham Palace, the Queen dictated to Princess Beatrice:

'How pleased my darling husband would have been at the whole thing, and who knows but that his pure bright spirit looks down upon his poor little wife, his children and children's children, with pleasure, on the development of his work. . . . Dear Bertie, who was most kind throughout . . . kissed my hand. What thoughts of my darling husband came into my mind, who was the originator of the idea of an exhibition. . . .' [269]

§ III — 1886–1887

THE PRINCE OF WALES had been eager with suggestions when Lord Salisbury formed his new Government in July. When he knew that his friend Lord Randolph Churchill was to be in the Cabinet he was elated, although Lord Randolph was himself 'rather nervous of the promotion.' [270] The Prince sponsored three more politicians of lesser talents: Lord Cadogan, who was appointed Lord Privy Seal; Lord Londonderry, who was appointed Viceroy of Ireland; and Lord Charles Beresford, who became Fourth Lord of the Admiralty. The Prince's recommendations were urged by affection and friendship as much as by good judgment. The appointments of Lord Cadogan and Lord Londonderry were successful, and Lord Salisbury thanked the Prince for 'the kindness and efficiency' with which he had assisted him over the appointment to Ireland. But the choice of the boisterous Irish sailor, Lord Charles Beresford, was not happy. An aptitude for practical jokes at Sandringham and witty telegrams did not recommend him to the sages of Whitehall. For two years he aggravated the Admiralty with his breezy efforts at reform. Like most Irishmen he was 'agin the Government,' even if it was his own party, and the time came for him to go to sea again. The Prince wrote to him,[271] 'You should apply for a ship before long so that you may put in your sea time, and it will be a change also after the House of Commons and London Society.' Lord Charles did not greet the hint. He exasperated the Admiralty, and he strained the friendship of the Prince of Wales by waiting one more year before he went seafaring again, 'Rather than pace up and down, Any longer London town.'

The appointment in which the Prince might have felt full confidence—that of Lord Randolph Churchill—ended disastrously at the close of the year. Lord Randolph's brilliance was already acknowledged, but he was still young and impatient. He was thirty-six years old when Lord Salisbury imposed the two great honours upon him, hoping that his talents would find maturity in office. On September 17th, Lord Salisbury wrote to Lady Salisbury of his self-willed protégé: 'When Randolph hints that, if I go, he is capable of all kinds of monkey tricks, I feel he can be as good as his word.'

281

In August, Lord Randolph was opposed to England's taking a share of the responsibility over the kidnapping of Prince Alexander. This difference of opinion was followed by his irritation over dealings with France in the control of the Suez Canal. Youth and unbridled talents loosened Lord Randolph's tongue at the first Cabinet meeting in November. 'It is an idle schoolboy dream to suppose that Tories can legislate,' he told the Ministers. '... I certainly have not the energy and courage to go on struggling against cliques, as poor Dizzy did all his life.'[272] Lord Salisbury tried to pacify Churchill with restraint and patience which drew blame upon himself. He was, his colleagues said, too self-effacing. But the master's hand was certain, if his voice was quiet. Lord Randolph resigned from the Chancellorship on December 23rd, the accumulation of dissent culminating when the Cabinet refused to sponsor his proposal to reduce the Naval and Military Estimates. There was too much talk of war abroad to make the plan attractive to the Cabinet.

The resignation interrupted a graceful scene. Hatfield was gay with the music and lights of a Christmas ball, and among the guests were Princess Mary of Teck and her daughter, Princess May. Princess Mary was sitting upon a sofa with Lord Salisbury when their talk was interrupted by the arrival of a box. The Prime Minister paused to read the letter of resignation, which was a terrible blow to his Government. Then he turned to the Princess and went on with the conversation as if nothing untoward had happened.

The Queen read the 'startling' news in *The Times*.[273] Lord Randolph had dined at Windsor only a few nights before when there had not been 'a symptom of resigning.' That *very night*, while he was a guest *at the Castle*, after hoodwinking her with talk of the coming *Session,* he had written his letter of resignation to Lord Salisbury.[274]

The friendship between the Prince and Lord Randolph was not affected by the Ministerial mishap. They continued to appear together at race meetings and the Prince ignored his mother's reproaches against a friendship with one who was 'so changeable and indiscreet.' The Prince's loyalty, often pursued with stubbornness, did not falter under Lord Salisbury's dilemma or his mother's disgust. He made an ill-chosen attempt to pacify his mother by suggesting that he might reconcile the Prime Minister and his unruly pupil with a view to Lord Randolph's joining the Cabinet again.

The weakening of the Government alarmed both Queen and Minister. Before Lord Salisbury had accepted office in July he had approached Lord Hartington, hoping that he would join him together with those Liberals who had deserted Mr. Gladstone over the Home Rule Bill. The first overture had been unsuccessful, partly because Lord Randolph was to be in the new Government. Now that this obstacle was removed, the Queen approached Lord Hartington again, together with his colleague, Mr. Goschen, entreating them to agree to the formation of a Coalition Government. Her appeal to Lord Hartington failed, but Mr. Goschen, whom Lord Randolph confessed that he had 'forgotten,' consented, while remaining a Liberal, to accept the office of Chancellor of the Exchequer. The Conservative ship was thus saved, but it was to suffer one more disaster before Lord Salisbury's Cabinet settled down to a semblance of equanimity.

Lord Iddesleigh, a devoted adherent if not always successful as Foreign Secretary, had been warned by his doctor that the glass 'was cracked,' and that it might 'break at any moment.' In the reshuffling of offices, forced upon Lord Salisbury by the retirement of Lord Randolph, Lord Iddesleigh resigned office to facilitate the inclusion of the Liberal Unionists. This sad end to his career was turned to tragedy by his sudden death in the ante-room of No. 10 Downing Street, while he was waiting to see the Prime Minister, who arrived just in time to see his friend die.

The year 1887 began in confusion. Lord Randolph's secession turned the kaleidoscope of the Cabinet rather violently. Lord Salisbury added the Foreign Office to his burdens. Mr. W. H. Smith was appointed First Lord of the Treasury and Leader of the House of Commons, and, after a few weeks, Mr. Arthur Balfour became Chief Secretary for Ireland.[275]

Chapter Twenty-Nine

§ 1 — 1887

THE DOCUMENTS which are left from 1887, the year of the first Jubilee, reveal a tussle between glory and depression. The story of Ireland increased by one more chapter, contributed by Mr. Arthur Balfour, the new Secretary for Ireland, who was destined for greatness under three sovereigns. Mr. Balfour was a nephew of Lord Salisbury, and he inherited the cloaks of scholarship and statesmanship, wearing both with honour. Balfour had accompanied his uncle to Berlin for the celebrated Congress in 1879, and he had linked this first experience of diplomacy with the writing of his erudite and thoughtful *Defence of Philosophic Doubt*. From these varied experiences he had faded into the manner of a dilettante for some time, associating himself with the elegant coterie of intellectuals called the *Souls,* and hiding his strength and ability behind academic abstraction.

For some years Mr. Balfour had not been considered seriously as a politician, although his personal qualities had won him many friends. The Queen thought him 'singularly charming and agreeable' [276] and she recorded the steps of his progress in the House with pleasure. His first legislation was the Crimes Bill, passed in renewed hope that the darkness upon Ireland might pass. The Bill was subjected to obstruction from Mr. Gladstone, as vehement as the attacks upon his own Home Rule Bill had been in the previous year.

The *Freeman* had greeted Mr. Balfour's election to the Irish Secretaryship with phrases which were amusing to those who are aware of his final achievement.

'It seems like breaking a butterfly on the wheel to extend Mr. Balfour on the rack of Irish politics. He is an elegant, fragile creature, a prey to that aristocratic languor which prevents him from assuming any but the limpest attitude. We are convinced of his inevitable failure as we are of our own existence.'

But the 'lisping hawthorn bird' and 'scented popinjay' brought imagination into Irish affairs, even if he did not contribute the figure of a bruiser. 'He came to the conclusion that the cancer which was sapping away the vitality of Ireland was not so much political injustice as the extreme poverty and wretchedness of its people. He satisfied himself that its evils were mainly economic, and he determined to subordinate and direct his whole policy to the end of bringing a comfortable livelihood within the reach of the Irish peasantry.' [277]

This high and noble ambition was not to be realised in Balfour's lifetime. But his Crimes Bill, which braved and survived the storms of opposition, made it possible for the Viceroy to write a reassuring letter to the Queen in December.[278]

He had waited long enough for the Bill to be 'given a fair trial,' he wrote. He feared to take a 'too sanguine view,' but he could not conceal from himself that law and order were being gradually restored even in the most disaffected districts. He wrote, 'Further improvement may be hoped for.' Lord Londonderry regarded the improvement as due to the administering of Mr. Balfour's act, 'with firmness,' and the policy of attacking the leading agitators instead of the 'small men.'

Mr. Balfour's name was not the only new one, 'shining with the first promise of success' in the political story of the year. On February 8th, Sir Edward Grey 'made a maiden speech of much promise and interest,' [279] and on March 24th, Mr. Asquith, 'a new member, spoke with considerable ability.' [280]

The most important step in foreign policy for the year was Lord Salisbury's secret understanding with Italy and Austria for common defence in the Mediterranean and the Near East. Bismarck viewed the arrangement with satisfaction. It was not against his plans that the three powers should combine to strengthen defences and assure a semblance of peace in the Mediterranean.

§ II — 1887

IN JULY of 1887, Letsie, Chief of the Basutos, wrote to Queen Victoria:

'Many of my people don't understand that a person can live so many years as Queen, and many even go so far as to say that she must long ago have gone to her rest, and that it is her fame and glory which remain. . . . For us, it is a curious thing that a woman should be a Queen. . . .' [281]

The habit of fifty years had caused many people to forget that it was 'curious' that a lonely woman should rule half the world. On June 20th millions upon millions of people trembled with excitement at the sudden realisation of the Queen's achievement. The newspapers of the time have recorded the pageantry of London and the wave of devotion which swept over the Empire. The celebrations were too closely wrapped up with human need for security to be affected by politics or discontent. The first

Jubilee festivals were in India, in February. There was
an element of truth in the suggestion that the people of
India, so 'passionately fond of pyrotechnic displays,'
might have been better governed with such brave shows
and entertainments than by soldiers and bureaucrats. On
the 16th, the Hindus 'were shown fireworks far superior
to any they had ever seen before.' Lord Dufferin wrote,
'The principal feature was the outline of your Majesty's
head, traced in lines of fire, which unexpectedly burst on
the vision of the astonished crowd. The likeness was ad-
mirable. . . .'

From this first tribute there grew waves which touched
every corner of the Empire. They surged back to England
and to Windsor, where, day after day, the Queen was
surrounded by glory. It is curious in the records of an
industrial age, and in the history of a material people, to
happen upon the romantic story of the Jubilee. The
Princes from India, heavy with jewels, came to Windsor
and held out their swords for the Queen to touch. Some
bowed before her with their hands held as if in prayer.
Her Indian servants, dressed in scarlet with white tur-
bans, kissed her feet in the morning when she sat down
to breakfast. The Kings of Denmark, Greece, Saxony and
Belgium came, and the Queen of Hawaii, with a gift of
precious feathers. The Crown Princes of Germany, Austria and Portugal and Princes from Persia, Japan and
Siam. For ten days the Queen lived through an orgy of
colour and tribute.

One afternoon, the Thakore of Morvi rode up to Windsor Castle, where the ghosts of Elizabethan and Plan-
tagenet gallants might have observed him. He was
mounted on a young horse, covered by a coat of mail,
splendidly caparisoned, with heavy ornamented tassels

hanging down and an amulet on one leg. The Queen met the Prince at the Castle entrance. He had brought his horse all the way from the banks of the Machhu to greet her. The Thakore leapt to the ground, bowed, and begged the Queen to accept his noble charger. It was all part of a fairy tale.

The great day was June 20th. The Queen wrote in her Journal:

'The day has come, and I am alone, though surrounded by many dear children. I am writing ... in the garden at Buckingham Palace; here I used to sit so often in former happy days. Fifty years to-day since I came to the throne!'

She had 'hurried' her dressing in the morning at Windsor, so that she could go down to breakfast at Frogmore, before travelling up to London where more than thirty Royal Princes were waiting at Buckingham Palace to greet her. The morning of the 21st

'was beautiful and bright with fresh air. Troops began passing early with bands playing, and one heard constant cheering.... Received many beautiful nosegays and presents.... Then dressed, wearing a dress and bonnet trimmed with white point d'Alencon, diamond ornaments in my bonnet, and pearls round my neck, with all my orders.

'At half-past eleven we left the Palace ... it was really a magnificent sight.... The crowds from the Palace gates up to the Abbey were enormous, and there was such an extraordinary outburst of enthusiasm as I had hardly ever seen in London before; all the people seemed to be in a good humour. The old Chelsea pensioners were in a stand near to the Arch.... We Princesses went into a little waiting-room.... When all was ready, the procession was formed.... *God Save the Queen* was played, and then changed to Handel's *Occasional Overture,* as I walked slowly up the Nave and Choir, which looked beautiful, all filled with people....

'I sat *alone* (oh! without my beloved husband, for whom this would have been such a proud day!) where I sat forty-nine years ago.... My robes were beautifully draped on the chair.... When the service was concluded, each of my sons, sons-in-law, grandsons ... and grandsons-in-law, stepped forward, bowed, and in succession kissed my hand, I kissing each....

'Only at four did we sit down to luncheon, to which all came. ... I felt quite exhausted by this time and ready to faint, so I got into my rolling chair and was rolled away to my room. Here I lay down on the sofa and rested, doing nothing but opening telegrams....'

In the evening the Queen travelled down to Windsor. Just as she was beginning dessert she heard that a torchlight procession of Eton boys had arrived in the quadrangle of the Castle.

'...Off we hurried, as fast as we could, to the corridor from whence we could see it beautifully.... Then we all went down to the Quadrangle, and I said, in as loud a voice as I could, "I thank you very much...." The Round Tower was illuminated with electric lights.... The town was also illuminated, but I was too tired to go and see it....'

In October the Prince of Wales unveiled a statue of the Queen at Balmoral, and, on the 10th, he left the Castle. The Queen again turned to her Journal and wrote:

'An early luncheon, after which dear Bertie left, having had a most pleasant visit, which I think he enjoyed and said so repeatedly. He had not stayed alone with me, excepting for a couple of days in May in '68, at Balmoral, since he married! He is so kind and affectionate that it is a pleasure to be a little quietly together.' [282]

Chapter Thirty

§ 1 — 1887–1888

QUEEN VICTORIA could not resist the appeal which had been made to her during the celebration of her Jubilee in 1887. There are a hundred little stories to show that the expressions of affection awakened an enthusiastic response in her. She was drawn more closely into the lives of her people, and, instead of greeting age as a reason for further retirement, she threw off more of the sable trappings of bereavement, and life at Court became almost gay again. The Jubilee celebrations at Buckingham Palace may have stirred the Queen's memory of the careless years before her marriage, when she sometimes danced until daylight crept over the garden wall and into the ballroom.

A few days before her sixty-eighth birthday the Queen held a drawing-room at Buckingham Palace, for the first time allowing certain 'poor divorced ladies,' who had had to 'divorce their husbands owing to cruelty, desertion, and misbehaviour,' to appear before her.[283] There were crowded days in London during this month, so very different from the dismal seasons at Windsor. On the 11th she had driven to Westminster Abbey to see the preparations for her Jubilee service, walking among the masses of boarding and lumber, placing flowers upon Lady Augusta Stanley's tomb, and pausing to see some of the monuments. Afterwards she had received Lord Salisbury, to talk over the plan for opening the People's Palace, which was to be one of the functions in the week of her

Jubilee. She had agreed to take tea at the Mansion House, which she would not have dreamed of doing two years before. From her interview with her Minister, she had hurried off to Earl's Court to see 'a very extraordinary and interesting sight—a performance of Buffalo Bill's Wild West,' and then, with no complaint of tiredness, she had returned to dine at Windsor.

Plays and tableaux were among the signs of her increased happiness. The Queen busied herself about these entertainments with joyful fuss over every detail. When she drove with her Ladies the tableaux would be discussed. One day a young and nervous Lady sat next to her in the carriage, and the following conversation ensued:

> The Queen: 'Have you any suggestions for your next tableau?'
> The Lady (harassed by the sudden question): 'Well, Ma'am, could we not have the scene of the execution of Mary Queen of Scots?'
> The Queen: 'Certainly not. How could you think of such a thing? You must suggest something better than that.'
> The Lady: 'Well, Ma'am, do you think we could do some scenes from the life of the Pretender?'
> The Queen: 'We never speak of the Pretender. You mean Prince Charles Edward.' [284]

The Queen's journeys abroad also widened her field of interests beyond the garden and woods of Windsor. She made a yearly habit of spending some of the cold months in the South of France or in Florence; and her increasing lameness did not deter her from the little journeys which she loved. Her Journals contain many records of expeditions from Aix-les-Bains or from her villa in Florence. In April of 1887 she had visited the monastery at the Grand Chartreuse, threading her way through the country in which the monks gathered the herbs and flowers from which they distilled their liqueur.[285]

'The Monastery nestles in among the high mountains. As we approached, we could see a monk standing under a doorway. . . . Just inside the Monastery the Grand Prieur General received us, a stout, burly, rosy-cheeked man, wearing spectacles. . . .

'We were shown where the cells were, and told I should see a young *compatriote,* an Englishman, who had been there for some time. The Grand Prieur unlocked the cell . . . and the young inmate immediately appeared, kneeling down and kissing my hand, and saying, "I am proud to be a subject of your Majesty. . . ." I remarked how young he looked, and he answered, "I am 23," and that he had been five years in the Grand Chartreuse, having entered at 18. I asked if he was contented, and he replied, "I am very happy." '

§ II — 1888

QUEEN VICTORIA's feelings had always been torn between the diplomatic needs of her country and her personal anxiety for those of her relatives who were ruling Princes in Germany. Glory came to her as the revered mother of the Courts of Europe, but also anxiety when the ambitions of these Courts did not agree with the aims of her own Government. She had realised this parting of the ways many times as Prince Bismarck forced his mighty plans upon Central Europe. The invasion of Schleswig-Holstein had divided her heart between her daughter and her daughter-in-law. The humiliation of Hesse-Darmstadt had divided her daughters (one married in Prussia and one in Darmstadt), and the ambitions of Russia threatened to estrange her from the wife of her son, Prince Alfred. Nobody else in the world, living or dead, had existed upon such a domestic volcano as the Queen. Some magic quality in her influence made it possible for her to survive the eruptions which continually shook her reign.

Prince Bismarck had been such a fiery Wotan in the story of the advance of Prussian influence, that the German Emperor, his son, the Crown Prince Frederick, and his grandson, Prince William, were overshadowed for more than twenty years of German history. Emperor William I had been relegated to picturesque ineptitude by the powers of his first Minister. His gentle qualities were drowned in the crashing symphony of Imperial Germany.

Prince Bismarck was master of all power except life and death. For cynics and philosophers there was something comical in the dire changes which followed the passing of the German Emperor in March of 1888. At the time of his death, his son, Prince Frederick, was also fatally ill in Charlottenburg.

In April Queen Victoria went to Berlin to see her daughter, then German Empress. The Queen arrived at the Palace on the morning of April 24th, and went to her rooms, 'charmingly arranged and done up by dear Vicky. They were the rooms of Frederick the Great, and have never been lived in since....' [286]

'After I had tidied myself up a bit,' wrote the Queen, 'dear Vicky came and asked me to go and see dear Fritz. He was lying in bed, his dear face unaltered; and he raised up both his hands with pleasure at seeing me, and gave me a nosegay. It was very touching and sad to see him thus in bed.'

The Queen drove from Charlottenburg into Berlin, to see the Dowager Empress. '... there was the Empress, in deep mourning, with a long veil, seated in a chair, quite crumpled up and deathly pale, really a rather ghastly sight. Her voice was so weak it was hardly audible....'

Next day Prince Bismarck was brought to the Queen, unmistakably nervous and ill at ease when he asked, before going into the room, whether the Queen would be 'seated or standing.' She was 'agreeably surprised to find him so amiable and gentle,' but, if there was victory for either of these rulers, it was for the Queen. Prince Bismarck could not resist the temptation to boast of Germany's army. They talked of the powers of Europe as of cards upon a playing table before them. The final gesture of graciousness was from the Queen. She hoped, she said, that Princess Bismarck would come to see her at the British Embassy in the afternoon, '...this seemed to give him much pleasure.' [287] One courtier who saw Bismarck after he withdrew from the Queen's presence said that the Chancellor wiped sweat from his forehead and remarked, 'That was a woman! One could do business with her!'

When the Queen left Berlin, her daughter went with her to the train and burst into tears. '...it was terrible to see her standing there...while the train moved slowly off, and to think of all she was suffering and might have to go through.' [288]

As the Queen was sitting at the cottage of one of her friends at Balmoral, in June, Princess Beatrice brought her a telegram telling of the Emperor Frederick's death. 'My poor dear Vicky, God help her,' the Queen cried. Nine days afterwards the young Emperor William II spoke at the opening of the Reichstag, 'of a leaning towards Russia,' but he made 'no mention of England.' [289]

Chapter Thirty-One

§ 1 — 1889

THE WILD behaviour of the young Emperor disturbed the serenity of many lives in 1889 and 1890, and the pretensions with which he assumed the Crown lost him the affection and trust of his relatives in England. He soon proved himself unfit for the role of Constitutional Monarch, attacking the problems of his country in the theatrical manner of an insecure ruler in the Balkans rather than an Emperor in Europe. The rift between the English and German Royal families widened in October of 1888, when the Emperor accused his uncle, the Prince of Wales, of not treating him with the respect due to him as an Emperor. The Queen expressed the general reaction to this pathetic complaint by describing it as 'too *vulgar* and too absurd, as well as untrue....'[290]

The story of the young Emperor's hallucinations is too well known to call for more than an outline of the incidents which brought so much misery to his relatives, and, in the end, disaster to Bismarck's dreams and power. The exchange of angry messages between the Emperor and Prince, always through third persons, culminated in a ridiculous scene in Vienna when the Prince of Wales was obliged to leave because his nephew did not wish to meet him there.

This affront drew the Queen and her son together more closely than ever, and when the Emperor later expressed his wish to visit England the Queen said that he 'must make some sort of apology, before he comes, to the Prince of Wales.' [291] To her son she wrote, 'William must *not* come *this* year; *you* could not meet him, and I could *not* after all he has said and done.' [292]

Perhaps the Emperor momentarily regretted the pompous declaration he had made to his grandmother in regard to the Emperor of Austria. He had written to her: 'We Emperors must stand together.' [293] At least he realised that his wounded pride as a nephew could not be allowed to stem his progress as an Emperor. In March, after the tiff had been patched up largely because of the Prince's chivalry and patience, the Emperor again pressed his wish to visit England. This time the Queen was obliged to swallow her pride and resentment in the cause of international peace. She accepted Lord Salisbury's suggestion that her unruly grandson had perhaps 'awakened from the temporary intoxication of the summer.' 'It is your Majesty's interest,' wrote Lord Salisbury, 'to make his penitential return as easy for him as possible.' [294] It was agreed therefore that the Emperor should visit the Queen in the summer, at Osborne, where irritated Londoners could not express their resentment.

The Queen began what was almost a campaign of favours for her heir about this time. Her whole-hearted support of his grievance was followed by graceful gestures of affection, and in April she spent four or five days at Sandringham, which she had not visited since her son's illness in December, 1871.

In his own home the Prince entertained his mother after his elegant and amusing fashion. Sandringham had put on its gayest feathers for the Queen. 'It was a very pretty sight,' she wrote. 'Everything came back to my mind, as we drove in at the gates. ... All was the same as

at that terrible time, and yet all was so different....
Bertie and Alix then took me upstairs to the well-known
old rooms, which have been freshly done up....'

On the last evening the party went down to the ballroom which had been converted into a theatre. When the
Queen went to her sitting-room, at one o'clock in the
morning, she wrote in her Journal:

'We sat in the front row, I between Bertie and Alix. The stage
was beautifully arranged, and with great scenic effects, and the
pieces were splendidly mounted, and with numbers of people
taking part. I believe there were between sixty and seventy, as well
as the orchestra. The piece, *The Bells,* is a melodrama ... and is
very thrilling. The hero (Irving), though a mannerist of the
Macready type, acted wonderfully. He is a murderer, and frequently imagines he hears the bells of the horses in the sledge,
in which sat the Polish Jew, whom he murdered.... *The Bells*
was followed by the trial scene from *The Merchant of Venice,*
in which Irving played the part of Shylock extremely well, and
Miss Ellen Terry that of Portia beautifully.... I waited a moment
in the drawing-room to speak to Irving and Ellen Terry. He is
very gentlemanlike, and she, very pleasing and handsome.'

Next morning the Queen returned to Windsor, after a
'very pleasant time under dear Bertie and Alix's hospitable
roof.' She was 'greatly touched by all their kindness and
affection.' [295]

§ 11 — 1889

THE FALSE domestic peace which followed the Emperor's
quarrel with his uncle made it possible for him to carry
out his plan to visit the Queen in August. She had written him a 'civil letter' in May, 'accepting his disclaimer
of having had anything to do with the Vienna incident.'

In June she conferred the rank of British Admiral upon him, as a courteous answer to his offer of an Honorary Colonelcy of the 1st Regiment of his Dragoon Guards. The Emperor's acknowledgment of the honour, sent to Sir Edward Malet, gives some idea of his state of mind on the eve of his visit to his grandmother.

'. . . the last sentence of your letter fairly overwhelmed me! What a surprise and an agreeable one too! Fancy wearing the same uniform as St. Vincent and Nelson; it is enough to make one quite giddy. I feel something like Macbeth must have felt when he was suddenly received by the witches with the cry of "All hail, who are Thane of Glamis and of Cawdor too." '

There was a gay postscript to the letter. 'I beg to be allowed to remark that I do not look upon you as a witch, but more as a good fairy.' The Emperor might have read on, turning over but one page of *Macbeth*: '. . . have eaten of the insane root, That takes the reason prisoner?'

§ III — 1889

THE QUEEN was seventy years old when the added domestic tumults of the German court were thrust upon her. She was bent upon vindicating her son. Her physical courage, of which one cannot write too often, lent an heroic touch to her devotion during June and July. The interests of her country obliged her to hide her true feeling for her grandson, but she did not allow either her duty as queen or her miserable health to prevent her from paying every possible tribute to the Prince of Wales after his humiliation in Vienna. On June 15th, when the unkindly inroads of age were already making her lame and tired, she wrote, 'Still in pain, and have to be carried up and down stairs, which is too tiresome.' Next day she was 'able to walk alone with a stick from room to room.' In this sorry state the Queen received her Ministers, and she sat up until late at night over her letters and her documents. On July 4th, as further manifestation of her devotion to the Prince, she went up to London, in great pain, to meet his guests at a party in the gardens of Marlborough House. She returned to Windsor in the evening, and she had 'a dreadful night.' Next day she sat in the garden at Frogmore, writing her letters in the little teahouse which she had built among the trees. When her letters were finished, she went over to the Mausoleum, past the cedar tree beneath which she used to take tea with Prince Albert and her mother. When she came to the far side of the lake she was so tired that she had to be carried up the steps into the Mausoleum. In the afternoon, she held a Council in the Castle, and, with evident pleasure, she declared her consent to the marriage of her grand-daughter, Princess Louise, to the Earl of Fife.

Chapter Thirty-Two

§ 1 — 1890

THE CONFLICTS and changes in Germany were so dramatic in 1890 that home affairs seemed to be dwarfed in importance for the Queen. Lord Salisbury's Government usually came to decisions which pleased her. 'Ireland had greatly improved, and Mr. Balfour was an immense strength, having done wonders.' This note in the Queen's Journal [296] indicates the calm policy by which Mr. Balfour guided his legislation. There were troubles enough in Ireland, Africa and Canada, but they were overshadowed by the resignation of Prince Bismarck in June. The Emperor's high-handed dismissal of the Chancellor shook every Court and Government in Europe. To the spectator, the action seemed to be disastrous. But the Emperor excused his decision on account of the Chancellor's age and ungovernable temper. Also he said, 'I have been educated politically by the Prince, and now I must show what I can do.'

His appointment as an Admiral in the British Navy had turned the Emperor William's head ridiculously. He inspected ships of the Queen's Navy whenever he could and he sent his grandmother letters which were heavy with advice as to how her Navy might be improved and strengthened. 'Admiral Hoskins must be reinforced,' he wrote, after he had lunched on board H.M.S. *Dreadnought,* and raised his eyes to see *his* Admiral's flag hoisted. Perhaps the Queen made a mistake in elevating him to such high rank in her Navy. In his own words it made him 'giddy,' awakening in him the ambition that Germany too might have an iron-clad fleet to carry terror across the oceans of the world. Wishing to be just, one seeks among the records of the time for some redeeming aspect of the Emperor's conduct. In his dismissal of Bismarck 'the other side of the story' is revealed in the account of the Emperor's convincing interview with the British Ambassador.[297] But one searches in vain for an explanation of his treatment of his English relations.

The silence of the Prince of Wales during his nephew's exhibitions of effrontery must endear him to those who respect the phlegmatic but dignified English tradition. In private the Prince did not mince his words, and he declared his nephew to be a braggart, a liar, and a menace to the peace of Europe. But the healthy outbursts of feeling within the walls of Marlborough House were curbed in public. In March the Prince declared his peaceful intentions by accepting the Emperor's invitation for both himself and his second son, Prince George, to visit Berlin.

Prince George was now twenty-five years of age. For some years he had been serving with the Navy, in the Mediterranean, on board the flagship of the Channel Squadron, and then in command of a torpedo boat in the naval manœuvres of 1889. He was well equipped to talk of sea-faring to his cousin if the conversation had tended that way. Somewhere else it has been observed that Coburg blood possesses a chameleon quality which has permitted the Princes of the family to assume the character of the country of their adoption with ease. The last drop of German blood had faded from the English Royal family before Prince George was born. He was more English than the English. If his ancestors had

thriven upon Goethe and Schiller he had pledged himself to Surtees and Whyte Melville, and his nature was
divided between the trusty, bluff officer in the Navy and
the English squire, devoted to his own acres. Every
modest, solid quality of British character was exemplified in him. Prince George's feelings for Germany had
never been a matter for doubt. It is said that he once
deplored the time he spent in Heidelberg, 'learning their
beastly language.' We have no record of what he said or
thought during the visit to Berlin. Both father and son
accepted every peaceful gesture from the Emperor with
gallant regard for their country, and no show of resentment for the unfortunate incident in Vienna the year
before. 'William did all in his power to make it very
agreeable and interesting,' the Prince of Wales wrote to
his mother.[298]

For three days after the official visit was over the
Prince of Wales and Prince George remained in Berlin
to pursue their own wishes and pleasure. Their spell of
festive days had been haunted by a dynamic incident.
Forty-eight hours before their arrival in Berlin, the young
Emperor had dismissed Prince Bismarck from office.
While the Prince of Wales was watching his nephew's
magnificent soldiers, observing the new rifles and the
new smokeless powder at the School of Musketry,
Prince Bismarck, a virulent veteran of seventy-five, was
realising a degree of anger never aroused in him before.
The mighty designer of Imperial Germany had been dismissed by the very man upon whom he had staked his
faith. The Prince of Wales hid his excitement during the
grand programme which the Emperor had arranged for
him, but when he was free, for the last three days in
Berlin, he straightway sought an interview with the dis-

missed Chancellor. He found Bismarck terrible with anger. Alone with him, the old man (who had not always been kind or generous to the Prince of Wales) heaped abuse upon the character of his Emperor. 'The old Prince was terribly hurt and pained,' the Prince wrote to the Queen. In England, where the news of the Prince's reception in Berlin was received with satisfaction, a states-man wrote of the young Emperor, to one of his colleagues, 'It is not a pleasant prospect to have Europe left at the mercy of a hothead who seems also to be a fool.' [299]

§ II — 1890

THE DEMOCRATIC Government of Britain has slowly lessened the direct power of Royalty, but, with this loss, British Sovereigns have gained a more subtle influence over the increasing millions of their subjects. The influence began towards the end of the last century, when the 1887 Jubilee brought the thoughts of a scattered Empire home to England in loyalty and affection. The Queen was never wholly conscious of her influence, and when expressions of devotion were forced on her she was often surprised. She expected and demanded loyalty, because she was Queen of an Empire. But personal tributes were not expected. When she drove in a closed carriage to place a wreath on the grave of Lady Ely at Kensal Green, she wrote in her Journal, 'There were crowds out, we could not understand why, and thought something must be going [on], but it turned out it was only to see me.' [300]

The Queen, who was devoid of vanity, never allowed the popularity of her later years to lessen her hold upon her position as a monarch. She clung tenaciously to every symbol of relationship with her people as Sovereign, inde-

pendent of the power of Parliament. She agreed that
democratic legislation was good for industry, colonisation,
civic responsibility and society, but she never admitted the
right of politicians to step in between herself and her
Army. This conception of the relationship between
Sovereign and Army (proved to be right in almost every
chapter of military history) caused the Queen deep resentment in the spring of 1890, when the Hartington
Commission recommended that the office of Commander-
in-Chief should be abolished. The Commander-in-Chief
was the Duke of Cambridge. The Queen pleaded, not in
her name, but in that of her successors.[301] She must, she
said, 'hand down to her son and grandson her crown un-
impaired.' The Cabinet rejected the proposal, but not
before the Queen, with the support of soldiers as distinguished as Lord Wolseley, had declared a principle which
the Government did not dare to shake. She wrote, 'One
of the greatest prerogatives of the Sovereign is the *direct
communication,* with an immovable and non-political
officer of high rank, *about the Army....*' [302]

§ III — 1890–1891

THERE WERE many dismal events in the New Year to keep
the Queen at her desk through long and anxious hours.
The scandal of 'Mr. Parnell's divorce [303] and the consequent split in the Irish Nationalist Party caused by Mr.
Gladstone's reaction to the moral outrage, the death of
Mr. W. H. Smith, the leader of the House, and a rising
of the Hindus in the hill state of Manipur, called for endless correspondence. But a deep-rooted spirit of happiness
appeared in the Queen's Journal, and she no longer
courted the release of death. The entry in her Journal on

305

January 1st is the most significant evidence of the change:

'...May God enable me to become worthier, less full of weakness and failings, and may He preserve me yet for some years!'

Twenty-nine years before, she had written, 'The things of this world are of no interest to the Queen...*her* thoughts are *fixed above*.'[304] But there were signs of joy in 1891. A few weeks before the end of the year the Queen had joined in an evening party at Balmoral. They had 'pushed the furniture back, and had a nice little impromptu dance.' Although she was already lame and obliged to walk from her room with a stick, she danced in a quadrille with her grandson. 'I did quite well,' she wrote, 'then followed some waltzes and polkas.'[305] The Prince's theatrical company at Sandringham stimulated the Queen to revive her patronage of the stage, and twice in March of 1891 she received players at Windsor. The cold spaces of the Waterloo Chamber rang with the jolly music of *The Gondoliers*. The Grand Inquisitor was 'most absurd' and Miss Jessie Bond, 'a clever little actress,' sang 'quite nicely.' In July, Paderewski, 'pale with a sort of aureole of gold hair,' played at Windsor, and on another day, the de Reszkes and Melba sang for the Queen. On March 17th, Mr. Hare presented *A Pair of Spectacles* in the Waterloo Chamber. It was 'extremely good.' Afterwards, the Queen received the actors in the drawing-room, noting that Mr. Hare was 'a gentleman as so many [actors] are nowadays.'[306]

§ IV — 1891

THE PARNELL divorce scandal and Mr. Gladstone's moral indignation and recoil from the Irish Nationalist Party

306

gave Mr. Balfour a rich opportunity for legislation in both sessions of Parliament in 1891. While the Irish were quarrelling, neglecting the English Tyrants in the Commons to exchange shafts among themselves, Mr. Balfour's Land Bill was passed; also the Tithe Bill which provided that the responsibility for the payment of tithe should be transferred from tenants to landowners. A third blessing was added to the legislation, with the support of Mr. Chamberlain, in the Education Bill, which afterwards gave free tuition to eighty-three per cent of the children attending English schools. Mr. Balfour, who at the Queen's suggestion succeeded to the Leadership of the House when Mr. Smith died in October, had justified the faith placed in him by both Sovereign and Prime Minister. The dilettante, who had attracted so much abuse to himself when he was appointed Secretary for Ireland, enjoyed triumph after triumph: largely because he attacked the problems of Ireland as a sane, sympathetic human being, and not as a professional politician. Even the Irish members admitted his success. 'The tone of the Irish members towards Mr. Balfour has much changed,' the Queen wrote to Mr. Goschen, who was temporary leader of the House of Commons when Mr. Smith was ill. 'Though they are occasionally violent, they do not care to conceal their admiration for his great ability, and appear to enjoy his retorts and replies to their arguments and suggestions.' [307]

So popular did Mr. Balfour become among Irish peasants that one old woman was heard addressing her pig as 'Arthur James.'

§ v — 1892

NOT MANY of the Queen's eighty years passed without some private sorrow or public disaster to mar her happiness. It is the lot of most people to be plunged into bereavement perhaps four or five times in their life. But the Queen spent few years without legitimate reason for mourning, and these melancholy occasions were most often in the years when there was a change of Government or a war. The year 1892 began with the personal unhappiness over the death of the Duke of Clarence, and it ended with what the Queen viewed as a disaster, the return of a Liberal Government under Mr. Gladstone. The death of her grandson was made increasingly sad because his betrothal to Princess Mary of Teck had been announced only a few weeks before. Prince Albert Victor had been waiting at Windsor one day when the Queen returned, with the shy request that he might speak to her alone. 'I suspected something at once,' wrote the Queen. 'He came in and said, "I have some good news to tell you; I am engaged to May Teck."' The Queen had been delighted, for she had 'much wished' for the marriage.

In January, the grandson whom she loved and understood was buried in the Chapel in which his wedding had been arranged. Prince George was now heir to the throne, after his father. The feelings of the people, plunged from the anticipation of marriage to death, slowly turned towards the new eldest son. His courage and diligence became matters of congratulation, and the adapting of his life and training to the new object of ruling the country was one of the problems which arose out of the tragedy of his brother's death.

Chapter Thirty-Three

§ 1 — 1892

IN MAY Mr. Gladstone spoke in the House of Commons
for more than an hour, 'with a vigour and animation
most remarkable in a man of eighty-two.' [308] When he
was not in the House, or speaking to the big audiences in
the provinces over which he wielded a magic, inexplicable power, Gladstone retired to Hawarden. There he
enjoyed his indignation against Lord Salisbury: there he
turned to his scheme for Ireland, and to the physical exercise which was to fit his body for his last battle. His
leadership of political thought had been shaken but in no
sense destroyed. His followers still pledged themselves to
him as their prophet.

The slow pendulum of political favour swung back,
and in July of 1892 the sixth year of Lord Salisbury's Parliament ended. In May a meeting had been held at
Devonshire House and Salisbury announced to the Queen
that it had been decided to dissolve Parliament at the end
of June. The Queen was at Balmoral, dividing her days
between the moors which she loved and the desk which
she loved less. She received Lord Salisbury's letters and
wondered again, as she had so often wondered, what the
impending change would bring. Her first thought in the
event of the Conservative fall was to send for Lord Rosebery. She had long thought of him as her next Liberal
Prime Minister. But, in the moment of being favourite
among the least favoured party, he had risked losing the

309

Queen's patronage by attacking Lord Salisbury in a speech at Edinburgh.[309]

The Queen said this made her sending for him *impossible*. The alternative was more than impossible. '...the G.O.M.[310] at eighty-two' was 'a very *alarming look-out.*' The Queen added in her letter to her Secretary that she feared 'a great deal of trouble.' The only compensations on the eve of the drastic political changes were in her family life. The Prince of Wales was tender and helpful and Prince George came and talked to her after breakfast. She thought him to be 'a dear boy with much character and most affectionate.' [311]

In July the Queen was at Osborne, near enough to London for every snippet of political gossip and every wave of anxiety to reach her. The results of the July elections came in slowly. On the 6th, the Conservatives had lost twelve seats but they had gained five. On July 7th, Mr. Gladstone 'got in' for Midlothian with four hundred less majority than before. On July 20th, Sir Henry Ponsonby reported to his mistress that the Parliament which has just been elected was 'far more democratic than the former one' and that the Labour Party 'must have a representative in the Government.' The Queen saw no compensations in the disaster. She clung to the grim hope that the 'small and divided majority,' and 'Mr. Gladstone's eyes and excitability,' might keep them all in a state of uncertainty. She continued in her letter to Sir Henry Ponsonby, 'As for the trouble and fatigue to the Queen, which she feels particularly unfit for, not one of these greedy place-seekers...care a straw for what their old Sovereign suffers. This is a very bitter feeling....

'...Lord Rosebery she *must* see and talk to *before* seeing *anyone else,* if there is an adverse vote. The Queen is glad that Mr. Gladstone is determined about his Home Rule, as that is sure to bring him into great difficulties. . . . Mr. Gladstone has brought so much personal violence into the contest, and used such insolent language, that the Queen is quite shocked and ashamed.'

In her despair the Queen turned to her son. Lord Rosebery would not be her Prime Minister, but he must be given the Foreign Office. Lord Rosebery was away on board a yacht and there was no way of bringing him into the grim shuffle of appointments and honours. The Queen suggested that the Prince of Wales might communicate with Rosebery, as a personal friend. The excitements crystallised into decision on August 11th, when the Government was defeated by a majority of forty votes. In the afternoon of August 12th, Lord Salisbury travelled down to Osborne to resign, and when the audience was over Queen Victoria wrote a bitter and chilling letter to his inevitable successor:

'Lord Salisbury having placed his resignation in the Queen's hands, which she has accepted with much regret, she now desires to ask Mr. Gladstone if he is prepared to try and form a Ministry to carry on the Government of the country.

'The Queen need scarcely add that she trusts that Mr. Gladstone and his friends will continue to maintain and promote the honour and welfare of her great Empire.'

The Queen left the subtle duty of inducing Lord Rosebery to accept the Foreign Secretaryship entirely to the Prince of Wales. It was the first independent commission of this magnitude she had given him. '. . . It would not do for me to press Lord Rosebery to join this Government,' the Queen wrote to the Prince.[312] She had heard that Lord Rosebery did not wish 'to *throw in his lot with these people,* as if he did so *now* he could never free himself from them and it would naturally ruin his career.' The Queen wrote, 'If I tried to press him and he did it *merely* to *oblige me against* his *own* wish and convictions, it would put me under obligations to him, and I might find myself in a very awkward position.'

On the same day the Prince wrote a letter to Rosebery which might be quoted almost in full because of the pleasant glimpse it gives of the writer's friendly candour:

MY DEAR ROSEBERY,—Nobody dislikes more than I do to interfere in matters which not only do not concern me, but which might be looked upon as indiscreet; but as we are such old friends and have so freely talked on so many subjects, especially regarding politics, the probability of a Liberal Government coming into power which has now become a fact, you will, I am sure, forgive my writing to say with what deep concern I have learnt from public rumour that you are disinclined to accept office in Mr. Gladstone's Government. That you may differ with him in many salient points I can easily understand and appreciate; but I, for one, who have my country's interest so deeply at heart, would deeply deplore if you were unwilling to accept the post of Secretary of State for Foreign Affairs—a post which you have filled before with such great ability, which has not only been appreciated at home, but by all foreign countries.

Though I know that the Queen has no desire to press you to accept this post, which for reasons best known to yourself you are disinclined to take, still I know how much she wishes for it; and I for one do most earnestly hope that you will reconsider what I understand is your present decision.... Let me, therefore, implore of you to accept office (if Mr. Gladstone will give you a free hand in foreign affairs, and not bind you to agree with him in *all* his home measures) for the Queen's sake and for that of our great Empire!

Forgive me bothering you, my dear Rosebery; but I should not write so strongly if I did not feel the grave importance of your accepting office in the present serious political crisis. Ever yours very sincerely,

ALBERT EDWARD.

312

On August 15th Lord Rosebery answered the letter. He agreed to accept office and he thanked the Prince for 'this fresh proof' of his 'constant friendship.' The two letters [313] marked an achievement in the life of the Prince of Wales. The Queen had allowed him to speak for her in one of the grave moments of her political experience and, in a sense, the Prince had appointed his first Minister.

Lord Salisbury's Government went to Osborne for its last council—the Prime Minister 'could hardly speak' as he gave the Queen the Foreign Office seal and thanked her for her kindness. Gladstone had already been received —the audience did not last very long. 'Mr. Gladstone sat close up to me,' wrote the Queen,[314] 'as he said he had grown deaf, but that I need not raise my voice, as it was clear. It is rather trying and anxious work to have to take as Prime Minister a man of eighty-two and a half, who really seems no longer quite fitted to be at the head of a Government, and whose views and principles are somewhat dangerous!!'

Mr. Gladstone bore his eighty-two years with courage. Two weeks after his first audience, while he was at Hawarden, 'a wild cow which had escaped into the woods actually rushed at him, throwing him upon his back whilst it stood over him; but he never for a moment lost his presence of mind, and, though having little breath to spare, he managed to get up and sheltered himself behind a tree, when he had the relief of seeing the cow, losing sight of him, walk away.' [315]

The Liberal régime began again and Queen Victoria clung to the hope of Lord Rosebery's calm control of foreign affairs and influence in the Cabinet. She watched the unfolding of Mr. Gladstone's policy with alarm: she deplored the lowering of Britain's name abroad and she wrote to Lord Rosebery, 'The fate of Gordon is not, and will not be, forgotten in Europe, and we must take great care in what we do.'[316]

§ II — 1892

THE PRINCE OF WALES flourished more willingly than his mother under Mr. Gladstone's Government, and the Prime Minister, Lord Rosebery and other members of the Cabinet encouraged his increasing links with the Administration and his interests in organised societies. In December, to the gratification of the Ministers, the Prince agreed to serve on the Commission formed to investigate the subject of relief for the aged poor.[317] His immediate wish was to include representatives of the working classes on the Commission. He presaged the changes of the times by inviting both the workers' representatives to Sandringham for week-ends. The sincerity of his approach to these new duties is indicated in the attendance figures of the meetings of the Commission. Out of forty-eight sessions, the Prince appeared at thirty-five. We are given a picture of him at one of the meetings in the reminiscences of James Stuart.[318] 'The Prince attended very regularly, and asked, when his turn came, very good questions.... I soon found out that they were of his own initiative, and that he really had a very considerable grasp of the subjects he dealt with.... He, like many other people when they are sitting on a committee, drew with a pencil on a piece of paper for a considerable part of the time. He drew Union Jacks, and he had two pencils, a red and a blue, besides his black one, which lay beside him always.'

Chapter Thirty-Four

§ 1 — 1893

THE EGYPTIANS made many mistakes as they floundered along under the ægis of the British Government, and early in 1893 their intrigues led them into new mischief. Railways, street lamps, theatres, plumbing and bathrooms had been introduced into Cairo before the Anglo-French occupation, so that it was in neither comforts nor amusements that the Egyptians were to learn from their British overlords. The benefits which Lord Cromer bestowed upon the country were through the science of administration, in which the Anglo-Saxon's reputed honesty had always given him an advantage over other colonising countries. But the Egyptians did not take kindly to the dull, reliable policy which had been imported from Whitehall. The Oriental becomes fuddled as a tipsy man when he smells intrigue, and in spite of Lord Cromer's firm hold on Egyptian affairs in the nineties, the palace of Khedive Tewfik was full of whisperings, sly *billets doux* and plots.

Tewfik, who seems to have been egged on by the Sultan, dismissed his Prime Minister in January in favour of a man who was the enemy of British influence. Lord Cromer wished to frighten the Egyptians by showing the mailed fist, but Mr. Gladstone forgot the lessons of Majuba and Khartoum and he again held back from action. The strength of the Queen's character must be insisted upon again at this point, where we find a dreary Cabinet

awakened by her reproaches and her persistence. Lord
Cromer had asked for reinforcements to remind the Egyptians of the power they were foolishly defying. He had
insisted on Tewfik's dismissal of the new minister and
upon an appointment which pleased him. Thus far the
Cabinet concurred, but Mr. Gladstone's pacifist tradition
prevented the Government from sending reinforcements
to Egypt. It was 'inconceivable' to the Queen 'that a
handful of men sitting in a room in London, the greater
part knowing little about Egypt, should pretend to say
whether there is danger or not!' [319]

Again the Queen's letters forced the Cabinet to action.
On the night in 1885 when news of Gordon's death arrived in England, Gladstone had been seen in a London
theatre. He had never been allowed to forget this clumsi-
ness, nor did the Queen neglect to remind him of Gordon
at the time of Cromer's desperate predicament. There was
panic among the Europeans in Egypt and the crazy Egyptians were pasting offensive hand-bills on the houses of
Cairo. The intrigues of both Turkish and French agents
added to Tewfik's bewilderment. British soldiers and their
intimidating rifles flashing in the sunshine beside the
Canal were the only means by which the Queen's power
could be impressed upon the country and she wrote to
Mr. Gladstone: [320]

'It is surely unjustifiable to leave a British representative ignorant of whether the Government wish to maintain the occupation of Egypt or to suffer their garrison to scuttle or be driven
out of it. The moment that necessity arises is the moment too late
for action, as must be remembered in the sad and terrible case of
Khartoum and cruel fate of Gordon. If troops are now sent to
Cairo the necessity will not arise and any danger of war will be
averted.'

The Queen won, and two days after the above letter reached Mr. Gladstone, he wrote to assure her that the battalion which was to leave Egypt should remain and that a troop-ship which happened to be on the way home, was to be detained in the Canal.

Two short notes end the story. The Queen wrote to Mr. Gladstone that she could not 'sufficiently express her relief and satisfaction at the decision now come to by her Government,'[321] and Sir Henry Ponsonby wrote to his mistress '... this awakening of spirit in the Cabinet is entirely due to your Majesty's pressing remonstrances.'[322]

§ II — 1893

THE BRILLIANCE which attended the marriages of the Queen's relatives into European Courts has faded sadly in the twentieth century. The descriptions of the wedding of the Duke of Edinburgh in St. Petersburg in 1874 seem to belong to the theatre rather than to life when we read the story in the light of existence in Soviet Russia to-day. And the high hopes which went with the Princess Royal when she married the son of the Crown Prince of Prussia in 1858 seem to end dismally among the woods at Doorn.

If the ambitious Leopold of Coburg, who formed connections with half the countries of Europe, were alive to-day, he would look wide-eyed upon the scenes of the twentieth century. His own Belgium remains loyal to his descendants because of the liberal policy which he planted in the country. In England, Prince Albert's descendants have raised the crown higher and higher, increasing their influence, until to-day constitutional monarchy is secure: the most secure power in the shifting tides of British affairs. But monarchy in other countries affected by the Coburgs is as good as dead.

To ramble among theories is dangerous, but a study of British domestic life and political history proves to us that the family security of the last three generations of the British royal family has contributed largely to the Empire's happiness. Wars in other countries ruled by Queen Victoria's relations always brought domestic conflict in time of battle. Because of the foreign marriages contracted by their rulers, the people of the countries became suspicious of their imported consorts. The isolation of the Empress Frederick in Prussia might have driven a weaker woman to the fate of the Empress of Mexico.

In the early years ambition and foreign policy may have urged the Queen to favour the marriages of her children into foreign Courts. Perhaps she came to suspect the wisdom of these alliances in the nineties, when she contemplated the unhappiness of her daughter in Potsdam and the diplomatic failure of the marriage with a Russian Grand Duchess.

If it is true that the Queen changed her ideas about royal marriages, Britain can thank heaven for the good fortune which urged her to favour the marriage of Prince George to an English Princess in 1893. The influence of this union upon British life, especially during the years 1914–1918, cannot be fully realised in this generation. The perspective of a hundred years will perhaps allow some scholar to write of the confidence, domestic security, moral courage and allegiance to duty which have flowed from Buckingham Palace and permeated the lives of the mass of British people since 1910.

The Queen was delighted when she was told that Prince George had proposed marriage to Princess May and been

THE QUEEN'S SITTING-ROOM AT BALMORAL CASTLE

accepted. The young Prince came to her to talk over the arrangements for the wedding and her comment after the interview was, 'It is a pleasure to do so with him, as he is so sensible.' The betrothal of her grandson stirred the Queen to displays of interest and vitality, all the more enchanting when one remembers her age, with the attendant weakening of sight and activity. Her birthday in May, celebrated at Balmoral, evoked a pathetic revolt against time. 'My poor old birthday,' she wrote,[323] 'my seventy-fourth. I wish now it was instead sixty-fourth. . . .'

There had been few signs of life in Buckingham Palace for thirty-three years. On the dreaded occasions when the Queen opened Parliament she had stayed there for a few hours and when the Shah of Persia came, the rooms were opened up for the strange oriental company which came with him. It is said that he looked out of his window one morning, saw a sheep and sent for it to be brought in and sacrificed on the drawing-room carpet. And in 1887 the dust-covers had been whirled off the beautiful gilt chairs for the celebrations of the Jubilee. But for the most part the shutters were closed and the stillness of death was upon the heart of London. Again in 1893 the warm July sunshine burst into the vast rooms of the palace. The Queen had come up to London for the marriage of Prince George and Princess May.

The Queen's own Journal gives a more simple and enchanting picture of the 'great day' than any paraphrase:

'. . . the crowds, the loyalty and enthusiasm were immense. Telegrams began pouring in from an early hour. Was rolled to our usual dining-room, to see from the window all that was going on. . . . Already, whilst I was still in bed, I heard the distant hum of the people. I breakfasted alone with Beatrice. Began to dress soon after eleven. I wore my wedding lace over a light black

319

stuff, and my wedding veil surmounted by a small coronet. While I was dressing, Mary (herself very handsome) brought in May, who looked very sweet. Her dress was very simple, of white satin with a silver design of roses, shamrocks, thistles and orange flowers, interwoven. On her head she had a small wreath of orange flowers, myrtle, and white heather surmounted by a diamond necklace I gave her, which can also be worn as a diadem, and her mother's wedding veil.'

The wedding was to be in the Chapel of St. James's Palace where the Queen herself was married in 1840.

'...I was the first to arrive and enter the Chapel, which was not intended, but which I was glad of, as I saw all the processions, which were very striking and dignified. There was a flourish of trumpets, followed by a march played outside, and then taken up by the organ, as the Royalties slowly entered.... The Bridegroom's procession followed rapidly, being supported by his father and uncle Affie, all in naval uniform. They had to wait a very short time, when the Bride appeared, followed by her ten dear bridesmaids.... I could not but remember that *I* had stood, where May did, fifty-three years ago, and dear Vicky thirty-five years ago, and that the dear ones, who stood where Georgie did, were gone from us. May these dear children's happiness last longer!'

The Queen returned to Buckingham Palace 'before everyone else.'

'The heat was very great, quite overwhelming. Went to the middle room, with the balcony, overlooking the Mall, and stepped out amidst much cheering. Very soon the Bride and Bridegroom arrived, and I stepped out on the balcony with them, taking her by the hand, which produced another great outburst of cheering.'

When luncheon was over, the Queen went into her own room and when the bride and bridegroom had been photographed, Princess May went to see her, 'looking very pretty in her dress of white poplin, edged with gold, and a pretty little toque with roses.' When Princess May left her, the Queen was 'rolled over to the middle room looking down the Mall, and found all the family assembled there.' Outside, thousands of Londoners were staring at the door through which the bride and bridegroom were to appear. Within, the Queen turned in her rolling chair and 'Wished the young couple affectionately good-bye.' [324]

§ III — 1893–1894

MR. GLADSTONE devoted the last year of his power as Prime Minister to his old love, the Home Rule Bill for Ireland. Not even the support of the Irish Nationalists was enough to bring him success in this last dramatic experiment in legislation. The support which he inspired in the House of Commons was swept aside when the Bill came before the House of Lords. The Irish Home Rule Bill had changed during its last seven years of incubation. Gladstone wished the Irish members to retain their seats in the British Parliament with the power to vote on Imperial questions but not on those affecting Britain alone. Ireland again dominated British affairs, and Mr. Gladstone neglected the many other members of the Empire family through his devotion to the one, recalcitrant brat. All through the summer Westminster wrangled, sometimes with brilliant oratory and sometimes in angry, undignified scenes. At eighty-three, Mr. Gladstone dominated the House: he was still a giant and his voice retained its beauty. But there were other speakers rising at the heels of the veteran, and the Queen noted with pleasure that they made fierce attacks upon the 'impracticable measure.' On February 13th the Queen was delighted because the Bill was 'pulled quite to pieces' in a splendid speech by Mr. Balfour.[325] After two years of silence Lord Randolph Churchill rose to support Mr. Balfour's arguments.[326] When they were not attacking the Bill at Westminster, Lord Salisbury and Mr. Balfour went into the provinces with almost the zest of Gladstone's own mission in Midlothian.

At times the Queen feared that the 'unfortunate' Bill might be carried. Mr. Chamberlain was already free of his radical swaddling clothes and his opinions showed that vision was being added to his inherent powers. The Queen noted his 'splendid speech' when the Bill was read the first time. But she wrote that it was 'sad to think' that the Bill was to be read once more. She ended the entry for the day in her Journal, 'Please God, in committee it will be much altered. But I am much disturbed about this. . . .'[327]

Almost five months afterwards the Queen wrote, still haunted by the endless debates, 'The House of Commons seems to be going from bad to worse, nothing but wrangling and quarrelling. . . .'[328] Two more months were to pass: many days were squandered and many tempers lost before the fearful second of September when Mr. Gladstone's Bill was carried in the Commons by a majority of thirty-four. Seven days afterwards it was rejected in the House of Lords by a majority of three hundred and sixty-eight. To the Queen it was all in the manner of coming into a haven after a storm. What was most 're-markable' to her was that the crowd of Londoners waiting outside the House of Lords 'cheered very much' when the news of the crushing majority filtered out to them.[329] They cheered again when Lord Salisbury appeared. The fickle public, loyal to ideas but seldom to leaders, surrounded Salisbury with glory again and, with the remnants of his rejected Bill in his hands, Mr. Gladstone retired into the background. But he still held the control of the Commons in his hands and it was not until March of the new year that the undermining of the leader's power brought about his final fall. There was something magnificent about the deaf, half-blind father of Liberalism living through the failure of the Bill to which he had devoted the last fine energies of his life. There was no phrase in the Queen's letters to show that she relented before the picture of an old enemy, magnificent in defeat, his senses failing, still stumbling on into battle. It was not until March 2nd, 1894, that Mr. Gladstone stood up to speak in the House of Commons for the last time. He still spoke of war rather than peace. His last words were a protest against the Lords for their treatment of the Commons. He was so deaf that he could not hear any voice that spoke against him: so blind that he saw both friends and enemies through a mist. The senses had closed in on him and his fierce life in the Commons was ended.

Three days before, Mr. Gladstone had sent for Sir Henry Ponsonby. 'It was about nothing more nor less than his resignation.... He is growing blind,' wrote the Queen, 'and is already very deaf, so that his decision is not to be wondered at.' The 'secret' was already the talk of London, but nobody dared to talk of it to the Queen at dinner at night, nobody, 'except Bertie.' [330]

Mr. Gladstone went down to Windsor on March 3rd with his resignation. There was talk of his failing eyes. They were obliged to sit very close as the Queen listened to him. There was no mention of the dissatisfaction in the Cabinet, the division of opinion over Gladstone's cheese-paring tricks with the navy. There was no show of tenderness for the veteran: no relaxation from the old rigidity and coldness. The Queen's Journal shows no tenderness for the old man's plight, no attempt at compassion which she did not feel. '... he would take an early opportunity of retiring from Parliament. He then kissed my hand and left.' [331]

When Mr. Gladstone had gone, the Queen went to her desk and, without consulting Minister or friend, she wrote to Lord Rosebery, 'urging him to accept the Premiership, if even only for a short time, for the good of the country.' [332] Lord Rosebery did not want to be Prime Minister but he sent his acceptance to the Queen. One fear haunted him as he wrote the letter. He told the Queen that he set 'the greatest value on the character of his relations' with her. 'Anything that changed it would cause him deep pain.' The Queen's 'constant goodness to him,' more especially at the time of his wife's death, had 'inspired him with the deepest feelings of loyal gratitude and affection' and he was afraid lest, at a time when he might pursue a policy to which his honour bound him, he might find himself in 'acute conflict' with his Queen.[333]

Queen Victoria soothed him. She thought it hardly possible, 'or at any rate probable,' that there would be trouble which might alienate him from her. In her letter [334] the Queen wrote:

'She does not object to Liberal measures which are not revolutionary, and she does not think it possible that Lord Rosebery will destroy well-tried, valued, and necessary institutions for the sole purpose of flattering useless Radicals or pandering to the pride of those whose only desire is their own self-gratification.'

Thus Mr. Gladstone withdrew from the service to his country and from the long, chilly association with his

Queen. There was no kindly scene and even her letter of farewell seemed to be wrung from her unwillingly. She thought he was right in wishing to retire, 'after so many years of arduous labour and responsibility....' She trusted that he would 'enjoy peace and quiet, with his excellent and devoted wife in health and happiness,' and that his eyesight might improve.

Early on the morning of March 3rd, before her husband's visit, Mrs. Gladstone had travelled down to Windsor to plead with the Queen. Few more pathetic interviews are recorded in the Queen's Journal. Mrs. Gladstone sought the Queen early, after breakfast. She was 'very much upset, poor thing.' She asked to be allowed to speak because her husband 'could not speak.' Mrs. Gladstone talked through tears. She knew the grim battles of Gladstone's life: she knew what the weight of his Sovereign's persistent frustration and dislike must have been to him. She pleaded with the Queen to believe that 'whatever his errors might have been,' Gladstone's 'devotion to Your Majesty and the Crown were very great.'

The Queen recorded the unhappy scene. 'She repeated this twice, and begged me to allow her to tell him that I believed it, which I did; for I am convinced it is the case, though at times his actions might have made it difficult to believe....I kissed her when she left.' [336]

The years of life still vouchsafed to Mr. Gladstone were not lightened by any gentle gestures of commiseration from the Queen and when he died, in May of 1898, she remained rigid: she did not unbend, even in the face of death.

The Prince of Wales was less censorious. When Mr. Gladstone resigned in 1894, there had been an exchange of gracious letters and the Prince had expressed his hope that Gladstone would count him as one of his 'many friends and admirers.' He said that both the Princess and himself had valued the friendship of the Prime Minister and Mrs. Gladstone for many years. When Gladstone died, the Prince acted as a pall-bearer and, when the coffin had been lowered into the grave in the Abbey, he crossed to the place where Mrs. Gladstone was seated and, after speaking a few sympathetic words, he kissed her hand. The Princely gesture set the seal upon a friendship which had endured for half a century.

The Queen had received Gladstone once, at Cimiez, before his death. Even then, when he was no longer a danger to her peace of mind, when he was old and blind and tired, she held back and gave no sign of friendly pity or forgiveness. A year afterwards, when Mr. Gladstone died at Hawarden, the Queen turned to one of her Ladies, regretting the necessity of writing a letter of sympathy to Mrs. Gladstone. 'How can I say that I am sorry when I am not?' she said.[337]

Chapter Thirty-Five

§ 1 — 1894

WHITE LODGE is a simple and beautiful house standing in Richmond Park. The house was built by George the First as 'a place of refreshment after the fatigues of the chase.' The ground upon which it stands has an older story to tell —a keeper's lodge belonging to Wolsey once stood there. It was Caroline, the clever wife of George the Second, who made White Lodge into a busy and beautiful place. She kept a dairy there, and she came to love the gardens so much that the King added to the house, building curved galleries on either side of the tall, central rooms.[338]

The house was like this in June of 1894 when the first son of Prince George and Princess Mary was born, in a room which caught the sun from the east. It first shone upon him at ten o'clock in the morning. Outside the window was a line of flaming rhododendrons: a copper beech shone upon the lawn and before the house there was a noble cedar beneath which the Prince was to play when he grew older. It was beneath this cedar that Princess Mary of Teck used to take tea. Here too, Prince Albert Edward of Wales sat with his tutors, in the fifties, when the days were warm. The magnolias on the white walls flowered in celebration of the Prince's birth, and through the warm June days the bees made themselves drunk and heavy with pollen among the ivory petals.

Two grandmothers were in the bedroom when a Prince was born. An hour afterwards he was carried into the sitting-room where his grandfather and the future Tsar of Russia were waiting. The Russian Prince had hurried across Europe so that he might be present to sponsor the new baby.

When the little Prince was two days old his great-grand-mother travelled over from Windsor to see him. There were great crowds as the carriages rolled up the Richmond Hill. 'After tea,' wrote the Queen, 'I went in to see the baby, a fine, strong-looking child.' [339] On July 16th the Queen went to Richmond again, for the Prince's christening.

'The dear fine baby, wearing the Honiton lace robe (made for Vicky's christening, worn by all our children and my English grandchildren), was brought in ... and handed to me. I then gave him to the Archbishop and received him back.... The child was very good. There was an absence of all music, which I thought a pity. When the service was over I went with Mary to the Long Gallery, where, in '61, I used to sit with dearest Albert and look through dear Mama's letters. Had tea with May, and afterwards we were photographed, I, holding the baby on my lap, Bertie and Georgie standing behind me, thus making the four generations.' [340]

The child was called 'Edward' after his grandfather and his names included the four Patron Saints of the United Kingdom—George, Andrew, Patrick, David, the last being the name commonly used by his family and intimate friends.

Every now and then the young Prince was taken to see his great-grandmother at Windsor or in London. Her eyes were so tired that she saw him only hazily when he appeared at the far end of the long room. She complained very often now about her failing sight. Her Ministers were asked to write their letters in big, clear script so that she could read what they had to say. Her secretaries too were obliged to write their reports in schoolboy, copybook letters, with strong black ink. So that the writing should not be dimmed by blotting, Colonel Bigge, her younger secretary, had a small copper oven made. In this his memoranda were dried before they went to the Queen to be read.

No other Queen had ever been able to contemplate three generations of Princes who would rule after her. As a child she had been able to recall three Kings who ruled before her. We are told that when the young Prince was two years old he was playing at his great-grandmother's feet one day with the little Grand Duchess Olga of Russia. The little girl lost her balance and fell: the Prince helped her to her feet and kissed her. Queen Victoria leaned forward and whispered to her companion. But the day was passed for planning royal marriages before Princes and Princesses could walk.

§ II — 1894

THERE WERE times when Queen Victoria might have regretted her independent appointment of Lord Rosebery as Prime Minister. Long association with the Court had bound the Primrose family to the Queen, but the young peer had radical notions of his own about the rights of the aristocracy and the sanctity of the House of Lords. When the Queen went for her yearly holiday to Florence or to the South of France, she did not permit any slackening of vigilance or any fading of interest in the moves made on the chessboard of Westminster. Her personal faith in Lord Rosebery had been shaken several times since he became her first minister and in March she sent him a scolding letter, from the Villa Fabbricotti. The attacks upon the House of Lords had been renewed and Lord Rosebery had been guilty of supporting the reformers, although his language had been 'in a much less strong degree' than most. The Queen wrote:

'The House of Lords might possibly be improved, but it is *part* and *parcel* of the *much vaunted* and *admired British Constitution* and CANNOT be *abolished*....It has, and with truth, often been said that there are Peers whose personal character render them unfit to remain in the House of Lords. But who is to be the judge of this? And if one comes to that, are there not quite as many very bad characters and very many disloyal ones, of whom the House of Commons would be much the better to be rid?' [341]

Lord Rosebery replied with the old argument against the Lords: that they were a Conservative body, accepting the legislation of a Conservative Government 'without question or dispute.' But when a Liberal Government was in power, the Second Chamber ceased to be 'harmless.' It became active and it exercised its powers to oppose the legislation of a Government with which it had little sympathy.

Rosebery declared his deepest wish to the Queen. If the Ministry fell, he hoped to 'extricate himself from politics for ever.' But while he remained in power, he clung to his convictions and he voiced them abroad, to the chagrin of the Queen. He continued his campaign against the Lords and in June the Queen spoke *'very* openly' to him about his speeches *'out* of Parliament.' They should take 'a more serious tone and be...less jocular, which is hardly befitting a Prime Minister.' [342] She added, 'Lord Rosebery is so clever that he may be carried away by a sense of humour, which is a little dangerous.'

It was a sense of conviction rather than a sense of humour which drove Rosebery on in his campaign against lazy and ineffectual members of his own class, and in October he reached the zenith of indignation in a speech at Bradford. Two days before this the Queen had been so distressed by his threat to lay his policy before the country that she had strained her constitutional vows by appealing for help to Lord Salisbury. She declared the proposed action to be 'mischievous in the highest degree ...and disloyal.'[343] The mass of the people were not drawn into the conflict. They were too well satisfied with the action of the Lords in rejecting the Irish Home Rule Bill to be drawn into a purely political squabble. But the Queen would not be calmed. Lord Rosebery let off his rockets of indignation in the provinces, and she appealed next to the Prince of Wales for help. Perhaps through his friendship with the charming Prime Minister who unfortunately had such radical tendencies—perhaps he might curb him! 'Can you not convey your feeling on this dangerous policy to him? I think he behaved very ill to me.'[344]

The Prince shared his mother's anxiety. But this time he offered her little help. 'Fear anything I write or say will avail nothing,'[345] he telegraphed, in reply.

Lord Rosebery's violent language in his speech at Bradford brought the last, agitated reproofs down upon him. The Queen accused him of ignoring the opinion of his Sovereign and she plucked phrases from his address to support her protests. Lord Rosebery was not intimidated. But he accompanied firmness of will with gracious assurances of his loyalty. 'If by any conceivable means he could relieve your Majesty he would gladly do so,' he wrote. But he had inherited a weight of promises from Mr.

Gladstone's régime and he was obliged to go on. 'Did he believe that his resignation of office would assist your Majesty, he would ask your Majesty's permission to retire to-morrow.'

The Queen revealed a liberal and patient frame of mind in her innumerable letters. In answer to one of Lord Rosebery's communications, she wrote:

'He is mistaken ... in thinking that "*any dealing with the H. of L.*" is *distasteful* to her. The Queen fully recognises the necessity for its reform. ...' [346]

When she had given Lord Rosebery this glimpse of her personal thought about the Second Chamber, she added a sentence which shows with what tenacity the Queen clung to her trust as Monarch:

'... the Queen would ask Lord Rosebery and his Cabinet to bear in mind that fifty-seven years ago the Constitution was delivered into her keeping, and that, right or wrong, she has her views as to the fulfilment of that trust.'

The letter ended with one more significant sentence:

'She cannot but think Lord Rosebery will feel that his position is not the only difficult one in these democratic days.'

Lord Rosebery pursued his dream of a refreshed and reformed House of Lords and the Queen clung to the obligations of her Constitution. But the tussle did not evoke feverish interest outside the Court and the Cabinet. The change of Government in the new year brought an end to the agitation. The anxiety of the Queen, her government and her people was drawn into a wider arena in 1895 through unsettlement in Africa, America, India

and Germany, and the old ghost of Lords reform was
allowed to rest.

§ III

ONE ENCHANTING impression which remains after reading
Queen Victoria's letters and journals is her freedom from
jealousy and her child-like admiration for beauty in other
women. The Queen was never beautiful, although the
poise of her head, the grace of her walk and the charm of
her voice and laugh gave an illusion of beauty, especially
when she was young. Nor did the Queen revel in clothes
or furbelows. Indeed, as she grew older, she tended to
dowdiness, preferring comfort to fashion. But her delight
over prettiness and clothes of other women never abated
and every now and then one comes upon a sentence to
prove this, written in her Journal late at night, when her
own homely black dress had been put away. 'Mrs. Chamberlain looked lovely, and was as charming as ever' when
she dined on March 8th in '94. By this time Mr. Chamberlain was also 'very agreeable,' and the day in '83, when his
'dangerous and improper language' offended the Queen,
was forgotten.

Sometimes the Queen commented on her own lack of
beauty, in a joking fashion. The comment was often the
prelude to a generous message to one of her guests or one
of her Ladies. Would she please wear such and such a
dress with such and such jewels, because she looked so
pretty in that ensemble? The Queen's relations with her
Ladies were mostly happy. Her instinct for people with
character usually saved her from unfortunate appointments and although being "in waiting" was a hard task
and not always comfortable in winter, because of the

Queen's love for cold and fresh air, the Ladies were drawn to her with a deep and personal devotion which never wavered. Her sense of justice was the key to the Queen's relationships with servants as well as courtiers, and if ever she spoke in anger and found afterwards that she was wrong, she would never hesitate to send for the person she had blamed, however humble, and say, 'I am sorry, I was wrong.' This justice permeated the Court and the staffs of the several palaces. If there were occasional displays of temper or intolerance (so naïvely confessed in the pages of her diary) they never left rancour or spite behind them.

While dwelling upon the 'goodness' of the Queen, it might not be irrelevant to deny a story of her childhood which has been told a thousand times in books and newspapers. It has been said that when Baroness Lehzen told her, as a girl, that she would some day be Queen of England, she had answered, 'I will be good.' The Queen denied this story one day, late in her life. She vowed that it was an invention. 'I never said such a thing. How could I?' she said.[347]

§ IV — 1894–1895

WHEN LORD ROSEBERY became Prime Minister after Mr. Gladstone's retirement, he described his seat as 'the most uneasy throne in Europe since that of Poland.' Many circumstances contributed to his discomfort. He had inherited Mr. Gladstone's policy and a sheaf of his promises. His rival, Sir William Harcourt, was Leader of the House of Commons, and it was not long before Prime Minister and Leader disliked each other so violently that they never spoke and seldom corresponded. Lord Rosebery sometimes poured out his woes to the Queen, and although she sympathised, she begged him to act 'as a check and a drag upon his Cabinet.' But Rosebery's position became more and more ridiculous. Sir William Harcourt's bitter hostility to him and the narrow majority by which the Government's bills were passed, only to be rejected by the Lords, created a state which tied his hands so that 'for all practical purposes,' he wrote to the Queen, he might as well be 'in the Tower of London.'

The end came in June. The Queen was on a train, travelling south from Balmoral. She took out her Journal to record the extraordinary circumstances. 'Heard with astonishment by telegraph, which I got at Carlisle, that ... the Government had been defeated.' The crisis had followed the announcement in the House of the retirement of the Duke of Cambridge from the office of Commander-in-Chief, a reform and change which is described in detail in the letters of the Queen for 1894. A few hours after the announcement had been made the Government had been defeated by seven votes, 'on a charge of keeping an insufficient reserve of cordite ammunition.'

Lord Rosebery's Government resigned and the Queen sent for Lord Salisbury again. What was an excitement in the lives of politicians was now no more than a grim duty to the Queen. For almost sixty years she had been summoning new Ministers and saying good-bye to old ones. But this was to be the last occasion upon which a Prime Minister went to Windsor to kiss her hand and accept the seals of office. Lord Rosebery withdrew, to his 'immense relief,' after his short, harassed season of power. There was a faintly Disraelian touch about the manner of his going. He had been an unruly Prime Minister, but he had never lacked the little gestures of chivalry which

335

pleased the Queen. There had been a touch of gallantry, here and there, to excuse his blundering attacks on the Lords. None more welcome than his letter of farewell:

'...I would ask leave with humble duty to write a word that I could not speak.

'I can say with absolute truth that my only regret in laying down my office is the cessation of my personal relations with your Majesty. May I then, once for all, and from the bottom of my heart, thank your Majesty for your abundant and gracious kindness to me? Whether in public or private life I shall always remember it with the deepest gratitude and pray for the continuance of your Majesty's health and glorious reign.' [348]

The Queen opened her heart to this pledge of Rosebery's devotion. She sent him an answer, beginning, 'Dear Lord Rosebery,' and at the end she wrote, 'I wish to offer you a little souvenir, which I hope will recall me to your memory, and that you will not forget me.' [349] The souvenir was an 'exquisite statuette.'

Chapter Thirty-Six

§ 1 — 1895–1896

IF THE achievement at the close of Queen Victoria's reign is to be appreciated, the number of her years and her increasing physical infirmities must be recalled. At an age when widows were inclined to take to their sofas, she ruled an Empire, wrestling with the changes of government, the wave of troubles which swept over the world in the nineties and, in the end, the tragedy of the South African war. She contributed force and decision to every cause and, in the last five years of her life, lame, tired and barely able to read, she almost guided the world. Those who refused her guidance were at least intimidated by her will.

The Queen was seventy-seven years old. On January 2nd of the new year she wrote in her Journal, 'Beatrice read me telegram after tea, as my sight is so bad, and I have not yet succeeded in getting spectacles to suit.' [350] Five days afterwards she complained again, 'So much to do, and my troublesome eyes make everything much more difficult.' [351]

The year had not been tranquil. There had been war between China and Japan and in the repercussions there had been a new strain in the relations between Britain and Russia. French and German ambitions in Africa added another problem to the weight upon her and the sins of Abdul Hamid aroused her once more, in defence of the massacred Armenians. There had been the passing

337

of Rosebery's Government and the establishing of Salisbury's solid Coalition to increase her burdens. Almost as soon as Lord Salisbury assumed office there had been friction with America over the boundary between the South American Republic of Venezuela and British Guiana. A bombardment of letters and despatches had followed and feeling in America had become so wild that President Cleveland had appealed to the national emotions of his people. The result had been panic and collapse in Wall Street. The whole world seemed to be shaking with changes. In South Africa, Kruger was astir. He had celebrated Emperor William's birthday by pleading for deeper friendship between Germany and the Transvaal.

In Europe, naval tacticians had been aroused by the opening of the Kiel Canal in June of 1894. The Emperor had led squadrons from the navies of Europe (even the navy of France) through the new water-way. His fatal pompousness had been inflated, and when he visited Cowes in the summer of 1895, he so bullied Lord Salisbury [352] (by this time Prime Minister and Foreign Secretary) that both the Queen and the Prince were furious. Lord Salisbury, being the only gentleman present at the interview, merely remarked to a friend that the Emperor apparently forgot that being the Queen's Minister, 'he could not work for the King of Prussia.' [353]

Here were mighty burdens for a woman of seventy-seven to shoulder. The failure of her eyes did not lessen the Queen's activities. She had made a significant gesture in February of 1894, when she gave a final proof of her devotion and trust in her heir after a long and unrelenting apprenticeship. She proposed that while she was abroad on holiday he should be appointed Guardian of the Realm. The first letter of a series upon the subject was written by Lieut.-Col. Bigge to Lord Rosebery. 'The Queen desires that you should make the proposal to the Prince of Wales regarding the Guardianship of the Realm, as her Majesty prefers not suggesting to H.R.H. what she thinks will be inconvenient and what he might find difficult to decline coming direct from her. And the Queen does not want to prevent his going abroad.' [354]

Lord Rosebery had already written to the Queen, agreeing that the Prince was the 'proper person to be entrusted with the formal guardianship of the Realm.' [355] He approached the Prince with the Queen's suggestion on February 13th. The Prince was 'ready and willing' to undertake the duties imposed upon him and, wrote Lord Rosebery, he would 'greatly curtail, if not altogether forgo, his trip abroad.' [356]

The project was abandoned for political reasons, on the advice of the Cabinet. But the spontaneous suggestion had come from the Queen and it provides an important and welcome fact in the long and often agitated relationship between mother and son.

§ II — 1896

WHEN LORD SALISBURY formed his Coalition Government in July, 1895, he had the support of a stalwart company of representative politicians. He himself undertook the duties of Foreign Secretary in addition to those of Prime Minister. The Duke of Devonshire, leader of the Liberal Unionists, became President of the Council, Mr. Balfour the First Lord of the Treasury, and Mr. Chamberlain, the typical Radical Imperialist, controlled the Colonial office.

§ III — 1896

THE NOTORIOUS Jameson raid was the first startling episode in this, the last stage of the Queen's reign. The story of the raid needs no more than a sketchy outline in these pages. Dr. Jameson, who was Administrator of the British South Africa Company's territory, invaded the Transvaal with about five hundred followers, to support the Uitlanders who were oppressed by Kruger. They were denied franchise and other civil rights, and Jameson's romantic but hopeless gesture ended in his own destruction. He went on, in spite of British intervention, and after hours of disastrous fighting at Krugersdorp, he surrendered. The events which followed are in every history book. An adventure in arms loses its brave colours when it is translated from African sunshine to the grey light of London. The penmen of Whitehall cannot buckle on their swords in a crisis. The news of Jameson's invasion and surrender caused panic in Westminster and at Windsor.

The incident which matters in this story is the sending of the famous telegram of congratulation to Kruger by the German Emperor. To enumerate the follies of the Emperor is to dwell on the pranks and mischief of a child. Queen Victoria had tried, more than a year before, to excuse 'this impetuous and conceited youth.' Unfortunately the 'youth' possessed the powers of an Emperor. The Kruger telegram was the most spectacular but not the most dangerous step in the sequence of events which culminated on the disastrous day in 1914.

The previour year had widened the gulf between the Emperor and the Prince, and one must leave the crises over the Jameson raid to trace the history of their enmity since 1894. The Prince had proved his patience many times and his actions show that he tried to place the interests of his country before the healthy dislike with which he contemplated his ridiculous nephew. In the summer of 1895 the Emperor had been openly insulting to his uncle at Cowes, taunting him because he had never been on active service and referring to him, among his friends, as 'the old peacock.' Here, if anywhere, the homely adage about the pot and the kettle had its fullest application. The Prince of Wales had long before realised that the way to appease his nephew was to give him fine feathers rather than food for argument. The Highland uniform which he had presented to him, many years before, had made the Emperor long for the right to wear a kilt, not as a figure at a fancy dress ball, but as Colonel-in-Chief of a Highland Regiment. The hint had been dropped in Berlin and the Prince had tried to induce his mother to grant the Emperor the honour he craved. 'It would please him immensely,' he pleaded. The Queen was dubious. The Emperor was already an Admiral in the British Navy. If honours were showered upon him in this way, what would there be 'left for him when he is older?' she wrote. The Prince's increasing influence over his mother won in the end and, in April of 1894, the Queen consented. But the Emperor was not given the coveted kilt. He was granted the 'traditional British "Red Coat,"' and he appeared in it, ludicrously enough, during the visit to Cowes when he described the Prince of Wales as an 'old peacock.' These incidents occurred before the Jameson raid and they remained within the limits of a family quarrel, with only hints at international conflict. But the enmity sprang into flame and came perilously near to war when

341

the Emperor took the chair at a conference in the Foreign
Office in Berlin, after news of the Jameson disaster reached
Europe. The Emperor proposed measures so drastic that
his Chancellor said, '... that would mean war with England.' The Emperor, through aberrations which cannot be
explained, said, 'Yes, but only on land.' Then followed
the drafting of the fatal telegram to Kruger.[357]

The *Morning Post* announced the train of thought
which was to run through British policy for the next
eighteen years. 'The nation will never forget this telegram and it will always bear it in mind in the future
orientation of its policy.'

The old, wise hand of the Queen was raised. The anger
of the Prince was young and healthy. He wished his
mother to give the Emperor 'a good snubbing.' Her answer came back:

'Dearest Bertie, I send you here the answer I received yesterday
to my letter from William. ... It would not do to have given him
"a good snub." Those sharp, cutting answers and remarks only
irritate and do harm, and in Sovereigns and Princes should be
most carefully guarded against. William's faults come from impetuousness (as well as conceit); and calmness and firmness are
the most powerful weapons in such cases. Lord Salisbury's great
strength is his great calmness and energy, both of which Mr.
Chamberlain possesses. ...' [358]

The Prince of Wales failed to lessen his nephew's blunders by friendly approach and the only good which came
of the quarrel was a clearer understanding with his
mother. His peaceful policy showed no harvest in the
German Court, but, later in the year, there was a little
compensation for him in the visit of the Tsar and Tsaritza
to Balmoral.

Queen Victoria planned a simple reception in her Highland home, viewing the visit as a domestic rather than a diplomatic event. This time she succumbed completely to her son's will. He wished for great ceremonies and pomp, such as would bring not only the sovereigns but the people of the two countries together, in a semblance of harmony. The Prince was at Homburg when the plan for the Russian visit was announced to him. He wrote a long memorandum, with a plan for suitable celebrations. This he forwarded to the Queen's secretary with a letter. 'I know the Queen expects the visit to Balmoral to be a private one,' he wrote, but he was sure that she would 'wish all honour to be done to them in the eyes of the world, especially in those of Russia. I am so anxious that the arrival should be marked with every possible compliment for the Emperor.' [359] The Queen accepted the Prince's change in plans and she wrote to him, 'We are trying to carry out your suggestions as much as possible.' [360] Eight days afterwards she telegraphed to him, 'The more I think over the question the stronger is my conviction that in order to do as much honour as possible to the Emperor on his landing for the first time in this country as such, you should receive him on my behalf. Trust that you will be able to do this. . . .'

The Tsar and Tsaritza arrived in Britain in great glory. There were conciliatory talks as the two sovereigns walked and drove in the balmy Deeside air, and when the Tsar left for Paris almost the last words the Queen said to him—words which are interesting in the light of later history—were '. . . tell France not to be so hostile to England.' [361]

The meeting at Balmoral was celebrated by an astonishing device. The Queen recorded the event in her Journal:

VICTORIA, THE WIDOW

'At twelve went down to below the terrace, near the ballroom, and we were all photographed by Downey by the new cinematograph process, which makes moving pictures by winding off a reel of films. We were walking up and down and the children jumping about. . . .' [362]

Chapter Thirty-Seven

§ 1 — 1896–1897

THE QUEEN was consoled for the troubles in Africa and India by the calm administration at home. Her thankfulness overflowed in March when she wrote to Lord Salisbury, 'Every day I feel the blessing of a strong Government in such safe and strong hands as yours.'[363] The plots of Kruger and the duplicity of her grandson at Potsdam were less formidable when she was surrounded by statesmen who were willing to sink their party differences and pet theories in the service of the country. Mr. Chamberlain had been very 'firm and sensible'[364] over the Jameson raid, and when Mr. Balfour came to see his Sovereign in September she wrote in her Journal, 'I am struck, as is every one, by Mr. Balfour's extreme fairness, impartiality, and large-mindedness. He sees all sides of a question, is wonderfully generous in his feelings towards others, and very gentle and sweet-tempered.'[365] The debates at Westminster were not lit by the brilliance of the seventies and Lord Salisbury's chivalry was of a sterner kind than that of Lord Beaconsfield. But the calm restrained character of her Cabinet was suited to the closing years of the Queen's reign.

Queen Victoria's domestic circle had been bereaved many times in recent years. In January Prince Henry of Battenberg had died at sea, on his way home after being invalided from the Ashanti expedition. His wife, Princess Beatrice, was suddenly bereft of domestic happiness as her

345

mother had been, thirty-five years before. The shadows of mourning hung over almost every month of the last five years of the Queen's life and both the exalted and the humble fell away from the company of her friends. Her secretary, Sir Henry Ponsonby, was dead; 'good old Mrs. Symon,' who kept the shop at Balmoral, and many of the Queen's servants died of old age in the nineties. The nearness of death only increased her wish to live on. There were no phrases of pious sadness in her Journal. She sat at her writing table, her eyes fortified with belladonna, 'guiding the land, the nation, the world almost, with her venerable influence.' [366]

The manifestations of life excited her too much for mournful pondering over death. She found increasing delight in the concerns of her grandchildren. Of Prince George and his wife she wrote, 'Every time I see them I love them more and respect them greatly. Thank God! Georgie has got such an excellent, useful, and good wife!' [367]

There was little that was sentimental about the ageing figure of the Queen. She rose with the splendour of a monarch in an heroic age to receive the trophies which Kitchener brought back for her from Dongola. She added the Sudanese drum, the Crusader sword which he had found, and the flag from the tower of Dongola to her collection of soldiers' plunder: the Zulu shields and the crowns of the Indian princes which she held at Windsor.

Kitchener sat next to the Queen at dinner and he told her the story of Dongola. Perhaps in a year or two he would go back and lead her soldiers as far as Khartoum and 'wipe out the stain on England's character.' [368] When dinner was over and when the Queen went to her sitting-room, she wrote her impressions of the 'striking, energetic-

346

looking soldier.' He had 'rather a firm expression,' but he was 'very pleasing to talk to.' [369]

The great century was ending. Every decade has brought its changes and the last mechanical surprise was the telephone. The Queen was able, if she wished, to speak with Lord Salisbury from Windsor to London. The new-fangled motor cars were already startling timorous villagers in remote places and on November 23rd, the Queen had sat in the Red Drawing-room at Windsor to see the 'so-called *animated pictures*' which had been taken when the Tsar was at Balmoral. It was '...a wonderful process, representing people, their movements and actions, as if they were alive.' And there were social changes which even the Queen admitted. Thirty years before she had been anxious when the Prince of Wales had entertained Americans at Marlborough House. Now she invited them to Windsor and she was especially pleased by Mrs. Curzon, 'very handsome and lady-like,' when she and her husband dined in December.

§ II — 1897

THE QUEEN was at Windsor on June of 1897. On the 20th she wrote in her Journal: 'This eventful day, 1897, has opened, and I pray God to help and protect me as He has hitherto done during these sixty long eventful years. ...God will surely help me on! How well I remember this day sixty years ago, when I was called from my bed by dear Mama to receive the news of my accession!' [370]

The rulers of Europe and the Princes of India had paid their tributes to Queen Victoria during her Jubilee in 1887. But the Diamond Jubilee of 1897 was more of an Empire celebration, to which her Colonial troops and Premiers came home. The words *Imperial England* matched themselves with *Imperial Rome,* for there has never been such homage paid to a ruler since the days of the Cæsars. Only time can give fullness of form and colour to history. Perhaps a thousand years must pass before a likeness can be seen between Kitchener invading the Sudan and Agricola crossing the border into Scotland. Perhaps then, Tacitus and the Correspondent for *The Times,* waiting in Cairo, will seem to be brothers, and the Roman Governor of Judæa and the Viceroy of Ireland not so very far apart.

One of the first suggestions was that Queen Victoria's Jubilee celebrations in the city of London should include the Monarch being drawn into St. Paul's Cathedral in her carriage by six cream horses. The idea was dropped, like an asp, because of Christian sensibilities. But the spectacle would have been one with the arrival of a Cæsar among the marble and porphyry columns of the Forum.

The anniversary of the Queen's accession fell upon a Sunday and the morning service in St. George's Chapel was perhaps the most solemn and inspiring occasion in the week of celebrations. The Chapel, built within the walls of Windsor Castle, is the shrine of British chivalry. Almost every sovereign from Edward the Third onwards has worshipped at its altar: Kings of every dynasty are buried within its vaults. Scenes as glorious as the marriage of Prince Albert Edward and as mournful as the stealthy burial of Charles the First have been enacted beneath its Gothic arches. Yet the glory of Kings has never displaced the simple dignity of worship or the sweet odour of sanctity with which the Chapel was endowed, five hundred years ago. The service on the morning of June 20th, 1897, was simple and quiet. The Queen sat facing the

348

altar at which her son was married in 1862. She wrote, 'I was much touched and overcome, especially when all my children and grandchildren came up to me and I kissed them, just as I did ten years ago at Westminster Abbey.' In the afternoon, the Queen went to St. George's once more, to listen to Mendelssohn's *Hymn of Praise*. 'Mme. Albani came down on purpose to sing in it.'

The Queen drove back to her rooms in the castle, feeling 'rather nervous about the coming days.' On Monday morning she travelled to Paddington by train. The doorway of her carriage had been widened to admit the wheeled chair in which she sat. When the Queen arrived at Buckingham Palace she rested for a little while and then she was taken round in her chair to the Bow Room, where all her family waited for her. Again it is in her Journal that the most simple record of the day is found. 'Seated in my chair, as I cannot stand long, I received all the foreign Princes in succession.' (Among them was the Archduke Franz Ferdinand who was shot at Serajevo in 1914.) 'I got back to my room a little before four, quite exhausted. Telegrams kept pouring in. It was quite impossible even to open them....'

'Dressed for dinner. I wore a dress of which the whole front was embroidered in gold, which had been specially worked in India, diamonds in my cap, and a diamond necklace, etc. The dinner was in the Supper-room, at little tables of twelve each.... I sat between the Archduke Franz Ferdinand and the Prince of Naples. After dinner went into Ballroom, where my private band played and the following were presented to me: the Colonial Premiers with their wives, the Special Envoys, the three Indian Princes, and all the officers of the two Indian escorts, who, as usual, held out their swords to be touched by me.... It was only a little after eleven when I got back to my room, feeling very tired.

There was a deal of noise in the streets, and we were told that many were sleeping out in the parks.' [371]

June 22nd was the 'never-to-be-forgotten day.'

'The night had been very hot, and I was rather restless. There was such a noise going on the whole time, but it did not keep me from getting some sleep.'

The Queen wore a 'dress of black silk, trimmed with panels of grey satin veiled with black net and steel embroideries, and some black lace.' Her bonnet was trimmed 'with creamy white flowers and white aigrette and some black lace.' Before she drove away from Buckingham Palace she touched an electric button which sent her message of thanks 'throughout the whole Empire.' The sun burst out as the carriage rolled out of the courtyard into a scene which London had never known before. Soldiers had come from all her dominions to escort her upon the six mile drive to St. Paul's by the north side of the river and home again along the south bank. The millions of people pressed into the streets of the route and sang as she passed. There was no question of their loyalty now. Their glory, their riches, their pride and their safety were symbolised in the little old figure which had ruled the land since the days when their grandfathers were young and gay. Few remembered a time when she was not their Queen. She was part of the eternity of Britain's existence. First came that magnificent company...the procession, mile upon mile. Then the six cream horses, then the carriage upon which perhaps ten million eyes were to gaze before the day was over. Once she looked up and saw a house in which the survivors of Balaclava were assembled to cheer as she drove past. In front of St. Paul's

350

Cathedral the carriage stopped. The Archbishop and the Bishops were waiting for her, their gorgeous copes radiant against the smoke-darkened stone. A *Te Deum* was sung in the open air. There was a prayer and a benediction and then the procession rolled on, across London Bridge, to the dimmer streets of the poor. Here too the houses blossomed and the singing went on. It seemed that London was a choir, six miles long, chanting the glory of her name and the venerable story of her reign. The Queen was very tired when she returned to the Palace. But it was truly a 'never-to-be-forgotten day.' She wrote, 'No one ever, I believe, has met with such an ovation as was given to me, passing through those six miles of streets.... The cheering was quite deafening, and every face seemed to be filled with real joy. I was much moved and gratified.'[372]

§ III — 1897-1899

IN THE two years following the celebration of her Diamond Jubilee Queen Victoria enjoyed influence over a wider sphere than perhaps any ruler in history. It was not only in Britain and the dominions that her name inspired awe and reverence. The civilised world had been deeply stirred by the events of the Jubilee and in America, France, Germany, Spain and Austria, the Queen's great age and her mellowed character endowed her with something of the power of an oracle. Perhaps the power was more personal than that of an oracle, for she seemed to come nearer to the every-day interests and common tasks than when she was younger. She was, in a sense, the mother of her century. Wherever she went she was acclaimed. The Queen Regent of Spain appealed to her for guidance and the Queen of Holland deferred to her judg-

ment. Hers was the only hand that could stay the mad
onrush of her grandson in Germany. When his duplicity
with Britain and Russia was at its height, she wrote to
the Tsar [373] exposing the German Emperor's tricks. Her
old hands juggled with the courts of Europe. When the
President of the French Republic waited upon her at
Cimiez ('so *grand seigneur* and not at all *parvenu*'),[374] he
avoided politics and graciously told her that she was
aimée par la population. During the same holiday visit to
Cimiez she went to a parade of the troops of the garrison.
The Governor, who was inspecting the soldiers, asked
that the salute should not be for him but for the little
stooping figure in the carriage. The influence of the
Queen's visits to France was so important that the British
Ambassador in Paris informed Lord Salisbury that it was
a 'simple truism' to say that 'whatever may be the condition of the official relations between the two Governments, the veneration and respect entertained by
Frenchmen towards the Queen of England are never
affected or prejudiced thereby.' [375] The power was purely
personal: in the early years of her widowhood the people
of Paris had hissed as she drove out of the gates of the
British Embassy. She was so old that the romance of
history seemed to touch her. The other giants of the
century were dead (Bismarck and Gladstone both died
in 1898), and the Queen was almost isolated, surrounded
by a younger generation of monarchs and statesmen. 'All
fall around me,' she wrote, 'I become more and more
lonely.' [376]

The Queen's personal power in Britain was amazing
during the last few years of her reign. It was to her that
the three hundred and thirty-six thousand Protestant
women appealed for the public control of convents. It

was her letter to the Duke of Norfolk which elicited the reassuring report on Catholic Institutions. When the Queen wished to soften the anger of the London newspapers against Germany, Sir Theodore Martin went to the editors of nine London daily journals, in her name, to ask them to 'adopt a quite altered tone' [377] towards the German Emperor and the German people. All agreed (including *The Times*) to follow her wish. Even the editor of *Punch* was willing to censor the humour of his caricaturists when it was aimed too fiercely at the Emperor and his statesmen. It was largely because of the Queen's interest, backed by the ultimate strength of public opinion, that Sunday newspapers were abandoned, at any rate for a while. This proof of the Queen's power in Fleet Street is remarkable to any student of newspaper history, for neither *The Times* nor *Punch* had been afraid to discuss the Queen and her domestic life with brutal candour in the early days of her reign. *The Times* had been one of the sharpest thorns in Prince Albert's side during all the twenty-one years of his life in England.

In September of 1898 one of the Queen's deepest ambitions was realised. Her horror over Gordon's death in Khartoum had never abated and she had already seen in the 'striking, energetic-looking' Kitchener the possible vindication of England's name. On September 5th, Kitchener telegraphed to his Sovereign from Nasri, 'This morning the British and Egyptian flags were hoisted on the walls of Gordon's Palace at Khartoum.' He had led her soldiers through the thrilling battle of Omdurman and the dervish army had been almost destroyed. When the troops reached Khartoum, they cheered *her* name and they prayed for *her,* during the memorial service which

353

was held upon the ground where Gordon was killed. She was grimly pleased by the victory and there was no sentimentality in her comment, 'Surely he is avenged.'

On her eightieth birthday the Queen was at Windsor. The wish to live was stronger than ever. There had been a nosegay for her from Princess Beatrice, first thing in the morning. This tribute from her devoted daughter had seldom been missed, in forty years. Her presents were laid out for her. There were silver candelabras for the Durbar room at Osborne, a miniature of George the Third set in diamonds, and a miniature of Prince Charles Edward from Lord Rosebery. The singers from Windsor and Eton and the choristers from Eton and St. George's Chapel serenaded her as she ate her breakfast and all day tributes poured into the Castle: almost three thousand telegrams, a bouquet in the shape of a harp from the Madrigal Society of Eton and Windsor, eighty roses from the Officers of the Scots Guards, flowers from her daughter in Germany. After lunch, 'Georgie and May came with their two little boys,' who gave her a bouquet.[378] The Queen, who had been among the first of her generation to applaud Wagner's music, selected three acts of *Lohengrin* for the evening celebration of her birthday. She was 'simply enchanted.' She wrote in her Journal, 'It is the most glorious composition, so poetic, so dramatic, and one might almost say, religious in feeling and full of sadness, pathos, and tenderness.... The whole opera produced a great impression on me.' The Prince of Wales sat near to his mother during the opera. He turned to her once and said that he had never heard a better performance.

The months of 1899 passed by in success, honour and celebration. When Mr. Balfour travelled down to Osborne to see the Queen in August, he said that the last session of Parliament had been 'the most successful and the quietest he ever remembered....' Everything was 'most satisfactory excepting the Transvaal.'[379] There was this one shadow over the year. The last day of 1898 had ended with thankfulness. It had been 'full of victories' and even her 'failing eyesight' and 'lameness, from rheumatism and the result of accidents' had not prevented the Queen from recording her wish to live on. But the closing months of 1899 were dark with foreboding. The first sign of disaster had come in May when the 21,684 Uitlanders of the Transvaal sent a petition to the Queen. Her secretary reported the contents of the desperate appeal of her people, twenty times more numerous than the Boers, yet intimidated so that they had no voice in the government of the rich mining country. He wrote, 'Promises made after the Jameson Raid have never been fulfilled; there is no liberty of the Press; British subjects can be expelled at the will of the President; the Uitlanders ... are overtaxed ... They are not allowed to meet together, or even to present petitions; the police are entirely composed of Boers, and behave in the most arbitrary and indeed oppressive manner, and are responsible for the murder of one British subject....'[380]

The imagination and industry of the British had brought prosperity to the Transvaal, especially through the development of the gold mines, yet the Boers placed the heaviest burden of taxation upon them with none of the compensations or privileges of citizenship. The inquisition was at last carried beyond the calm fields of compromise and conference. Kruger's relentless policy, the breaking of the promises which he had made after Majuba, and the failure of Sir Alfred Milner's conference with the Boer leader brought about a disastrous state of

355

affairs in the summer of 1899, and it was obvious that the only solution of the Transvaal problem lay in battle.

§ IV — 1899

THE RETROSPECT of thirty years allows us to view the South African war dispassionately and many contemporary historians have belittled both the cause and the achievement of the British soldiers. Germany and France rang with recriminations while Britain was preparing for the conflict in 1899. The breadth of the Channel allowed them to study our warlike mien dispassionately, and in the German and French newspapers Britain was represented as a great and powerful nation setting out to crush a minority. The Prussians forgot their own invasion of Schleswig-Holstein and they denounced Britain with as much moral indignation as we had denounced them, when we pleaded for 'poor little Denmark.'

While Germany and France moralised, Britain prepared for battle. Ten thousand soldiers from India and the Mediterranean poured into Natal; farmers and citizens in Australia, Canada and New Zealand turned from their peaceful occupations to offer their allegiance and service to England, in case of war. On October 4th Lord Wolseley announced the extent of his preparations to the Queen. There would be '70,000 men of Your Majesty's Army, the largest number *ever* sent from the United Kingdom for any war.' [381]

Kruger, dour and mighty, had dominated the policy of the Transvaal for many years, through vicissitudes which had hardened his heart and narrowed his vision. He waited until early October of 1899, when British troops were pouring into the country, before he flung down the gauntlet. His ultimatum was sent to the British Government on October 9th. The terms were refused and, two days afterwards, the two years and seven months of the South African War began.

Queen Victoria was at Balmoral. Sir Redvers Buller had travelled north to see her on October 5th, and he had told her that he did not think that 'there would be much hard fighting.' The soldier's optimistic prophecy, told to her in his 'blunt, straight-forward way,' [382] was not wholly reassuring to the Queen. Too many times during her life she had been the victim of over-optimism among her Ministers and Generals on the eve of war. She rose in this, the last tragedy of her reign, to give her armies the encouragement and compassion they needed. The moral issues which were to be dissected by historians in later years did not disturb her: nor the indignation of Germany and France. The strain and anxiety seemed to restore her energies rather than to weaken them, as she encouraged her Ministers or pored over maps with her Generals. She drove about the country to wish Godspeed to her soldiers and to show them that she was no sentimental stranger to the grim disaster of war. She left the quiet gardens of Balmoral to drive over, through Ballater, to the barracks. Her guard of Gordon Highlanders was drawn up, ready to join the rest of the regiment in Edinburgh and sail for South Africa. She spoke to them, 'May God protect you! I am confident that you will always do your duty, and will ever maintain the high reputation of the Gordon Highlanders.' They cheered her and she drove away with 'a lump in her throat.' But there was no pausing for emotional indulgence. Even Deeside was darkened by the foreboding and the sons of her old Highland friends were buckling on the trappings of war. News came to

Balmoral from the four corners of the earth. While Sir George White led the Indian forces through their first minor successes only to be shut up in Ladysmith, and while other troops were besieged in Kimberley and Mafeking, passions and danger shook the calm of Canadians, Australians and New Zealanders. Even when the Government in Canada held back carefully from any spontaneous pledges, the emotions of the mass of people were so strong that they swept all political apathy aside. The Canadian contingent sailed from Quebec on October 30th. Every detail of the gallantry of her soldiers was sent to the Queen: news of the nursing associations, the preparation of comforts, the arrangements to care for the women who were left behind. The Governor of Canada told her of the 400 Canadian soldiers who knelt in the Cathedral in Quebec to take the Sacrament before they sailed. The Governor of New Zealand wrote of the 'magic spell' which her name had cast over the people. Troopships sped across the seas towards the harassed country. In England, Sir Henry Campbell-Bannerman, who had inherited the cloak of Mr. Gladstone, made faint protests against the Government in the name of Liberalism. But the time was one for heroics rather than safety or reason and the noises of war soon drowned the voices of the few who demurred. In November and December the Queen drove down to the barracks at Windsor to inspect the troops before they departed. She noted their new khaki uniforms, much less picturesque than the uniforms worn by her soldiers when she sped them on their way to the Crimea, but much more 'practical.' When the troops were asked to give her three cheers, 'they gave many more and would hardly stop.' [383] On November 29th, she went to the barracks again to inspect the battalion of Grenadiers, 'drawn up without arms.' She drove down the line, unable to leave her carriage because of her lameness. Then the wives were brought up for her to see. One, with a baby in her arms, held back because her husband had only sailed that morning. She did not feel that she had the right, yet, to come near to the carriage. But she was pressed forward and, with the others who were close to the Queen, she saw that there were tears in her eyes.

In November, while the forces were still besieged in Kimberley, Mafeking and Ladysmith, Lord Methuen triumphed in three engagements, at Belmont, Enslin and Modder River. The good news of Modder River had barely reached England when the failure of a night attack on Stormberg plunged the country into gloom again. The 'black week' had begun.

General Gatacre's failure at Stormberg was followed by Lord Methuen's losses at Magersfontein and then, on December 15th, Sir Redvers Buller was attacked and was repulsed while attempting to cross the Tugela, on the way to relieve Ladysmith. The succession of calamitous telegrams reached the Queen at Windsor: one when she was in the room where Queen Anne had received the news of Blenheim. The news depressed Westminster and even Sir Redvers Buller faltered in the face of defeat and he telegraphed suggesting that he should 'let Ladysmith go.' The Cabinet rejected his suggestion and urged him to force his way on to Sir George White's relief. But the 'black week' drained the courage out of the Government and some even dared to talk of a truce or even of defeat. The fountain of courage was at Windsor. Forty-five of the Queen's eighty years seemed to fall away from her. She was again on the balcony of Buckingham Palace, with Prince Albert beside her, waving her handkerchief as the soldiers passed on their way to the Levant. When Lord Salisbury went down to Windsor he found an old woman sitting in her chair. The Queen's eyes were so dim that their weakness was apparent as he looked into them. The wrinkled hands upon the arms of the chair were old, but they moved energetically when there was any suggestion of failure. 'All will come right,' she said, again and again. When she was alone her hands were seldom still. Woollen comforters and caps grew beneath her busy needles and there was a note of anger in her voice when she learned that they were given to the officers and not to the men. She thought and felt with the mass of her people. One of her first messages to Lord Salisbury at the beginning of the war had been, 'I sincerely hope that the increased taxation ... will not fall upon the working classes....' [384]

Through the last depressing days of the year, when melancholy letters came from Westminster to Windsor, her spirit was magnificent. When Mr. Balfour came to her in December, unhappy before the news from Africa, she was almost angry as she interrupted his gloomy references to defeat. 'Please understand that there is no one depressed in *this* house,' she said, 'we are not interested in the possibilities of defeat; they do not exist.' [385] Never once did she waver in this last courageous proof of her greatness. Mr. Balfour went back to London after the proud reprimand and he said that it had been *splendid* to pass from 'the clamorous croakers in clubs and newspapers into the presence of this little old lady, alone among her women at Windsor, and hear her sweep all their vaticinations into nothingness with a nod.'

Chapter Thirty-Eight

§ 1 — 1900

THE PRINCE OF WALES had celebrated his fifty-eighth, birthday in November of 1899. On the eve of his accession he was a mature man, almost past middle-age and endowed with the honoured name of 'grandfather.' For the greater part of the Prince's life the Queen had denied him a share of her constitutional power: at least she had given it to him in niggardly doses, until she came to the autumn of her reign. But it is not from the throne alone that a constitutional monarch rules his empire: the changes of the eighteenth century had demanded that a new kind of sovereign should rise from the ashes of kingship: a sovereign who lived close to his people, no longer in the manner of the Prince of the story-book, without the common touch and fading away among aristocratic pursuits. The Prince of Wales may not have been allowed to share his mother's rights, but he had not wasted his time in repining or in kicking against a brick wall. He had thrown himself into the maelstrom of Britain's daily life, associating himself with philanthropy, education, health reforms, social welfare, fashion, society and harmless amusement. No other Prince ever approached the throne with such a full knowledge of and sympathy for the anxieties and frailties of his people. In this lay the secret of Prince Albert Edward's popularity. Sir Sidney Lee quotes in his honour the happy phrase, 'he saw life steadily and saw it whole.'

His early choice of Radical friends gives a singular insight into the Prince's character and mind. He clung tenaciously to the dignity and rights of his position, but he was always fascinated by men who did not lie down obediently under the royal heel. Unless they are popinjays, Princes must be tantalised by a wish for a personal triumph for the royalist cause, whenever they are face to face with violent reformers or socialists. The tributes of John Bright lingered in the Queen's memory, beyond the sweet adulation of proven courtiers. When a King receives a socialist minister, he engages in a fray which is centuries old: the conflict between the power of the individual to rule and the right of the mass to live. The deeply personal qualities of both are on trial. The King must yield a little and the socialist must yield a little, both towards the middle state of gentleness and reason. The Prince of Wales had learned this lesson through his friendships with Sir Charles Dilke, and Mr. Chamberlain, in the early phase of his radicalism. The mixed company at Marlborough House had not been so much of an error as the Queen supposed. The cosmopolitan contacts allowed her son, at the end of the century and on the eve of his accession, to speak in a language which the people understood. With the close of the Victorian era the tradition of nobly-born politicians ended: the tradition which had always stirred Bismarck to envy. There were to be no more Melbournes or Derbys or Salisburys to guide the land. The age of the great aristocrats was over and a new kind of blood was coming into Westminster. James Ramsay MacDonald was elected secretary of the Labour Party in 1900. James Henry Thomas was a young engine driver, twenty-five years old, dreaming his dreams as he travelled over the lines of the Great Western Railway.

David Lloyd George had represented Carnarvon in the Commons for ten years and Philip Snowden had retired from the Civil Service to enter politics. These were to be among the statesmen of the new century.

During the South African war the Prince came nearer and nearer to the cosmopolitan interests of his people and to the responsibilities which were awaiting him. His organisation of war philanthropy and his personal service to the wounded took him into new spheres of activity: his letters to and from the soldiers in Africa widened his knowledge and deepened his sympathies. One of his correspondents was Mr. Winston Churchill, who sent him colourful descriptions of his capture by the Boers, his imprisonment and his escape.

If the South African war drew the Prince nearer to the anxieties of British people, it also fed the bitterness which existed between himself and his nephew in Germany. The Emperor's letters, written to his grandmother and to his uncle during the months of the war, are nothing short of fantastic. He poured his emotional and silly advice upon them at almost every turn of the fortunes of the armies. In March, 1900, he wrote to the Queen, telling her that he could not intervene in the interests of peace. Her answer silenced him for a little time. She wrote, not directly, but through the British Ambassador in Berlin, to tell him that 'my whole nation is with me in a fixed determination to see this war through without intervention. The time for, and the terms of peace, must be left to our decision, and my country...will resist all interference.'

The Prince did not find it so easy to snub his nephew. The outstanding examples of the Emperor's interference were two sets of 'aphorisms on the war,' designed to teach Britain, through the Prince of Wales, how she should pursue the campaigns in Africa. The second series of *aphorisms* ended with an arch impertinence. The Emperor suggested that if England was demoralised by the Boer successes and obliged to accept defeat, she could do so without humiliation. He added an unfortunate and malicious parallel. 'Last year,' he wrote, 'in the great cricket match of England *v.* Australia, the former took the latter's victory quietly, with chivalrous acknowledgment of her opponent.'

The Prince paused before answering his nephew's letter. But an incident in January added enough irritation to inflame him into sending a candid reply. Dr. Leyds, Secretary of State for the Transvaal Government, was in Berlin and, on January 27th, he was invited to a dinner in celebration of the Emperor's birthday. The host was Chancellor von Hohenlohe. Sir Frank Lascelles, the British Ambassador, was obliged to be among the guests and to shake hands with Leyds. This last affront was too much for the Prince of Wales. He hoped, he said, that Sir Frank 'washed his hands with carbolic soap after having shaken hands with the Boer representative.' His letter to his nephew was phrased more cautiously. Acknowledging the Emperor's last set of *aphorisms,* he wrote, 'We, however, feel confident that in the end the result will be successful, though that opinion is not shared on the Continent or by Dr. Leyds, who, I perceive, has been received with open arms by all classes of Society in Berlin! ... The British Empire is not fighting for its very existence, as you know full well. . . .' [386]

The evil genius which guided the Emperor's policy led him to his deepest perfidy in January of 1900. In the midst of his letter writing to his grandmother, for whom he professed his admiration and love in grandiose terms, he went to the Russian Ambassador in Berlin [387] and proposed that this was the time, while Britain was harassed and weakened by the South African war, for the powers of Europe to combine in an attack upon England. The war against the Boers had made the British the most hated of all people in Europe: no more propitious moment would ever come to bring the arrogant Britons to their knees. Proof of that hatred came when Lord Roberts entered Bloemfontein in March, when the King of Sweden was the 'only Sovereign who telegraphed spontaneously' to the Queen. [388]

The German Emperor's voice was loud and his duplicity was without equal. But his influence was uncertain and distrusted in Russia and France and the lamentable plot against England went no further. If either France or Russia had been inclined to listen to the tempter, their hopes would have been weakened by the swift change which came to the fortunes of Britain's arms in South Africa early in the new year. Lord Roberts and Lord Kitchener had assumed control at the Cape on January 10th, and under their command the tide of favour and victory turned. The misfortunes of the 'black week' were slowly overcome and forgotten. On February 15th, General French, commanding horse artillery, cavalry and mounted infantry, dispersed the enemy and entered Kimberley. The good news was hurried to the Isle of Wight in time to greet the Queen at breakfast. She drove into Ryde in the afternoon and when she returned to Osborne there was another telegram. General French reported, from the relieved town, 'Have captured enemy laager, store depot of supplies and ammunition. Kimberley cheerful and well.' [389]

The Queen's courage had wavered for a moment a few

weeks before—the new year had begun 'full of anxiety and fear.' But she had admitted this only in the pages of her Journal. She had kept a brave face for her ministers and when they came down to see her, after the first news of victory, she was able to enjoy the pleasure of saying 'I told you so.' One pretty scene intervened between the relief of Kimberley and the next encouraging news from the war area. On February 19th, the Queen wrote in her Journal:

'Out with Beatrice, before which I had seen the little bugler, James Dunn of the Dublin Fusiliers, only 14 years of age, who was wounded in the arm and chest at Colenso. He swam the Tugela, and was then helped back to camp by a soldier and a sailor. He lost his bugle on the battlefield, so I gave him another with an inscription.... He is a nice-looking modest boy.'

Eight days afterwards, the second series of welcome telegrams reached the Queen, this time at Windsor. Lord Roberts informed her from Army Headquarters, 'General Cronje and his whole force capitulated at daybreak this morning, unconditionally. He is now a prisoner in my camp.' The second triumph came on the anniversary of Majuba. On February 28th, the troops relieved Lady-smith. The Queen was able to record another victory in her Journal. 'Before I got up Lizzie Stewart, my ward-robe maid, came in saying the telegraph boy had just come in with a telegram he was anxious I should have at once.' It was from Sir Redvers Buller, announcing the entry into Ladysmith. The Queen's 'joy was unbounded.' She let 'everybody in the Castle know, and telegraphed to the relations.' Her day was full and marvellous. Tele-grams poured into the castle all the morning and in the afternoon the Queen held an Investiture. Prince George stood by her and helped her to put on the decorations. She used *his* sword upon the shoulders of the knights, when they knelt before her.

§ II — 1900

THE PENDULUM swung back with the surrender of General Cronje and the relief of Kimberley and Ladysmith. The Boers were disheartened by the reverses, but they made a bold endeavour at compromise by telegraphing to Lord Salisbury that they were willing to make peace if the 'incontestable independence of both republics' was assured. They went further and petitioned the European powers to intervene on their behalf. But Britain's heart was hardened. There were the families of fourteen thousand dead officers and men of the United Kingdom and Ireland to stimulate her bitterness. The war went on, to the added chagrin of the nations of Europe. England suffered a less splendid isolation than Lord Salisbury desired. She was hated by the rest of Europe more than ever before in the Queen's reign. The focus for this outburst of anger was the Queen. The French and German newspapers derided her and challenged the morality of the cause in Africa. The abuse of the Queen became so bitter in April 1900 that the Prince of Wales poured indignation upon the French point of view and, as President of the British Commission, refused to attend the opening of the Paris Exhibition. Sir Arthur Bigge wrote, on his behalf, 'At the opening ceremony we would appear in the British uniform, and it is not improbable that he might be insulted by the Paris mob; and ... an insult to our uniform might lead to war.' The Prince said that his presence at the ceremony would 'be a positive slight to the

Queen, and would be regarded by Frenchmen as a proof that he was indifferent to the vile caricatures and lampooning of his mother by their Press.' [390]

The indignities and affronts of the French were drowned by acclamations all over Great Britain. Dissentient murmurs in Paris could not be heard by the cheering crowds outside the telegraph offices where they waited for news from Africa: few, if any, paused to read the Paris newspapers. The country was as dizzy with joy over victory as it had been mournful a few months before over the foreboding of defeat. On March 13th Lord Roberts entered Bloemfontein. The welcome telegram travelled from the captured town to Windsor within a few hours. 'By the help of God,' wrote Lord Roberts, 'and by the bravery of her Majesty's soldiers, the troops under my command have taken possession of Bloemfontein.' Her flag had been hoisted over the Presidency. The enemy had withdrawn from the neighbourhood and, he said, 'all seems quiet.' [391]

From Bloemfontein Lord Roberts advanced northwards, and after several combats he entered Kroonstad on May 12th. Five days afterwards, Colonel Baden-Powell and his troops in Mafeking were relieved by a mounted force under the command of Colonel Mahon. Slowly the advance of Lord Roberts's army became a march of glory. On May 28th, he crossed the Vaal river: three days afterwards he entered Johannesburg and, on June 5th, Pretoria. There were many minor battles to follow and many stubborn efforts at resistance on the part of the Boer leaders. But the war was won although it was not ended, and on September 1st the Transvaal was added to Queen Victoria's dominions.

§ III — 1900

ON THE morning of March 8th, the Queen travelled from Windsor to London. Between Paddington Station and the Palace the streets were crowded with people who had waited for her since early morning. Now, more than ever, she was the symbol of their courage and of the success which had come to the army in South Africa. The pavements were gay borders of smiling faces and thousands upon thousands of little flags. She drove into the palace quadrangle, 'through the principal gate, like for a triumphal entry.' Again London acclaimed her, more loudly than for the Jubilees. Then she had been their revered Queen, mysterious because of the accumulation of her years and wisdom. Now she drove past them bowing, forever bowing in acknowledgment of their cheers, more tangible to them because she too had been through the vale of anxiety over the war.

At night, while the Queen was dining in the palace, Londoners surged towards the railings as if upon a pilgrimage. Long after the last shafts of light had withdrawn from the sky, they pressed against the palace gates, waiting. When it was quite dark they still waited in thousands. Constitution Hill was dense with people. They spread down the Mall and along every street that led to the palace. They waited in silence at first, but suddenly, as if the pent-up emotions could be withheld no longer, they began to cheer. The palace rang with the sound of a million voices. About half-past nine, the curtains of a window parted. The Queen appeared, no more than a shadowy form, looking down upon them. Then

369

somebody carried a light across the room and held it behind her, so that the people could see her well. She stood
perfectly still until she was so tired that she turned and
went back to her chair.

Chapter Thirty-Nine

1900

ALMOST FORTY years had passed since the Queen's last visit to Ireland. Prince Albert had been alive then and they had been anxious as they drove through the streets of Dublin, for there had been occasional hisses, mingled with the cheering, as the carriage rolled on towards Viceregal Lodge. The Queen's love for the Irish had never been spontaneous or strong, partly because it was not in her nature to understand the emotional Celts. If there was indulgence for the distressful country up to the time of Prince Albert's death, it perished soon afterwards when the Dubliners mutilated his statue in Leinster Square. Deep-rooted resentment and bitterness followed, and through all the forty years of her widowhood, until the time of the South African war, there was no kindly word for Ireland in the Queen's letters or Journal. The Irish were law breakers and charlatans and they deserved neither help nor pity. The failure of constant attempts, both in and out of Parliament, to satisfy a race difficult to understand, and apparently impossible to govern, prevented the Queen from judging the Irish problems impartially or from making any real effort to help or comprehend. The Queen seldom allowed her responsibilities as a constitutional monarch to be overruled by her personal prejudices but, in regard to Ireland, she proved herself to be humanly frail. She poured her indignation upon the country as zealously as she poured her love upon Scotland.

When it was almost too late, the courage of the Irish soldiers in South Africa and her own softened character allowed her to make her first kindly gesture towards Ireland for forty years. Perhaps it was that the gentleness which came on the eve of death allowed her hands to unclench. So much that was poignant and sharp in the sixties was no more than a wistful memory in 1900. Prince Alfred had survived the Fenian's bullet and Prince Albert's name had not been besmirched by the foolish act of the Irish mob. Somebody told her that Irishmen intrigued only when they had nothing else to do, and that the wild energies they devoted to lawlessness would turn into constructive talents if only they could have had a royal lead and been shown the way. Maybe this was true. Perhaps the motives which made Irishmen struggle against her government and yet cross the seas to fight for her against the Boers were the same. The Queen read the despatches from South Africa until her eyes could bear the strain no longer. Then one of her daughters or one of her ladies would read to her. Many times there were references to the brave Irish. They had often been among the foremost in courage and fortitude. Perhaps there was a stirring towards self-reproach when the Queen telegraphed to Sir Redvers Buller in February, 'I have heard with the deepest concern of the heavy losses sustained by my brave Irish soldiers.' [392] In March, the Queen's graciousness swept all her old resentment away and her gratitude was expressed in an Army Order which tells its own story:

'Her Majesty the Queen is pleased to order that in future, upon St. Patrick's Day, all ranks in her Majesty's Irish regiments shall wear, as a distinction, a sprig of shamrock in their headdress, to commemorate the gallantry of her Irish soldiers during the recent battles in South Africa.'

As Lord Wolseley prophesied, her appreciation of the gallant services of the Irish had 'a magical effect upon that sentimental and imaginative race all over the world.' [393]

On the morning of March 3rd, the Queen had a long conversation with the Duke of Connaught. She had decided not to go to Cimiez this year. The animosity of the French and the impertinences they had written about her in the newspapers made her yearly visit quite impossible. There was, she told him, 'a possible idea of mine to go to Ireland.' [394] A friend who talked to her about this time wrote afterwards that the Queen 'desired almost passionately to be loved by the Irish.' [395]

Early in April the old Queen was wheeled on to her yacht, and on the morning of the 4th she accepted the salute of the Channel Fleet in Kingstown Harbour. At half-past eleven she went on shore. Her bonnet and parasol were embroidered with silver shamrocks and there was a bunch of *real* shamrocks pinned to her black dress. The procession of four carriages travelled from Kingstown to Dublin, and for two and a half hours the little figure bowed, backwards and forwards, acknowledging cheers such as Ireland had never given before. Some of the Irish women fell upon their knees in the roadway and cried as the Queen passed by. In their hours of allegiance the Irish were not less passionate than in their hours of indignation. They had swept in from the countryside to line the long road into Dublin. Bluejackets and soldiers and policemen guarded her way through the towns, but

in many parts of the country, 'there was scarcely a policeman or soldier' to be seen. She noted this and was pleased.
She drove under an arch upon which was inscribed:

Blest for ever is she who relied
On Erin's honour and Erin's pride.

The Queen was very tired when she came to Viceregal
Lodge. She was wheeled to the foot of the staircase in her
chair and then carried up to her room, where she rested.
But there was complete happiness as she wrote, 'Even the
Nationalists in front of the City Hall seemed to forget
their politics and cheered and waved their hats.' [396]

The Queen stayed in Ireland for twenty-two days. On
the first Saturday she drove slowly among fifty-five thousand schoolchildren in Phœnix Park. One mite called out,
'Shure you're a nice old lady,' as the carriage passed, and
two little girls came forward with a nosegay. There was
not one harsh intrusion; not one dissentient voice to mar
the scene. The Queen wrote that the cheering 'was quite
overpowering.'

The business of government was not allowed to relax.
There were letters every day from Lord Salisbury and
answers from the Queen. She protested because women
were travelling out to South Africa, occupying the rooms
which should belong to wounded soldiers. There was a
plea for Lord Roberts in the hope that he would not be
hampered by political meddling, and a protest when despatches were published describing the relief of Ladysmith to the detriment of some of the officers. 'I must
protest most strongly against any such important steps
having been taken without my knowledge and approval,'
she wrote. Such 'lamentable want of direction and judgment' was 'cruel and ungenerous' to the officers on serv-

ice. When she was not reading or writing, the Queen drove out from Viceregal Lodge upon some journey or other. One day she went to see the lions at the Zoo. Every day had its busy expedition. Convents were visited and the Mother Superior of the Sacred Heart kissed her hand. From the first day to the last, Ireland was courteous and charming to her. There was no hint of resentment over the forty years of neglect: no peevish wrangle over what was past. On April 26th the Queen returned to England. The Channel Fleet escorted the *Victoria and Albert* across the Channel 'but,' wrote the Queen, 'I unfortunately did not see much of it, as feeling very tired, I soon went below to rest.... I slept the greater part of the time.'

The Prince of Wales had remained in London during his mother's holiday in Ireland. The letters of both mother and son show that they were subconsciously aware of the violent changes that waited for them in the coming year. The Queen pleaded with him not to go to Paris in May. 'Dearest Bertie,' she wrote, 'I wish to express to you my earnest hope that you will not go to Paris.... We are all most anxious that your precious life should not be jeopardised.' [397]

When the Queen drove in London, crowds of people still waited for her and cheered. They formed the habit of lingering at the gates of Buckingham Palace, as if they sensed impending tragedy. She wrote again and again of her tiredness, but this did not prevent her busy journeys to and fro, to Wellington College, to hospitals and to exhibitions, and by railway between Windsor and London. In July she held her last garden party at Buckingham Palace. She drove among her guests in a low Victoria, 'in the most broiling heat,' and afterwards she took tea in the royal tent. Many old friends were brought up to her.

375

For the first time the Queen wore her spectacles on a public occasion. Her sight had become so dim that she could no longer recognise the faces of those with whom she spoke. The daily entries in her Journal became shorter and the paragraph describing the garden party ended, 'I was dreadfully hot and rather tired....'

In July the Queen's busy days were fraught with a new anxiety. There had been a hundred worries since her return from Ireland; the Boxer rising in Pekin and the outrages upon foreigners; the reports of mismanagement in the hospitals in South Africa; the continued guerilla warfare of which Lord Roberts sent her many harassing reports, and the news of Germany's growing naval ambitions. On July 31st the burden was increased through the death of the Queen's grandson, Prince Alfred, son of the Duke of Coburg. The news reached Windsor early in the morning. 'It is hard at eighty-one,' was the Queen's courageous comment. 'I was greatly upset, one sorrow, one trial, one anxiety following another. It is a horrible year, nothing but sadness and horrors of one kind and another....Felt terribly shaken and broken....'

Chapter Forty

§ 1 — 1900–1901

THROUGH NOVEMBER and December of 1900 the Queen bewailed her failing health in her Journal. She felt 'very poorly and wretched.' 'My appetite is completely gone, and I have great difficulty in eating anything.' The disgust for food continued and most of her nights were sleepless and haunted by a mass of troubles. On November 11th she had 'a shocking night.' No draught could make her sleep and constant pain kept her awake. Yet she plodded through the wearisome papers each day and saw her Ministers, refusing to yield to the rheumatic pain and increasing blindness. When there were changes in Lord Salisbury's Cabinet, following the victorious election in October, she watched every move and anticipated every danger. Lord Salisbury was also approaching death and the depletion of his powers forced him to abandon the Foreign Office in favour of Lord Lansdowne. The Queen still commanded. She would accept Lord Lansdowne 'on the strict understanding' that he should be under Lord Salisbury's 'personal supervision.' Remembering Lord Palmerston's pranks in the Foreign Office, she insisted that no telegram or despatch should be sent by the new Foreign Secretary without being first submitted to the Prime Minister. One reads the Queen's Journal for the last two months of her life in awe. She seemed to transcend human endurance. She would lie awake all night, torn by pain, and feel so tired next day that she could

377

do nothing but lie upon a sofa, but, when duty demanded it, she would force her tired body to immediate effort. On the last day of November she drove into the Quadrangle to inspect the Canadian troops home from South Africa. The men were brought up to her carriage, the officers were presented, and the especially lame and mutilated were offered a word of sympathy. She asked some of the officers to dine and she entertained the men to dinner in the Riding School. The troops of every Dominion went to Windsor in this way. She even went down to the Riding School to speak with the soldiers, seeing them through a haze, listening to their applause. The Australians were especially jolly. When they had cheered, a sergeant called for 'One more Colonial,' which was, wrote the Queen, 'apparently . . . a particular way of cheering in Australia.' She noted every passing event: the scandal over the housing of the poor in Windsor, the illness of Lord Roberts's daughter, and, at the end of December, the death of her beloved friend, Lady Churchill. All were dying: her daughter in Germany, her grandson in Africa, her friends, one by one. It seemed that with the end of the century the people who were identified with it were also to depart. On December 18th, the Queen travelled from Windsor to Osborne in great pain. On December 28th, she dictated for the pages of her Journal:

'I had a bad night though I got a little sleep at the beginning. Besides, I don't think I could have slept, as there was such a fearful storm. Then I thought of what would be going on. . . . The weather was so tempestuous that I got quite alarmed about it. I went to sleep again, after I had wished to get up, which was very tiresome. It rained and blew so hard that it was impossible to think of going out, so I did some signing, though I could hardly see a word I wrote.'

Early in the morning of January 2nd, Lord Roberts's ship steamed past the Queen's window and anchored in Southampton Water. Lord Roberts was to arrive at Osborne later in the day, and the Queen 'managed' to go out for half an hour to see the arch of welcome which had been built over the gates in his honour. In the late afternoon Lord Roberts arrived at the house. His return was perhaps the last, glorious episode in the Queen's life. She had always been thrilled by the return of her victorious servants and she rallied her strength to greet him and to talk to him. She received him 'most warmly' and then, when her own greeting was over, he knelt gallantly and kissed her hand. When he went from the room, the Queen drooped under the effort she had made. She was wheeled away in her chair to rest. She saw Lord Roberts once more, on January 14th, and she talked with him for an hour. Mr. Chamberlain, the last of her Ministers to see her, came to talk about South Africa, on the 11th. But her powers were fading quickly and on the evening of Tuesday, January 22nd, the Queen died. The last words she dictated for her Journal were of work. '...Did some signing, and dictated to Lenchen.' The last word she spoke coherently, on her death-bed, was 'Bertie,' her name for the new King, who was at her side.

§ 11 — 1901

THERE WAS not a breath of wind as the *Alberta* moved across from the island, past eleven miles of battleships and cruisers, to the mainland. The grey, sunless day deepened the majestic gloom of the funeral procession and the terrible reverberations of the cannon filled the Solent as the yacht moved on, through the rolling clouds of smoke.

Emperors, Kings and Princes had hurried across Europe to pay their last homage to their venerable grandmother. German and French battleships hovered off the coast of Ryde as the *Alberta* moved forward, following an advance guard of black-hulled destroyers. An admiral stood at the prow of the yacht and on the deck, at the corners of the white bier, four more admirals stood, stiff and still, guarding the coffin of the Queen of the Seas. The thousands of people standing upon the shore-line in silence were dressed in black or wore some sign of the dismal occasion. In London, millions of people waited...they had emptied the shops of the metropolis of every inch of crêpe and every black garment. An awful silence had settled on the streets of the city as the millions pressed in towards the route of the procession.

The hulls of the destroyers were painted black and the people of Portsmouth, dumb with sorrow, had pinned signs of mourning on their doors. But the coffin on the *Alberta* was covered with a fiery, crimson pall. The Queen's last wish had been that there should be no black trappings near her. She had asked instead that her wedding veil should be placed over her face. So it was as a bride that she moved slowly to the anchorage and then, in the morning, to London.

When the coffin was placed upon a gun-carriage at Windsor station, the horses became so restive after their long wait in the cold that the guard of honour hurriedly helped to unharness them and themselves took the shafts. The communication cord (in those days slung from carriage to carriage, outside the train) was hastily brought from the railway station so that the bluejackets could draw the gun-carriage up the steep hill. The white coffin was carried into the candle light of St. George's Chapel for the funeral service, and then into the Albert Memorial Chapel, where it rested all night. The scent of the thousands of wreaths was so heavy that one of the soldiers guarding the coffin fainted during his vigil.

Next day, none but the Royal family followed the coffin down to the mausoleum at Frogmore. The last ceremony had no touch with the outer world. The Queen who had lived so long that France had passed through two dynasties and into a republic, so long that the Kingdom she inherited had become an Empire, left a void when she died; a void so frightening that, for a moment, life seemed to stand still. There were strange echoes of sorrow from strange places. In Dublin, a newspaper boy bought a bunch of violets and hung them upon the funeral poster he carried as he scampered through the streets. In Zululand, a chief said, when he heard of the death of the White Queen, 'Then I shall see another star in the sky.'

As the last procession moved towards the mausoleum, light snow began to fall, as it had fallen two hundred and fifty years before, when the Cavaliers carried the coffin of Charles the First into the dark, silent Chapel at Windsor. The coffin was carried between an avenue of soldiers, past the pond upon which the Queen and the Prince had skated together, and into the mausoleum. The sarcophagus was open and Prince Albert's coffin lay there, and upon it, his sword.

One day, a few weeks before he died, Prince Albert had said to the Queen, 'We don't know in what state we shall meet again; but that we shall recognise each other and be together in eternity I am perfectly certain.' In all the forty

381

years of her widowhood, while the world about her moved restlessly towards doubt and cynicism, the Queen had believed what her husband had told her, with all her heart.

REFERENCES

Chapter One

1 To Earl Russell, January 10th, 1862.
2 The Earl of Derby.
3 To the Earl of Derby, February 17th, 1862.
4 Lord Grey to the Lord Mayor of London, February 19th, 1862.
5 The Queen to the Marchioness of Clanricarde, June 17th, 1862.
6 *A Victorian Dean: a memoir of Arthur Stanley, Dean of Westminster*, page 120.
7 *A Victorian Dean: a memoir of Arthur Stanley, Dean of Westminster*, page 124.
8 The Queen's Journal, January 29th, 1862.
9 The Queen's Journal, January 29th, 1862.
10 *Queen Victoria's Letters*, Vol. III, page 606.
11 The Queen to Earl Russell, January 14th, 1862.
12 Afterwards Dean Stanley of Westminster.

Chapter Two

13 *Dean Stanley's Letters*, the originals of which are in the possession of Lord Stanley of Alderley.
14 *Dean Stanley's Letters*, the originals of which are in the possession of Lord Stanley of Alderley.
15 *Dean Stanley's Letters*, the originals of which are in the possession of Lord Stanley of Alderley.
16 These extracts are from *Dean Stanley's Letters*, the originals of which are in the possession of Lord Stanley of Alderley.
17 These extracts are from *Dean Stanley's Letters*, the originals of which are in the possession of Lord Stanley of Alderley.
18 The Queen's Journal, June 14th, 1862.
19 The Queen's Journal, June 30th, 1862.
20 *Letters of Lady Augusta Stanley*, page 265.
21 The Queen to the Prince of Wales, July 9th, 1862.

22 *King Edward VII*, Lee, Vol. I, page 138.
23 The Queen's Journal, September 3rd, 1862.
24 *Her Majesty, The Romance of the Queens of England*, by E. Thornton Cook, page 378.
25 *Letters of Lady Augusta Stanley*, page 269.
26 *King Edward VII*, Lee, Vol. I, page 146.
27 *Letters of Lady Augusta Stanley*, page 258.

Chapter Three
28 *Letters of Lady Augusta Stanley*, page 281.
29 *Letters of Lady Augusta Stanley*, page 273.
30 *Letters of Lady Augusta Stanley*, page 273.
31 Afterwards Emperor William II.
32 *Letters of Lady Augusta Stanley*, page 282.
33 The Crown Princess to Queen Victoria, June 8th, 1863.
34 Laeken, September 21st, 1863.
35 To her brother-in-law, Duke Ernst of Saxe-Coburg-Gotha.
36 The extracts from the Queen's Memoranda in this chapter are from *Letters of Queen Victoria*, 1863.
37 Letter to the King of the Belgians, November 19th, 1863.
38 To the Queen, September 4th, 1863.

Chapter Four
39 *Her Majesty, The Romance of the Queens of England*, by E. Thornton Cook, page 375.
40 To Dr. Acland, November 23rd, 1862.
41 The Queen to the Prince of Wales, January 13th, 1864.
42 *Delane of 'The Times,'* Sir Edward Cook, page 146.
43 Sir John Hobart Caradoc, second and last Lord Howden, diplomatist (1799–1873).
44 To the Earl of Clarendon, June 4th, 1864. Maxwell's *Life of Clarendon*, Vol. II, page 292.

Chapter Five
45 A letter to Earl Granville, July 2nd, 1882.
46 The Hon. Emily Eden to the Earl of Clarendon, 1866.
47 The Crown Princess of Prussia to the Queen, April 13th, 1864.
48 During 1863 and 1864, Admiral Sir A. L. Kuper commanded the attacks upon Japanese positions. In 1863 the palace of the

Prince of Satsuma was shelled and half the town of Kagosima was burned. In 1864, when the Daimio of Nagato closed the Straits of Simonoseki against foreign ships, Kuper again commanded the reprisals when all the forts were silenced and stormed.

49 The Crown Princess to the Queen, April 13th, 1864.
50 The Queen's Journal, March 28th, 1871.
51 February 13th, 1864.
52 February 15th, 1864.
53 The Queen of Holland to Mary Marchioness of Salisbury, January 2nd, 1875.
54 Earl Granville to the Queen, May 30th, 1864.
55 The Crown Princess to the Queen, May 26th, 1864.
56 To the Queen, April 21st, 1864.
57 Quoted in letter from the King of the Belgians to the Queen, June 15th, 1864.
58 The Queen to the Earl of Clarendon, May 17th, 1864.
59 Sir Augustus Berkeley Paget was Envoy Extraordinary and Minister Plenipotentiary to Denmark from 1859 to 1863.
60 The Earl of Clarendon to the Queen, May 30th, 1864.
61 General Grey to Earl Russell, June 4th, 1864.

Chapter Six
62 From a letter to Sir Charles Fitzroy.
63 Wife of Sir Henry Layard, formerly Ambassador at Constantinople.
64 This story was related to the author by Commendatore Villari, the Italian scholar and historian.

Chapter Seven
65 The Earl of Clarendon.
66 To the King of the Belgians, October 20th, 1865.
67 To the Earl of Clarendon. *Life and Letters of the Fourth Earl of Clarendon*, Vol. II, page 300.
68 *Later Letters of Lady Augusta Stanley,* page 41.
69 The Queen's Journal, February 6th, 1866.
70 To Lady Augusta Stanley.
71 Quoted in the Introductory Note to Chapter V, *Letters of Queen Victoria*, 1862–1878.

72 January 1st, 1881.

73 *The Times,* July 24th, 1866.

74 The Crown Princess of Prussia to Queen Victoria, August 10th, 1866.

Chapter Eight

75 Earl Spencer.

76 *Later Letters of Lady Augusta Stanley,* page 111.

77 May 11th, 1885.

78 The Queen's Journal, October 14th, 1867.

79 The Queen to the Prince of Wales, March 9th, 1868.

80 *King Edward VII,* Lee, Vol. I, page 181.

81 Widow of General Bruce, his Governor, who had died after their journey to the Near East.

Chapter Nine

82 General Grey to Queen Victoria, February 24th, 1868.

83 Mr. Disraeli to the Queen, February 26th, 1868.

84 Mr. Disraeli to the Queen, February 26th, 1868.

85 General Grey to Queen Victoria, November 23rd, 1868.

86 Earl Granville to General Grey, December 5th, 1868.

87 *Queen Victoria as I Knew Her,* Sir Theodore Martin, page 50.

88 *Queen Victoria as I Knew Her,* Sir Theodore Martin, page 51.

89 The Queen's Journal, March 4th, 1869.

90 The Queen's Journal, March 23rd, 1870.

Chapter Ten

91 In 1846 the King of the French broke his promise to Queen Victoria, that the Duc de Montpensier should not be a suitor for the hand of the Queen of Spain's sister until the Queen was married and an heir was born. This was to exclude the Duc de Montpensier or his heirs from the throne in Spain: an increase of French power which would not have been welcome in England. The story is told in *Albert the Good,* Chap. XVII, and in other histories and records of the period.

92 Queen Victoria's memorandum, September 9th, 1870.

93 *Later Letters of Lady Augusta Stanley,* page 101.

94 Lord Cowley to Mary Marchioness of Salisbury, August 4th, 1868.

95 *Later Letters of Lady Augusta Stanley,* page 101.

96 The Queen to the Crown Princess, July 20th, 1870.

97 To the Queen, July 15th, 1870.

98 To the Queen, September 6th, 1870.

99 The Queen's Journal, September 5th, 1870.

100 The Queen's Journal, November 30th, 1870.

101 The Queen's Journal, March 27th, 1871.

102 The Queen's Journal, March 27th, 1871.

103 German Crown Prince to Queen Victoria, January 3rd, 1871.

104 The 15th Earl, son of Lord Derby, who had been Prime Minister.

105 *King Edward and his Times,* André Maurois.

106 *Memoirs of Sir Robert Morier,* Vol. II, page 153.

107 The Prince of Wales to the Queen, July 20th, 1870.

108 *King Edward VII,* Lee, Vol. I, page 310.

109 The Prince of Wales to the Queen, August 21st, 1870.

110 The Emperor of Germany to Queen Victoria, January 14th, 1871.

111, 112 & 113 *King Edward VII,* Lee, Vol. I, page 216.

Chapter Eleven

114 *The Times,* November 24th, 1871.

115 October 22nd, 1873.

116 The Queen's Journal, July 3rd, 1871.

117 The Queen's Journal, November 22nd, 1871.

118 The Queen's Journal, June 20th, 1873.

119 The Queen's Journal, December 13th, 1871.

120 *Later Letters of Lady Augusta Stanley,* page 149.

121 The Crown Princess to the Queen, October 4th, 1873.

122 King George V.

123 The Queen's Journal, February 27th, 1872.

124 Colonel Ponsonby to the Queen, March 21st, 1873.

Chapter Twelve

125 *King Edward VII,* Lee, Vol. I, page 336.

126 Newton's *Life of Lord Lyons,* Vol. II, page 29, quoted in *King Edward VII,* Lee, Vol. I, page 337.

127 Mr. Gladstone to the Prince of Wales, May 5th, 1870.

Chapter Thirteen

128 To the Rt. Hon. W. E. Forster, February 11th, 1874.
129 Diary, December 1st, 1873.
130 Prince Alfred, Duke of Edinburgh, afterwards Duke of Saxe-Coburg-Gotha, was married to the Grand Duchess Marie of Russia in St. Petersburg.
131 Memorandum, February 18th, 1874.
132 Mr. Disraeli to the Queen, April 17th, 1874.
133 Hitchman's *Life of Lord Beaconsfield,* Vol. I, page 134.
134 To Lady Bradford, 1874.
135 The Queen to Mr. Disraeli, July 11th, 1874.
136 Mr. Disraeli to Lady Bradford.

Chapter Fourteen

137 Quoted by Sir John Marriott in *Queen Victoria and her Ministers.*
138 Queen Victoria to Mr. Gladstone, August 11th, 1872.
139 The Queen to Theodore Martin, November 26th, 1875.
140 Mr. Disraeli to Lady Bradford, November 25th, 1875.
141 This and preceding quotations are from Mr. Disraeli's letters to Lady Bradford quoted in Chapter XII of Buckle's *Life of Disraeli,* Vol. V.
142 Lord Derby to Mr. Disraeli, May 4th, 1874.
143 Queen Victoria to Mr. Disraeli, May 7th, 1874.
144, 145 Mr. Disraeli to Montagu Corry, September 30th, 1875.
146 Queen Victoria to the German Crown Princess, June 8th, 1875.

Chapter Fifteen

147 To Lord Beaconsfield, October 6th, 1878.
148 *Letters of Lady Augusta Stanley,* page 162.
149 To Lord Northbrook, Viceroy of India, May 17th, 1875.
150 The Queen to the Crown Princess of Prussia, June 8th, 1875.
151 *King Edward VII,* Lee, Vol. I, page 374.
152 *King Edward VII,* Lee, Vol. I, page 374.
153 October 29th, 1875.
154 *Life of Disraeli,* Buckle, Vol. V, page 453.
155 The Queen's Journal, April 2nd, 1876.
156 The Prince of Wales to Mr. Disraeli, April 22nd, 1876.

157 Mr. Knollys to Mr. Disraeli, April 22nd, 1876.
158 Sir Henry James, Liberal Member of Parliament and sportsman.

Chapter Sixteen
159 *Letters of Queen Victoria,* second series, Vol. II, page 437.
160 Mr. Disraeli to the Queen, June 7th, 1876.
161 *Life of Disraeli,* Buckle, Vol. V, page 480.
162 *Life of Disraeli,* Buckle, Vol. V, page 488.
163 *Life of Disraeli,* Buckle, Vol. V, page 497.
164 Lord Beaconsfield to Lady Bradford, December 28th, 1876.
165 Article on 'The Character of Queen Victoria,' *Quarterly Review,* April, 1901.
166 July 24th, 1878. *King Edward VII,* Sir Sidney Lee, pages 367, 368.
167 Memorandum by Queen Victoria, October 17th, 1876.
168 *Life of Gladstone,* John Morley, Vol. II, page 552.
169 The Queen to Lord Beaconsfield, November 5th, 1877.

Chapter Seventeen
170 *Life of Gladstone,* Morley, Vol. II, pages 558–559.
171 Lord Beaconsfield to the Queen, December 17th, 1877.
172 Lord Derby to Lord Beaconsfield, December 17th, 1877.
173 December 19th, 1877.
174 December 18th, 1877.
175 *Life of Gladstone,* Morley, Vol. II, page 569.
176 Written from Downing Street, February 10th, 1878.
177 Lord Beaconsfield to the Queen, April 1st, 1878.
178 Princess Alice, Grand Duchess of Hesse, to the Queen, March 1st, 1878.
179 The German Crown Princess to the Queen, April 5th, 1878.
180 January 10th, 1878.
181 In November of 1876, Lord Salisbury had been the special envoy at a Conference in Constantinople. Lord Beaconsfield had paid a 'generous compliment' to the work of his colleague. But no brave decisions were achieved through the Conference. The Prince's blame, directed so personally at Lord Salisbury, was perhaps unjust; at least carelessly phrased.
182 This and subsequent reports of Lord Beaconsfield's experiences

in Berlin are from his diary, written for the Queen. The extracts are published in Buckle's *Life of Disraeli,* Vol. VI, Chapter IX.

183 Montagu Corry to Lady Ilchester, July 2nd, 1878.

Chapter Eighteen

184 Lady Augusta Stanley to her sister, Lady Francis Baillie. The original of this letter is in the possession of the Dean of Windsor.

Chapter Nineteen

185 *King Edward VII,* Lee, Vol. I, page 440.
186 *King Edward VII,* Lee, Vol. I, page 441.
187 To Lady Bradford, April 14th, 1879.
188 To Lady Bradford, November 19th, 1878.

Chapter Twenty

189 The Prince of Wales to Lord Beaconsfield, April 13th, 1879.
190 To Anne Lady Chesterfield, June 28th, 1879.
191 Lord Beaconsfield to the Queen, January 14th, 1880.
192 This and the two preceding quotations are taken from a letter written by the Queen to Sir Henry Ponsonby, April 8th, 1880.
193 April, 1880.
194 Memorandum by Queen Victoria, April 23rd, 1880.
195 *Life of Gladstone,* Morley, Vol. II, page 628.

Chapter Twenty-One

196 Earl Granville to Sir Henry Ponsonby, April 30th, 1880.
197 The Queen's Journal, April 28th, 1880.
198 The Queen's Journal, April 28th, 1880.
199 *Life of Gladstone,* Morley, Vol. III, page 22.
200 *Life of Gladstone,* Morley, Vol. III, page 26.
201 September 20th, 1880.
202 July 16th, 1881.
203 Queen Victoria to Earl Granville, August 8th, 1880.
204 Queen Victoria to Earl Granville, September 4th, 1880.

Chapter Twenty-Two

205 November 7th, 1880.
206 To Earl Cowper, December 5th, 1880.

207 *Life of Gladstone,* Morley, Vol. III, page 51.
208 Mr. Gladstone to Queen Victoria, April 6th, 1881.
209 The Queen to Earl Granville, August 17th, 1881.
210 May 27th, 1882.
212 From Osborne, January 1st, 1881.
214 The Queen's Journal, January 5th, 1881.
215 *King Edward VII,* Lee, Vol. I, page 450.
216 *King Edward VII,* Lee, Vol. I, page 451.
217 *King Edward VII,* Lee, Vol. I, page 451.
218 June 27th, 1881.
219 *King Edward VII,* Lee, Vol. I, page 452.
220 J. J. J. Tissot, the French painter who had left Paris under suspicion of being a Communist. He lived in London.
221 The Queen's Journal, October 30th, 1882.
222 The Earl of Dufferin to Earl Granville, December 11th, 1882.
223 The Queen to Earl Granville, December 12th, 1882.
224 Queen Victoria to Earl Granville, March 9th, 1883.
225 The Bill was rejected by the Senate although the Republicans afterwards passed a Bill (following on the royalist demonstration at the marriage of the Comte de Paris) forbidding any direct claimant to the throne of any of the three lines, Bourbon, Orleans and Bonaparte, to reside in France. For an account of the interest of the Prince of Wales in the expulsion of the royalist princes, see *King Edward VII,* Lee, Vol. I, page 462.
226 *Die Grosse Politik,* Vol. IV, page 31. Quoted in *King Edward VII,* Lee, Vol. I, page 477.
227 *King Edward VII,* Lee, Vol. I, page 485.
228 Quoted in *King Edward VII,* Lee, Vol. I, page 485.
229 & 230 *King Edward VII,* Lee, Vol. I, page 485.

Chapter Twenty-Four
231 Mr. Gladstone's Diary, September 11th, 1882.
232 Earl Granville to Queen Victoria, January 23rd, 1883.
233 Queen Victoria to Mr. Gladstone, January 5th, 1883.
234 The Queen to Earl Granville, January 20th, 1883.
235 The Queen to Earl Granville, February 8th, 1883.
236 The Prince to Lord Wolseley, December 5th, 1884.

237 The comment of the Commander-in-chief, quoted in *King Edward VII*, Lee, Vol. I, page 468.
238 *Letters of Queen Victoria*. Introductory note by George Earle Buckle.

Chapter Twenty-Five
239 The Queen to Sir Henry Ponsonby, March 27th, 1884.
240 The Queen to Sir Henry Ponsonby, May 17th, 1884.
241 The Queen to Sir Henry Ponsonby, May 17th, 1884.
242 Mr. Gladstone to Queen Victoria, July 25th, 1884.
243 The Queen to Mr. Gladstone, August 10th, 1884.
244 November 17th, 1884.
245 The Prince of Wales to Lord Wolseley, December 5th, 1884.
246 *Life of Gladstone*, Morley, Vol. III, page 209.

Chapter Twenty-Six
247 The Marquess of Hartington to Sir Henry Ponsonby, January 23rd, 1885.
248 Queen Victoria to Sir Henry Ponsonby, January 24th, 1885.
249 *Life of Robert, Marquis of Salisbury*, Vol. III, pages 128–129.
250 Mr. Gladstone to Queen Victoria, June 9th, 1885.
251 The Queen's Journal, June 23rd, 1885.
252 The Queen's Journal, June 24th, 1885.
253 The Queen's Journal, July 14th, 1885.
254 *Life of Robert, Marquis of Salisbury*, Vol. III, page 232.
255 The Queen to the Marquis of Salisbury, December 3rd, 1885.
256 *Life of Robert, Marquis of Salisbury*, Vol. III, page 290.
257 *Life of Robert, Marquis of Salisbury*, Vol. III, page 290.

Chapter Twenty-Seven
258 Mr. Gladstone's Diary, quoted in *Life of Gladstone*, Morley, Vol. III, page 310.
259 Lord Tennyson's *Life of Tennyson*, Vol. II, pages 445–446.
260 *Life of Gladstone*, Morley, Vol. III, pages 347–348.
261 The Queen to the Marquis of Salisbury, July 22nd, 1886.

Chapter Twenty-Eight
262 The Queen's Journal, November 19th, 1886.
263 Queen Victoria to the Marquis of Salisbury, September 1st, 1886.

264 From private information.

265 The Marquis of Salisbury, at the Guildhall, November 9th, 1886.

266 The Queen's Journal, December 8th, 1886.

267 The Queen's Journal, March 6th, 1887.

268 The Queen's Journal, May 4th, 1886.

269 The Queen's Journal, May 4th, 1886.

270 The Marquis of Salisbury to the Queen. *Life of Robert, Marquis of Salisbury,* Vol. III, page 315.

271 July 11th, 1888.

272 November 6th. *Life of Lord Randolph Churchill,* Vol. II, page 223, and quoted in *Life of Robert, Marquis of Salisbury,* Vol. III, pages 322–323.

273 Queen Victoria to the Marquis of Salisbury, December 23rd, 1886.

274 Queen Victoria to Mr. Goschen, December 24th, 1886.

275 Sir Michael Hicks-Beach was first appointed Chief Secretary for Ireland, but he was obliged to resign because of the failure of his eyesight.

Chapter Twenty-Nine

276 The Queen's Journal, March 5th, 1887.

277 *Arthur James Balfour,* Bernard Alderson, page 67.

278 The Marquis of Londonderry to Queen Victoria, December 10th, 1887.

279 *Letters of Queen Victoria.* Third series, Vol. I, page 271.

280 Mr. W. H. Smith to Queen Victoria, March 24th, 1887.

281 Chief Letsie to Queen Victoria, July 21st, 1887.

282 The Queen's Journal, October 10th, 1887.

Chapter Thirty

283 The Queen's Journal, May 10th, 1887.

284 The Queen's Journal, April 23rd, 1887.

285 The Queen's Journal, April 23rd, 1887.

286 The Queen's Journal, April 23rd, 1888.

287 The Queen's Journal, April 25th, 1888.

288 The Queen's Journal, April 26th, 1888.

289 The Queen's Journal, June 25th, 1888.

Chapter Thirty-One

290 Queen Victoria to the Marquis of Salisbury, October 15th, 1888.

291 Queen Victoria to the Marquis of Salisbury, February 27th, 1889.

292 Queen Victoria to the Prince of Wales, February 7th, 1889.

293 The German Emperor to Queen Victoria, July 6th, 1888.

294 The Marquis of Salisbury to Queen Victoria, March 9th, 1889.

295 The Queen's Journal, April 27th, 1889.

Chapter Thirty-Two

296 February 7th, 1890.

297 *Letters of Queen Victoria,* 1886–1891. Third series, Vol. I. See letter from Sir Edward Malet to Queen Victoria, March 22nd, 1890.

298 The Prince of Wales to Queen Victoria, March 31st, 1890.

299 Sir William Harcourt to John Morley, *Life of Sir William Harcourt,* Gardiner.

300 The Queen's Journal, June 27th, 1890.

301 Queen Victoria to Sir Henry Ponsonby, March 20th, 1890.

302 Queen Victoria to Sir Henry Ponsonby, April 30th, 1890.

303 Mr. Parnell had been concerned in a drab domestic scandal in the previous year. He died under the weight of his exertions and troubles in October, 1891.

304 Queen Victoria to Earl Russell, January 10th, 1862.

305 The Queen's Journal, October 11th, 1890.

306 The Queen's Journal, March 17th, 1891.

307 The Queen to Mr. Goschen, May 22nd, 1891.

Chapter Thirty-Three

308 Mr. Balfour to the Queen, May 28th, 1892.

309 May 12th, 1892.

310 The initial letters of the words 'Grand Old Man,' the popular name for Mr. Gladstone, used by both friends and enemies, were also used by the Queen.

311 The Queen's Journal, June 11th, 1892.

312 The Queen to the Prince of Wales, August 13th, 1892.

313 Printed in *Letters of Queen Victoria.* Third series, Vol. II, pages 144 and 145.

314 The Queen's Journal, August 15th, 1892.
315 Mrs. Gladstone to Queen Victoria, September 2nd, 1892.
316 Queen Victoria to the Earl of Rosebery, September 28th, 1892.
317 Mr. Gladstone to Queen Victoria, December 17th, 1892.
318 Quoted in *King Edward VII,* Lee, Vol. I, page 553.

Chapter Thirty-Four
319 The Queen's Journal, January 21st, 1893.
320 Queen Victoria to Mr. Gladstone, January 21st, 1893.
321 Queen Victoria to Mr. Gladstone, January 23rd, 1893.
322 Sir Henry Ponsonby to Queen Victoria, January 23rd, 1893.
323 The Queen's Journal, May 16th, 1893.
324 The Queen's Journal, July 5th, 1893.
325 The Queen's Journal, February 15th, 1893.
326 Mr. Gladstone to Queen Victoria, February 17th, 1893.
327 The Queen's Journal, February 19th, 1893.
328 The Queen's Journal, July 8th, 1893.
329 The Queen's Journal, September 9th, 1893.
330 The Queen's Journal, February 27th, 1894.
331 The Queen's Journal, March 3rd, 1894.
332 The Queen's Journal, March 3rd, 1894.
333 The Earl of Rosebery to Queen Victoria, March 4th, 1894.
334 The Queen to the Earl of Rosebery, March 4th, 1894.
336 The Queen's Journal, March 3rd, 1894.
337 Private information.

Chapter Thirty-Five
338 White Lodge is now the home of Lord Lee of Fareham and
   the galleries are the setting for his noble collection of pictures.
339 The Queen's Journal, June 26th, 1894.
340 The Queen's Journal, July 16th, 1894.
341 Queen Victoria to the Earl of Rosebery, March 17th, 1894.
342 Queen Victoria to the Earl of Rosebery, June 8th, 1894.
343 Queen Victoria to the Marquis of Salisbury, October 25th,
   1894.
344 Queen Victoria to the Prince of Wales, October 25th, 1894.
345 The Prince of Wales to Queen Victoria, October 26th, 1894.
346 Queen Victoria to the Earl of Rosebery, November 13th, 1894.
347 From private sources, recounted to the author.

348 The Earl of Rosebery to Queen Victoria, June 23rd, 1895.
349 Queen Victoria to the Earl of Rosebery, June 23rd, 1895.

Chapter Thirty-Six
350 The Queen's Journal, January 2nd, 1896.
351 The Queen's Journal, January 7th, 1896.
352 and 353 *King Edward VII,* Lee, Vol. I, page 670.
354 Lieut.-Col. Bigge to the Earl of Rosebery, February 12th, 1895.
355 The Earl of Rosebery to Queen Victoria, February 11th, 1895.
356 The Earl of Rosebery to Queen Victoria, February 13th, 1895.
357 This and subsequent details of the relationship between the Emperor and the Prince of Wales are taken from *King Edward VII,* Lee, Vol. I, Ch. XXXVIII.
358 Queen Victoria to the Prince of Wales, January 11th, 1896.
359 The Prince of Wales to Lieut.-Col. Bigge, August 26th, 1896.
360 Queen Victoria to the Prince of Wales, September 2nd, 1896.
361 *King Edward VII,* Lee, Vol. I, page 697.
362 The Queen's Journal, October 3rd, 1896.

Chapter Thirty-Seven
363 Queen Victoria to the Marquis of Salisbury, March 22nd, 1896.
364 The Queen's Journal, January 10th, 1896.
365 The Queen's Journal, September 11th, 1896.
366 *Shades of Eton,* Percy Lubbock.
367 The Queen's Journal, September 30th, 1897.
368 The Queen's Journal, December 5th, 1896.
369 The Queen's Journal, November 6th, 1896.
370 The Queen's Journal, June 20th, 1897.
371 The Queen's Journal, June 21st, 1897.
372 The Queen's Journal, June 22nd, 1897.
373 March 1st, 1899.
374 The Queen's Journal, April 13th, 1898.
375 Sir Edmund Monson to the Marquis of Salisbury, May 9th, 1899.
376 The Queen's Journal, March 10th, 1899.
377 Sir Theodore Martin to Queen Victoria, January 13th, 1898.
378 The Queen's Journal, May 24th, 1899.
379 The Queen's Journal, August 7th, 1899.

380 Sir Arthur Bigge to Queen Victoria, May 10th, 1899.

381 Viscount Wolseley to Queen Victoria, October 4th, 1899.

382 The Queen's Journal, October 5th, 1899.

383 The Queen's Journal, November 11th, 1899.

384 Queen Victoria to the Marquis of Salisbury, October 20th, 1899.

385 *Life of Robert, Marquis of Salisbury,* Vol. III, page 191.

Chapter Thirty-Eight

386 The Prince of Wales to the German Emperor, February 8th, 1900.

387 A full record of this incident, with authorities, is given in *King Edward VII,* Lee, Vol. I, pages 761–769.

388 The Queen's Journal, March 1st, 1900.

389 The Queen's Journal, February 16th, 1900.

390 Sir Arthur Bigge to the Marquis of Salisbury, March 25th, 1900.

391 Lord Roberts to Queen Victoria, March 13th, 1900.

Chapter Thirty-Nine

392 Queen Victoria to Sir Redvers Buller, February 27th, 1900.

393 Viscount Wolseley to Queen Victoria, March 1st, 1900.

394 The Queen's Journal, March 2nd, 1900.

395 Quoted in *Queen Victoria and Her Ministers,* by Sir John A. R. Marriott, page 224.

396 The Queen's Journal, April 4th, 1900.

397 Queen Victoria to the Prince of Wales, May 8th, 1900.

BIBLIOGRAPHY

Letters of Queen Victoria, edited by George Earle Buckle. Second series and third series.

King Edward VII, a biography by Sir Sidney Lee, Volume I.

Life of Gladstone, by John Morley, Volume II and Volume III.

The Life of Benjamin Disraeli, Earl of Beaconsfield, by George Earle Buckle.

Lord Rosebery, by the Marquis of Crewe, K.G.

V.R.I., Her Life and Empire, by the Marquis of Lorne, afterwards Duke of Argyle.

Arthur James Balfour, by Bernard Alderson.

Letters of Lady Augusta Stanley, edited by the Dean of Windsor and Hector Bolitho.

Later Letters of Lady Augusta Stanley, edited by the Dean of Windsor and Hector Bolitho.

Queen Victoria and Her Ministers, by Sir John A. R. Marriott.

Parliamentary Reminiscences and Reflections, by Lord George Hamilton, 2 Volumes.

Social Transformations of the Victorian Age, by T. H. S. Escott.

Queen Victoria, a biography by Sir Sidney Lee.

Life of Robert, Marquis of Salisbury, by Lady Gwendolin Cecil, 3 Volumes.

Queen Victoria as I Knew Her, by Theodore Martin.

Life and Letters of the Fourth Earl of Clarendon, Volume II.

Life of Lord Beaconsfield, by Hitchman.

King Edward and His Times (The Edwardian Era), by André Maurois.

Files of *The Times.*

INDEX

Abdul Aziz, Sultan of Turkey: visits London, 123; Prince of Wales visits, 125; dethroned, 161

Abdul Hamid II, Sultan of Turkey: accession of, 162; convention with Great Britain, 182; supports deposition of Khedive Ismail, 205; Armenian massacre, 337

Aberdeen, waterworks opened, 66

Abu Klea, battle of, 263

Adrianople, Russians enter, 179

Afghanistan—Great Britain: war, 196; policy, 216, 217; Russian action in, 195, 196

Africa, South—Basuto rebellion, 217; Boers: Transvaal rebellion, 217; independence guaranteed, 218; Kruger's plea for German friendship, 338; war against British (1899-1902), 355-360, 363-370, 374; Cape Colony: governor, 197; High Commissioner, first, 197; Jameson raid, 340-342; Kaffir rebellion, 197; Natal: governorship, 200-203; Transvaal: annexation, 198; governorship, 200-202; minerals and British policy: Lord Wolseley's statements, 218; Zulu war: see Zulu War

Africa, South-West: German annexation, 252-253

Albani, Mme.: sings at Albert Hall, 280; at Windsor, 349

Albany, Duke of: see Leopold, Prince

Albert, Prince (Duke of York), on Royal Family, 114

Albert, the Prince Consort: see Prince Consort, the

Albert Edward, Prince of Wales: early training, 5, 6, 9, 10, 16, 17; acquires Sandringham House, and

Marlborough House, 16; betrothal, 18; in Coburg, 18; to remain abroad, 20; wedding, 22-26; first child, 33; Knight of St. Patrick, 79; illness, 113-118; Accession, eve of: character, 361; Alice, Princess: relations, 18; visits, 125; Amusements, love of: attacked, 83-88; Aristocracy, defence of: 42; Balmoral statue: unveils, 290; Beaconsfield, Lord: relations, 107, 152, 153, 165, 166, 182, 183, 203; *Belle Hélène, La:* rebukes Lord Chamberlain, 42; Beresford, Lord Charles: friendship, 280; Berlin: visits, 124, 172, 302, 303; Berlin Congress: views, 183, 184; Bismarck, Prince: attitude of, 104; meets, 172, 303; Cabs, hired: use, 42; Canada, visit to, 150; Children, relations with, 83, 191; Churchill, Lord Randolph: friendship, 276, 283; Clubs: frequents, 39; Democratic sympathies, 85, 86; Denmark: sympathy, 50; visits, 124; Dilke, Sir C.: friendship, 167, 206, 231, 232; Diplomatic documents: request to see, 51, 108; golden key incident, 109; Queen's attitude changed, 171, 172, 173; Drama, patronage of, 298; Egypt and Palestine: visits, 6, 10-15, 94, 124; Eugénie, Empress: offer to, 105; Faces, memory for, 40; Foreign Office messengers: alleged use, 111; Foreign royalties: entertainment, 127, 128; Franco-Prussian War: attitude during, 103-105; French sympathies, 103-106; *Entente Cordial* phrase, 204; effect of Egyptian crisis, 231, 232, 233, 236;

INDEX

INDEX

CPSIA information can be obtained
at www.ICGtesting.com
Printed in the USA
BVOW09s2000070218

507536BV00012B/73/P